2

WITHDRAWN

# MEDIA AND THE RUSSIAN PUBLIC

# MEDiA
# AND THE
# RUSSiAN
# PUBLiC

## Ellen Propper Mickiewicz

PRAEGER

PRAEGER SPECIAL STUDIES • PRAEGER SCIENTIFIC

**Library of Congress Cataloging in Publication Data**

Mickiewicz, Ellen Propper.
    Media and the Russian public.

    Includes index.
    1.  Mass media--Russia.  2.  Mass media--Social
aspects--Russia.  3.  Public opinion--Russia.
I.  Title.
P92.R9M5          302.2'3          80-21544
ISBN 0-03-057681-4
ISBN 0-03-057679-2 (pbk.)

Published in 1981 by Praeger Publishers
CBS Educational and Professional Publishing
A Division of CBS, Inc.
521 Fifth Avenue, New York, New York 10175 U.S.A.

© 1981 by Praeger Publishers

123456789   145   987654321

Printed in the United States of America

*For Cyril*

"There is no fate, hence no accident—
only our inability to foresee circumstances."

Andrea Giovene
*The Autobiography of Giuliano di Sansevero*

# PREFACE

I have written this study with two goals in mind. The first is to provide as much information as is available about the exposure of Soviet Russians to the mass media and about their attitudes toward media communications. The second, broader goal is to enable the reader to see, through the prism of media attitudes and consumption, a picture of representative Russian public opinion. We have never before had the opportunity, nor have the Russians themselves, to survey the attitudes of the broad masses. In the West we have had to rely on various types of unrepresentative samples. In the Soviet Union the leadership has claimed to know the attitudes of its population without the need to survey it. These claims have been greatly weakened in the past decade or so with the advent of public opinion polling.

The wide range of subjects to which we in the West are accustomed, in particular of subjects of a partisan or political nature, is not considered appropriate for the Soviet opinion surveys. However, within the boundaries of what is permitted, there is a great deal we may learn about the opinions that Russians in Russia hold.* What is more important, we may see what affects those attitudes: the role education plays in creating satisfaction or dissatisfaction; how being disadvantaged in Russia relates to attitudes and participation; in what ways generational factors are associated with the propensity to adopt a critical stance; the difference in trust accorded the nation from that given the locality. These are some of those broader questions of opinions and attitude formation in Russia that we shall look at through the information gleaned from the media studies.

I approach these theoretical questions from two perspectives—that of the student of Soviet society and that of the analyst of media consumption in Western systems, in particular, our own. But I have tried to render my findings into language free of jargon. I have done this in order to convey the sense of everyday, average Russian life, which may be constructed from the surveys and which we in the West are least likely to see with the sources normally available to us.

---

*Most of the surveys on which this study is based were conducted in the Russian Republic; however, Estonian surveys have been among the most innovative, particularly with respect to the theater and film audiences, and these surveys are analyzed primarily in Chapter 6.

However, if we are to have any confidence in the picture that the surveys show us and the theoretical relationships they reveal, then their methods must be discussed in some detail. That is the function of the first chapter, "Probing Russian Public Opinion."

The next three chapters cover the varied dimensions of what has become a revolution in Soviet media: the belated, but massive, introduction of television throughout the country. The tremendous changes this revolution has ignited, many of which are familiar from our own experience, have not yet been completed, but the impact is there to read. Chapter 5 addresses itself to newspaper readers. In Soviet society the newspaper was virtually canonized by Lenin and continues to enjoy a prestige in official rhetoric that no other medium can approach. In fact, the readership does look to the newspaper for a number of functions, including that of public advocacy, but as an audience, it is by no means monolithic. Chapter 6 focuses on the film and theater audiences in Russia and, in a more limited way, on the audience for music.

The next two chapters treat two outlying cases of theoretical interest: people who are relatively impervious to the media and people who are excessive media consumers. The first, the isolates, are not easily labeled, but they are an increasing source of concern to specialists, both Soviet and Western, who study urban disorder. I am speaking here of unassimilated migrants who have moved to Soviet cities from the countryside and are locked into a pattern of disorientation and alienation; their world is the subject of Chapter 7. The heavy consumers of media communications are the members of the Communist Party, whose distinctive pattern of participation and activism is analyzed in Chapter 8.

In the last chapter I discuss relationships contributing to attitude formation and differences in exposure among different types or groups in the Russian media public. We may only speculate about some of the factors that seem to influence public opinion in Russia, since time and more (and different) surveys are needed; such, for example, is the case of attention to foreign radio broadcasters. Some factors are more stable and unambiguous and reappear across time and varied types of surveys. Taken together, these findings about attitudes and opinions enable us to address that most fundamental of all questions: How malleable is the Russian public?

During the course of my research I learned a great deal from the insights and information provided by a number of people, and I should like gratefully to acknowledge their help: Bradley Greenberg, chairman of the department of communication at Michigan State University; Wesley Fisher, of the department of sociology of Columbia University; Ken Wirt, of the communication research department of the Public Broadcasting Service; James Critchlow, a lifelong student of Soviet society, and planning and research officer for the United States Board for International Broadcasting; Gregory Guroff and James McGregor of the United States International Communication Agency; and Ludmila Obolensky of the Voice of America. For his prodigious bibliographic skills, I am grateful to Robert V. Allen of the Library of Congress, and to my colleague, Vladimir Shlapentokh, one of the most eminent of Soviet sociologists, I owe thanks for a number of interesting publications. Much of the writing of this study was supported by a grant from the Ford Foundation, which gave me the time and resources to complete a work that has been of central interest to me for several years. With her usual patient and expert perfection, Susan Cooley typed the successive drafts of the manuscript.

# CONTENTS

## DEFINITIONS AND TERMS

- Soviet Union:  "Soviet" is used throughout the text to denote that which
pertains to the country considered as a whole.
"Russian" is used to denote an ethnic Russian or that which
pertains to the Russian Republic.
- Levels of political administration:

All-Union—national

Republic—15 regional divisions, each named for the predominant indigenous
ethnic group.

|     |                      |
|-----|----------------------|
| 1.  | Russian Republic     |
| 2.  | Ukrainian Republic   |
| 3.  | Belorussian Republic |
| 4.  | Latvian Republic     |
| 5.  | Estonian Republic    |
| 6.  | Lithuanian Republic  |
| 7.  | Moldavian Republic   |
| 8.  | Georgian Republic    |
| 9.  | Armenian Republic    |
| 10. | Azerbaidzhani Republic |
| 11. | Turkmenian Republic  |
| 12. | Kirgiz Republic      |
| 13. | Tadzhik Republic     |
| 14. | Uzbek Republic       |
| 15. | Kazakh Republic      |

Oblast—province*

City

Raion—district or precinct.
- Social classes:  Officially the population of the Soviet Union is divided into
two classes: workers and peasants.

Workers include:

a. The intelligentsia, which is officially considered a stratum
(not a separate class), is made up of people with higher
education in jobs requiring higher education.
b. Agricultural workers on state farms, where the land is
nationalized and farmers receive a daily wage.
c. All others not employed on collective farms.

---

*Autonomous republics and autonomous oblasts are similar to the province, but have
official recognition that there are concentrations of particular ethnic groups in the area,
and thus have a greater and more specific ethnic identity than does the province.

xi

Peasants include:

> Workers on collective farms, where land is, in theory, held cooperatively and income depends on division of what is produced collectively.

# MEDIA
# AND THE
# RUSSIAN
# PUBLIC

# 1

## PROBING RUSSIAN
## PUBLIC OPINION

For the first time since Stalin rose to power, there is a genuine opportunity to look at the opinion of large publics in the Soviet Union. Over the course of the last ten years or so, Soviet academicians have been carrying out large-scale polls of the population of the Russian Republic, the most populous area in the country. Among the most interesting of the polls are those that examine attitudes and opinions relating to the mass media. Because what is transmitted by the media reflects a broad spectrum of priorities and information, the opinions probed by the mass media specialists similarly range over a wide variety of subjects. Although we may not be able to know "what Russians think of Brezhnev" or the "Communist system" because explicitly political polls are not permitted, we have been afforded, in these recent surveys, a glimpse at what Russians think of their communications media, whom they trust, what they prefer, and what leaves them satisfied or dissatisfied. Beyond that, we may extract an idea of what matters to large numbers of people: entertainment and escapism, politics, or culture, to name some obvious categories. In fact, it would not be a mistake to say that in order to learn about the attitudes and behavior of large segments of the population in Russia, we must study precisely this kind of information.

Other sources of information about public opinion in Russia, the ones we usually rely on, are certainly of value, but that value is circumscribed by well-known limitations. For example, the columns and books journalists produce must inevitably be based on the associations and events a single individual and his friends encounter. They are hardly representative of the opinion or behavior of large groups in Russian society. Interesting as a foreigner's impressions are—whether of a journalist, student, tourist, or businessman—they give us a limited range of information, and this information tells us much more about unusual individuals than about the "normal" patterns of society at large. The same problem inheres in the other major source to which students of the Soviet Union are accustomed to turning for information on public opinion: the testimony of former citizens, called at various times immigrants, refugees, and émigrés. The most socially varied group was the one that left the Soviet Union during World War II. This group, who described for the most part the Russia of the 1930s and earlier, was interviewed right after the war in European displaced persons' camps, and analyzed in the seminal works of the Harvard Project, a massive study sponsored by the Air Force. Since that time much has obviously changed in Russia, and there is now the testimony of Soviet citizens who have more recently left that country. The problem here is that though their testimony is dramatic, interesting, and often profound, it is, again, unrepresentative; that is, one cannot say anything about what forms attitudes for broad segments of Russian society. The reasons are well known. People who leave that society are not only those who are able to do so (a small minority of the population), but also those who have already formed negative opinions about the society. The overwhelming majority (perhaps more than 90 percent) of émigrés who have come to the United States have at least a college education, while only 4.5 percent of the citizens in the Soviet Union do. In addition, the émigrés are far more urban (and urbane); they are much more likely to live in the Western urban centers of Russia; they have a very narrow range of elite professions; and they have standards of living in the Soviet Union consonant with that socioeconomic status. In addition, they are, in terms of ethnic identification, to a great degree members of the minorities in Soviet society. When we study the growing literature emerging from recent arrivals, literature that is by no means homogeneous, we gain insights into the attitudes of interesting and talented individuals, but, again, we do not know what attitudes broad strata of Russians hold.

As is known from experience with surveys in the United States, the best way to tap reliable public opinion among large groups in society is the public opinion poll. No surrogate fulfills the requirement of representativeness. But why is representativeness so important? It is important only if one wants to go beyond an individual case to generalize either about a larger group in the population or about processes that underlie attitude formation in the society. Naturally, one may have in mind either the society as a whole or some segment of the society, for example, the college educated, or women, or farm families. But the important thing is that as a result of a properly designed public opinion poll, that kind of generalization may be made with some confidence. It may not be made if the opinions upon which the generalizations are based are drawn from sources that do not represent that larger population. What guarantees that the subgroup in fact represents that larger group for whom generalizations will be made is a complex question, and the science of sampling provides the guidelines. What that science tells us, however, is that construction of the sample should not be influenced or biased by the habits and predispositions of the observer. The observations of visitors and former citizens cannot meet that criterion. But those observations, interesting in themselves, would be made much more useful to the student of the Soviet system if they could be set off against the benchmarks or parameters that public opinion data for broader elements of the society could provide. Whether or not one may speak of a true public opinion poll or survey research in the Soviet Union is a matter that will be examined below.

Quite beyond helping to flesh out the conclusions of those who leave the Soviet Union, or whose works are smuggled out, public opinion research gives us some insight into the functioning of the everyday, "normal" communications process. It is not the exceptions we will look at here, but the rule: what characterizes the reactions of the typical, not the atypical. Although extremes may always be of immediate interest, the truer picture is drawn from that vast area under the bell of the normal curve, and it is this population to whom we turn in this study.

Underlying this study is the assumption that certain Soviet surveys may tell us something about the attitudes and behavior they claim to probe. This assumption maintains that the opinion studies conducted under the auspices of the Soviet Academy of Sciences, which I call "academic studies," do provide genuine information, or, the obverse, that they are neither fictional products of the manipulating bureaucrat nor propagandistic offerings for the disorientation of the Western observer. It should be said right away that there are surveys and surveys. There is now an ample literature in the West about the history of Soviet sociology: How it was brusquely suppressed by Stalin after creative beginnings in the 1920s and how it surfaced again during Khrushchev's regime.[1] There is, at present, no degree specifically in sociology; experts in the field usually have advanced degrees in philosophy or economics. However, there is a Soviet Sociological Association, sociology branches of the Soviet Academy of Sciences, and various publications, the most prestigious of which is *Sociological Research,* a scholarly journal published by the Institute of Sociological Research of the Soviet Academy of Sciences. It is estimated that at present there are between 2,000 and 2,500 sociologists working in the Soviet Union in about 120 cities. In this number are not only academic sociologists, but also industrial sociologists and party and trade union sociologists.[2] There are several central institutes or centers and their regional branches that sponsor public opinion research. Under the Soviet Academy of Sciences, for example, there is an Institute of Sociological Research, two sectors of which, the Sector of Public Opinion and the Sector of Sociological Problems of Mass Communication, coordinated much of the research cited in this study. In addition, the Moscow University Laboratory for the study of the functioning of the press, radio, and television—part of the school of journalism—has produced several noteworthy studies. For public opinion research geared to more clearly political questions, there is a Sector of Scientific Communism, under the Institute of Philosophy, and within the party's Academy of Social Sciences there is a Department of Theories and Methods of Ideological Work, and a new Section for Party Effectiveness Research. This last was formed at about the same time that a small information sector of the party's Central Committee was downgraded.

Not all surveys are methodologically sound enough to be cited with any degree of certainty. Especially in the days of Khrushchev, the polling that was touted with so much enthusiasm was, like so many of his hasty, ill-prepared measures of the crudest and most inaccurate kind, relying often on self-selected samples, such as providing clip-out coupons in newspapers for the activists to fill out. In no way could these results be called representative. In looking at Soviet polling, one should also be aware of the fact that outright, directly political polling does not take place for publication. The basic policies and personnel of the ruling Communist Party are not considered fitting subjects for public scrutiny, much less judgment. The whole area of what is considered appropriate for probing and reporting the public reaction in the Soviet system is circumscribed.

Still, there is a reasonably large and varied array of Soviet public opinion surveys that the discriminating observer may use to gain a glimpse of mass public opinion. One must pare away those early polls in which would-be respondents clipped and mailed in their newspaper opinion coupons, and one must eliminate the numerous amateur surveys conducted by all sorts of civic organizations or student groups in which the methods are unclear or faulty. Soviet academic sociologists are themselves uneasy about these kinds of surveys. Of the self-selected write-in newspaper sample, they have noted that although in the early 1960s it seemed a quick, easy, and inexpensive way to probe public opinion, it soon turned out that the results varied so much from year to year that the findings were too unstable to be trusted. Claims of representativeness are no longer made, and the method is rarely employed now. Only the magazine *Soviet Screen* still uses this method to any significant degree, and it gathers in about 50,000 questionnaires a year, from a total circulation of 2 million copies.[3] Equally disturbing for rigorous Soviet sociologists is the new enthusiasm for what they call "dilettante sociology": the work of volunteer amateurs busily carrying out surveys of their own devising as part of their public volunteer work (what the Soviets call "constructive leisure"), especially popular with activist youths polling their peers. This kind of haphazard activity results in what one dismayed scholar called "a pejorative view of professional sociologists."[4] That said, may one then look at the more rigorous of the Soviet studies as true public opinion polls? The answer to this more serious question must be detailed and complex.

To begin with, it should be stated that it is important to make sure one does not neglect sources of information emanating from the Soviet Union just because that particular source was not available in the past. Post-Stalin polling has had a short history, and scientific or academic polling goes back only a decade or so. The Soviets have good reason to conduct serious surveys. They have become increasingly aware of the problems in policy formation and analysis that lack of relevant data exacerbates. In their current Five-Year Plan, socioeconomic planning includes the development of sociological research, social indicators analysis, and the elaboration of the methods whereby comparability of results may be enhanced through standardization and unification of methodology, replication of studies, and the initiation of increased numbers of panel studies. They are doing this for the obvious reason that they need to know some basic tendencies in attitudes regarding family planning, moving to cities, labor transience, and communications behavior, in order to be able to plan for the future. The numbers of such studies are growing. For example, in the last five years, the number of publications containing empirical information about the functioning of the Soviet press increased fivefold over the previous five years.[5] This does not mean that the "push" of public opinion is expected to outweigh the "pull" of central policymaking activity, but only that the need to extract reliable opinion data has been articulated and funded by the Brezhnev regime. All widely circulated or official characterizations of public opinion research must emphasize the instrumental function of the research. Such analyses of attitudes and behavior are always said to further more efficient planning for control and direction of the Soviet public. However, whether the statements one continually sees to this effect constitute actual belief, lip service to the official doctrine, or some combination, is by no means clear. Regional reports published in small numbers of copies are often substantially different from the summaries of the same survey published in Moscow. The same author or research group will emphasize different kinds of conclusions depending on the audience. The actual results will not differ, but the stated purpose of the research and the use to which it may be put will be seen to differ drastically—whether to guide policymakers or to be shaped by them.

Some Western observers assert that the Soviets use public opinion in a purely manipulative way—that they intend to mold the public and therefore such research is fundamentally incompatible with Western notions of survey research. Of course, this coincides with the officially disseminated Soviet view, which stresses the guiding and expert role of the party in shaping and educating a still "immature" population. However, in fact, if not in theory, the East-West distinction may not be quite so clear and may be a false dichotomy. Much survey research is frankly manipulative in the United States as well. Market research, for example, is carried out by corporations for the more efficient shaping of public tastes and habits in order to sell a product. Politicians here commission surveys in part to find out what their constituents want, but also, in part, to plan how to shape and control public opinion. Major policy initiatives are preceded by campaigns to influence and change the public mind. It is the academic survey that is least likely to have a direct policy connection.

An important distinction between Soviet and Western surveys may be found in the kinds of subjects that are considered appropriate for research. As noted earlier, directly political polls are considered inappropriate for publication in the Soviet Union, since the "uninformed," "inexpert" judgment of average citizens about their rulers is considered illegitimate in terms of the official doctrine. On the other hand, there are areas of public opinion research that are more public in the Soviet Union than in the United States. For example, audience preference in television programming is, in the United States, largely a matter for research by the television industry itself. Surveys are conducted within the industry and the results rarely surface, except in the sense that changes in programming might reflect in-house survey findings. In the Soviet Union, this kind of research is part of what academic sociologists do, and the results are published by the academic press.

But even more basic is the question of efficiency. Certain attitudes and predispositions of the Soviet population are now considered by the leadership to be of great consequence in planning the economic development of the country. Just as a reassessment of efficiency considerations is visible in the new policies, so too have the leaders reassessed the impact of their communications policy. It is no longer assumed, as it seems to have been under Stalin, that blanketing the public with repeated messages necessarily results in the persuasion and "brainwashing" of that population. It is no longer assumed that just because a message has been broadcast, televised, or printed, it has been received, understood, and assimilated. As the following chapters will show, the Russian public, when examined scientifically, turns out to be much less homogeneous, monolithic, and malleable than the Soviets (and Western observers who were, perhaps, persuaded by the Stalinist theories of their communication efficacy) had thought. Once these assumptions have been made, the door is open to a consideration of the public's attitudes and demands. Greater efficiency, greater reach, and greater penetration may be accomplished only by utilizing that opening and thus, ipso facto, granting validity to those demands. Purely manipulative surveys cannot logically exist. The real question for the leadership is no longer whether public opinion should be listened to, but how much. The more the policies take account of opinions and attitudes, the simpler might be the task of implementation, but the greater the distance traversed from pure manipulation. It is a continuum, not a dichotomy.

A second reason why one may usefully study certain Soviet opinion surveys is that one finds that comparison of the media studies used here reveals the kind of internal consistency and theoretical comparability that gross falsification of results would not permit. Since most of the studies we use are published by academic centers in various regions of the Russian Republic, fairly distant from one another, this consistency seems even more impressive.

## THE TOO-POSITIVE RESPONSE

A more subtle question about the utility of analyzing Soviet media research may be put in the following way: Even if the academicians operate with maximum scholarly restraint and rectitude in the most acceptable fashion of sociologists everywhere (the maximal assumption), won't the average Russian citizen, given his experience of Stalinist terror and surveillance and his assumed fear of deviance from the official norm (the maximal assumption), feel constrained to give unrealistically positive answers to all the questions put to him?

One should be aware, first of all, that the overly positive response is a phenomenon present in virtually all opinion research everywhere. The Soviet case is a case on a continuum. A great deal of research has been done by Americans on the so-called "acquiescent" respondent, the respondent who wants to please the interviewer and say something agreeable. It is known that "people tend to give some edge of favor to responses that seem more, rather than less, socially acceptable, whatever their true situation. . . ."[6] Beyond this bias, there is another phenomenon that tends to exaggerate the weight of the positive response: when people are asked in a direct way to rate something, they tend to favor the positive side of the response. A series of indirect questions will, to some degree, reduce the bias of the positive. Then, too, in American opinion research, it has been found that, for example, marital satisfaction seemed unrealistically high in the face of rapidly increasing divorce rates, or that during the conflict both in Vietnam and in the streets, the feeling of "contentment" was reported as very high in the opinion pools. The seeming disparity between survey results and personal experience may be explained by the fact that "the visibility and even the genuine political influence of public discontent and protest usually registers in psychological magnitudes which vastly outweigh the fractions of a population which are actually feeling the discontent."[7] Even though vocal and important groups may feel deeply about certain issues, that intensity may not be present over vast areas of the population living their everyday life. The fact of an upward positive bias in opinion findings is a methodological constraint that may, to some extent, be countered by the judicious use of indirect questions. Yet, if there is an across-the-board bias, it may in a sense be simply accepted, and the important questions, that is, the *differences* among groups and their attitudes, will be relatively unaffected. "When we view objects from an angle under clear water, there is a very similar absolute displacement. Yet if the surface is calm, we see objects below in essentially their proper shape and proper relationship to one another."[8] As we shall see below, it is these differences that are of greatest theoretical interest in probing Russian attitudes.

The degree of positive bias may very well be much higher in the case of Soviet opinion surveys; that society may be much further along the continuum of the constraining pressure of the positive response. To the extent that it is a generalized bias, it does not remove the differences in responses among groups. The positive bias is a phenomenon with which the Soviet sociologists whose work will be analyzed here are very familiar, and certain techniques have been worked out to reduce its effect. These are the most important methods the Soviet sociologists use to counter the effect of a too-acquiescent respondent:

• Comparisons of responses with relevant democraphic data. For example, in 1966 the national newspaper *Izvestia* had a circulation of 7.9 million copies and received from readers some 469,000 letters to the editor. For every 100 copies, about six letters were sent in. In a readership survey it was found that about 7 to 8 percent of the respondents declared they had written such letters in the recent past. One has more confidence in the survey finding because it is very close to what was already known by other means.

• Reduction of value expectations by indicating acceptability of alternative responses; for example, instead of "Do you regularly brush your teeth?" the substitution of "Some people, because of the morning rush, don't always have time to clean their teeth. Has this happened to you?"

• Avoidance of emotional freight in questions like: "Do you spend time raising your children?"

• Presentation of several differing opinions and asking respondent for choice of a variant. To dispel fear of criticizing, instead of asking "How do you rate . . . ", present a number of variants preceded by "Some think. . . . "

• Use of indirect questions.

• Use and comparison of several questions, a positive answer to all of which would be internally contradictory.

• Variation in questions, so that a yes answer is not necessarily positive; for example, "Some people think that this film is not a success. Do you agree with this?"

• Explicit and emphatic explanation of measures taken to guarantee anonymity.

• Replication of study and comparison of results.[9]

It is too obvious to require restatement that the task of Soviet sociologists is extremely demanding and difficult; they walk a narrow line between official disfavor and scholarly integrity. Conditions there, both past and present, may hardly be said to favor frank, free, and open exchange of opinion. On the other hand, the surveys contain much valuable information for an analysis of Soviet society. The utility of the information exists because Soviet sociologists have tried to reduce the positive bias that to some degree inheres in all surveys, but is probably much more pronounced and serious in the Soviet case. Not only have they developed the techniques listed above, but also they avoided the use of any directly political questions.

By raising questions about survey research techniques that are derived from American experience, I do assume that the Soviet Union may indeed be compared at least in some ways to other political systems, and that some of the research techniques and findings encountered elsewhere will be of help in assessing the tendencies and dynamics of Soviet society. I would also suggest that in analyzing the Russian mass media audience, one should be aware of the methodological problems one might expect even in the most experienced and advanced media studies: those in the United States. Any analysis of media consumption and attitudes toward the media in socialist countries, regardless of the problems peculiar to those systems, will be unlikely to overcome the gray areas of conceptual and methodological difficulty present in most Western studies. It is essential in considering these questions to keep in mind the problems, constraints, and patterns involved in media research in general or in the United States, where it is most advanced and where most experience has accumulated, before one may look at the state of the art in socialist countries. Media research is a most imperfect thing even where most advanced, and seems to be subject to certain weaknesses or constraints. As will be seen below, however, the kinds of questions one asks about the media audience are of crucial importance in the validity and utility of the results—and that is true both of Western and of socialist systems.

## LOCAL AND NATIONAL POLLS

Must one have large, national studies with large samples in order to examine media audiences? In both the Soviet Union and the United States, there are relatively few studies that use national samples. Over 90 percent of the studies of the American television audience are based on local surveys with small sample size. National samples are used by Nielsen and Roper, as well as in some few, though important, academic studies.[10] Of the Soviet surveys I analyze, the majority also are local in scope. In the Soviet Union, as in the United States, the sociological study utilizing a national sample constitutes a very small proportion of the total number of studies conducted in the country. It was found that in all sociological publications from 1970 to 1973 in which level of research was reported, the national sample was used in not more than 1 percent of the studies, the republic level figured in 7 percent of the studies, and the province level in 8 percent of the studies. The rest were local, either rural or urban.[11]

A study based on a national sample is a very expensive project. Most studies conducted by scholars are not funded lavishly enough for the construction of a national sample. However, the question of funding should be considered apart from the conceptual difference between most local and national surveys. There is a theoretical reason why local studies are useful. Most studies, both in the United States and the Soviet Union, seek to relate media behavior to other variables. The hypotheses they pose do not involve estimates of, for example, the size of the national audience for a particular event or for a particular kind of programming. Rather, most studies formulate hypotheses concerning the relationship between media exposure and certain variables. The variables of theoretical interest to American and Soviet sociologists are similar: sociodemographic groups, such as the aged, the young, the poor, and others. The choice of variables and their theoretical import will be discussed below. Here the point is made that a small-scale or local survey is the typical media study, in both the United States and the Soviet Union, in large part because the questions posed by the investigator seek to uncover relationships between or among variables. In American television research

most academically conducted studies of audience viewing have
involved limited samples drawn from defined geographical areas.
Usually, the purpose has not been to measure program popularity,
but to relate the quantity and nature of exposure to television and
other mass media to other variables. . . . [A] methodological limit
lies in the use of samples representing specific areas of populations.
For example, one would not venture to estimate audience size for
educational television from Lyle's small Denver sample. . . . However,
his finding that the educational television audience is disproportionately drawn from the higher educated is not only not surprising, but
a relationship which probably can be considered applicable to other
urban populations.[12]

Similarly, the theoretical questions for the Soviet mass media audience are related
not so much to total size of audience for this or that program, but rather to the
way in which certain variables or characteristics relate to media consumption
and attitudes about the media. It is the effect of the variable that is of interest
both in the American and in the Russian cases, not the overall size or aggregate
number. One would not compare numbers of American and Russian audiences,
but the theoretical relationships that are revealed by studies in the two countries.
No prior claim is made, as will be seen below, that the two societies will be identical or even similar, grosso modo, in those theoretical relationships.

Since the bulk of American and Soviet studies of the media rely on small-
scale local surveys, how may one generalize beyond the single locale in which
the survey was conducted? The Denver study mentioned above was, in a sense,
validated or confirmed by other studies that compared data from still other
small-scale surveys from other communities. The comparison of results of other
local surveys is a way of solidifying one's conclusions and enhancing the reliability
and validity of one's generalizations. That is, in general, the method adopted by
media analysts in the United States in order to overcome a fundamental limitation
characteristic of media research, and the method is used to overcome the same
limitation in Soviet media research. Some of the surveys upon which this book
is based are national and a very few are drawn from non-Russian territories; the
preponderant majority of sources relate to Russian-language media and Russian-
Republic audiences. I have collected a number of extensively reported local
surveys, and comparing them strengthens the representativeness of the findings.
In fact, the method of comparing similar communities is increasingly a method
employed by the Soviet sociologists. For example, one social scientist found
that the results of six different studies (from six different locales) of leisure time
use were extremely close, and that research on the professional orientation of
youths in one urban school system had been supported by results of other studies
that had replicated the study in other locales and, similarly, with other major
studies.[13] The specific issue of Soviet sampling techniques will be discussed
below. Here, suffice it to say that the constraint inherent in the use of the local
sample will be treated as it is in American media research.

## THE QUALITY OF ATTENTION

> Viewing is an activity with a wide range of participator correlates, including rapt attention, discontinuous attention while engaged in other activity, occasional viewing in spurts while moving in and out of the viewing area, and passive, inattentive aural monitoring while remaining in the same room as the set. . . . The consequence is that the actual quantity of the television content consumed remains ambiguous. . . .[14]

Analyzing attention is a problem in all media studies. The quality of attention is unmeasurable. It is for this reason that the Nielsen ratings have limited utility, since they only measure the amount of time a television set is turned on, making no distinction between a set absentmindedly left on by the man walking his dog and a set playing to the concentrated attention of a family of six. It is true that recent work does attempt to distinguish between the consumption of television as primary activity and as secondary activity.[15] Some attention to this problem may be seen in the work of Soviet sociologists who noted, for example, that in rural settings the viewer turns down the sound for opera broadcasts, but does not turn off the set. In general, this book makes no attempt to infer a particular kind of attention or level of concentration from the media studies conducted in Russia; audience attention may well range from passive boredom to fascinated involvement. Increased or reduced amounts of exposure will, however, be important variables.

## PREFERENCE AND BEHAVIOR

American and Soviet media analysts do not use a single method to estimate media consumption. Several methods are used in each society, and an unavoidable consequence is noncomparability of results. For example, in television audience research in the United States, use of Nielsen methods, or Roper-type questionnaire methods, or the diary method will all yield somewhat different results. There is an inevitable problem of comparability in absolute levels of viewing as a function of the methodology employed. However, findings about within-sample differences would be comparable. The same inherent methodological constraint governs the Soviet studies.

The major American discussions of attitudes toward the media record what people think or say they think in response to various questions, and it is not possible to infer behavioral correlates from these statements. In fact, the whole area of audience preference is, in the United States as compared to the Soviet Union, underresearched. Most studies of television program preference in the United States are conducted by the television industry itself and are revealed only in the form of programming decisions. Similarly, in newspapers it is the advertiser who is responsible for the limited number of studies of content preference. In the Soviet Union, much greater attention is given to the question of subject matter and program-type preference in the media, and some Soviet sociologists have related preference statements to actual behavior in media consumption. As to methodology, the Soviet sociologists tend to follow that elaborated in the United States, with the consequent limitations. Of television preference research, a prominent American scholar noted, "There is also no well-developed methodology for studying preferences beyond tabulating expressed declarations in regard to program categories. . . ."[16] But in the Soviet Union, research about audience preference is often supplemented by and compared to actual bahavior in media consumption, thus providing an important additional dimension.

## FACTORS AFFECTING MEDIA CONSUMPTION

In this study, media behavior is related to other factors. The same factors appear to be of theoretical interest to both Soviet and American sociologists. The choice of these variables is based on empirical and theoretical grounds, and in spite of the differences in the two societies, there is reason to use these same variables. No inference is made that the effect of the variables, the intensity or direction of the relationship among the variables, is identical or even similar in the two societies. I *do* make the assumption that the Soviet Union may indeed be compared to other societies, that comparative theory may be utilized in analyzing Russian society, and that similarities as well as differences are salient issues.

The variables I relate to media consumption are the major social characteristics of education, age, occupation, social class, urban and rural residence, sex, and family and life-cycle variables. Empirically, it is evident that these variables do account for significant differences in media consumption both in the United States and in the Soviet Union. Theoretically, these variables stand for complex processes in the formation of the human being, his attitudes and behavior. "For example, persons of different ages, races, income, or urban-rural residence may have characteristically different ways of evaluating the same objective situations in no small measure because they bring different standards of comparison to bear upon these evaluations."[17] Other examples: theoretically, aging is linked to loss of mobility, reduced income, infirmity; "income is something of a reflector of differences in the objective comfort of situations. . . . Education is something of a reflector of differences in awareness of alternatives. . . ."[18] These variables may also be interrelated, although not necessarily pushing in the same attitudinal direction. In the Soviet case, some of these factors may figure far more importantly than they do in the United States, and other factors, such as membership in the Communist Party (which will be examined in a later chapter), are unique to the Soviet case.

## TIME FRAMES AND VALIDITY OF RESULTS

A serious question in any opinion research is raised by the passage of time. At what point are one's results out of date? For example, one sees routinely, in textbooks and other studies of the Soviet Union, the merging of the findings of the Harvard Project (where respondents are generally describing experiences in the Soviet Union of the 1920s and the 1930s) and descriptions of Soviet society of the 1960s and 1970s provided by travelers, émigrés, and Western reporters. There are no strict rules governing permissible or acceptable amounts of time during which the "warranty" of the data is in effect.

In part, the problem is a technical one. The survey is a difficult and time-consuming form of research, and from initiation of project through data collection to analysis and publication, several years are necessarily involved.

But it is also a theoretical problem that has two dimensions. First, on the one hand, the survey instrument may be designed to explore immediate and highly volatile attitudes. A Gallup poll that watches the weekly reaction to the president's initiatives is geared precisely to capture the volatile and momentary reaction, and the questions it poses to the respondent are appropriately designed. Weekly television ratings are products of similarly intended probes. On the other hand, the kinds of questions posed may be designed to capture more durable and stable attitudes or responses, and these surveys will pass out of date much later.

The second dimension of the theoretical problem is associated with exogenous or external variables. The durability of the findings of the survey will be related to the effect that changes have produced in the intervening time between the original collection of the data and the date on which they are being cited. We may suppose that between the Harvard Project and the present, significant changes in Russian society, attitudes, and behavior might have been produced by World War II, the continued reign of Stalin, the wartime and postwar purges, major demographic changes, the political leadership periods of Khrushchev and Brezhnev, changes in interactions with the West, and developments in communications technology and distribution. The variables are too numerous to catalogue, but they are of sufficient magnitude to warrant caution in the use of the survey that preceded them. Even though there is always change of some sort over time, we may more confidently assume greater durability and stability of results over periods in which less dramatic change relevant to the subject studied has intervened. In this study, greater stability of results may be assumed because of the kinds of questions to be explored (that is, complex relationships underlying differential consumption and attitudes) and because of the time period under review (the Brezhnev years). The major change in communications media during this time has been the belated, though massive, introduction of television for private household ownership. The steepest rise in density of television sets took place in the decade of the 1960s. After 1970 the rate of increase is markedly slower as saturation is approached, particularly in urban areas. It also is known that the effect of the television revolution was least felt in the consumption of newspaper communications, so that the durability of these surveys is greater than would be that of surveys that focus on radio, the leisure-time activity that was most seriously displaced by the introduction of television into the Soviet Union (as it was in the United States). The findings reported and the relationships in this book are likely to be among the more stable.

## SOVIET SURVEY METHODS

The methods used to collect the data and the format for the reporting are of great importance in determining the degree of confidence with which one may use survey results in a study of the Russian mass media audience. The question of representativeness was discussed above. A second methodological question—how error may be reduced—has been discussed in another context. The problem of the respondent prone to answer too positively is a problem of error, and the methods used to deal with it may be of broad utility for many kinds of error. The no-answer response is a distinct problem. Attention must always be paid to the weight of this response. It varies in frequency and may arise from lack of information about the subject, lapse of memory, or deliberate refusal to respond because of protest or lack of trust. The same methods used to reduce the too-positive answer have also been used to reduce the no-answer response when it is a negative response to questions perceived as too direct or threatening. Unless otherwise noted, I do not use survey findings in which the no-answer response may invalidate the conclusions.

Sampling methods in Soviet surveys have been found to vary quite widely. No survey based on a self-selected sample will be included in this study. Sample size is, if anything, greater in Soviet surveys than in comparable Western research. A study of virtually all Soviet academic sociological publications between 1970 and 1973 found that only 14 percent used samples below 500, 20 percent used samples of over 2,000, and almost 10 percent used samples of over 3,000.[19] As the science of sampling develops, smaller samples may reliably be constructed. The Soviets have been reducing their sample size, in part by applying sampling methodology worked out elsewhere. Particularly interesting in this regard are references to American procedures that have been built into Soviet surveys. For example, sampling methods used at the Institute for Social Research of the University of Michigan were applied in the *Literary Gazette* national readership survey, and such journals as *Public Opinion Quarterly* are cited as sources of procedures adopted in Soviet surveys.[20] Whereas the *Izvestia* survey used a sample of 8,000, the *Pravda* survey was able to reduce its sample to 4,000 with improved sampling techniques.

Although in the past it was common to conduct polls where people worked, this is changing. Now the use of territorial samples, polling towns, and precincts is growing, as it becomes apparent that only in the territorial sample will certain groups in the population (such as retired people, housewives, schoolchildren, college students) automatically be included. As one sociologist put it, only the territorial sample "can secure the simultaneous study of all strata and groups of the population."[21] Whether the sample is based on the territorial configuration or the place of work, the particular locus is determined by its demographic characteristics in terms of the subject to be studied. In looking at certain aspects of the small city, for example, sociologists found that Voronezh was to be one of the typical (for the Russian Republic) centers to be surveyed because in its population proportion of the able-bodied age group, the proportion of the student population, and other characteristics, it was close to the average for cities of that size in the Russian Republic. Studying a particular locale because of its characteristics is a technique commonly used in survey research everywhere. The Minneapolis-St. Paul area was the site of a study of television audiences because "it offered a fairly representative mix of broadcasting stations. . . ."[22]

How it is determined whether an individual is included in a sample is important for the validity of the results. As noted earlier, selecting oneself for inclusion is hardly likely to produce confidence in the results. Methods of determining or constructing the sample changed quite markedly over the course of the rebirth of Soviet sociology. As in other aspects of Soviet surveys, so too with regard to the sampling techniques: the early surveys tended to use less systematic and unbiased methods, while the more recent academic surveys, the ones that are examined in this study, have tended to use the basic forms of probability sampling in use in the West. In the survey of Soviet sociological publications between 1970 and 1973 cited earlier, it was found that three types of probability sampling are used most: 38 percent of the studies used systematic sampling, 25 percent used stratified sampling, and 22 percent used cluster sampling. A fourth type of probability sample, the simple random sample with and without replacement, was used in 8 percent of the studies.[23] With each of the four types statistical inference may be made, because the probability of any individual falling within the sample is essentially equal to that of any other individual. To put it another way, the probability that an individual will be included in the sample has not been determined by the personal bias of the researcher. Another type of sampling, found in 5 percent of the Soviet studies, is the sample that attempts to cover the universe of people to be studied. This is, of course, an extremely expensive and unwieldy form of research, one that may be replaced when small samples representative of that universe are substituted. Finally, in some 2 percent of the studies under review, the quota sample is used.[24] The quota sample, which was used extensively in the early days of the post-Stalin sociology renaissance, is a nonprobability sample. Probabilities are unknown and statistical inference may not legitimately be used. In the quota sample, the object is to survey certain percentages or "quotas" of particular interest, whether persons of a certain income range, age, place of residence, and so on. The problem, in terms of the kinds of generalizations one may draw, is that it is left to the pollster to fill up his quota, and he may choose people because he knows them, because they live or work nearby, or for any of a variety of reasons that might skew the results. Since probabilities are not equal, one cannot say whether or not, or to what extent, that sample "stands for" some larger group or process, and one may not draw conclusions beyond the given group of people in the quota sample. However, the results of a study using quota sampling may be extremely interesting and may tell us a good deal about those particular respondents, and we may compare the findings of such a study to others that use probability sampling techniques in order to assess its credibility. It is important to note that the use of quota sampling among academic sociologists in the Soviet Union has declined sharply in the last decade as the importance of reliability and validity has become recognized and has required, in turn, increasing attention to methodological rigor. In trying to make surveys more reliable and, therefore, more useful, it has also been recognized that categories of analysis must be standardized. In the past, survey researchers would make up their own demographic categories or subdivide their samples as they wished. As a result, findings of various surveys could not be compared. This problem, so common during the early days of post-Stalin polling, is less serious at present; replicated studies are more plentiful and the attention to comparability of categories of analysis is seen in articles dedicated to the problem and in the surveys themselves.

Soviet surveys are rarely reported with the completeness and detail the reader would like to see. When the publications come from a regional publisher, a province branch of the Academy of Sciences, the information is usually far more detailed and extensive than when the same surveys are reported in the national press or by the large Moscow publishers. However, the characteristic mode of reporting is the percentage distribution of responses (or, in some cases, time spent in a certain activity) by sociodemographic or other category of analysis. It is virtually impossible to perform statistical operations involving scaling of attitudes or to make fine distinctions concerning the interrelation of independent variables. The typical format in Soviet publications is what one normally sees in this country in Gallup and Roper polls or, for that matter, in most of the major sources of research into the American television and newspaper audience: the cross-tabulation of type of respondent and frequency of response in percentage or, occasionally, in absolute numbers.[25] Whereas more sophisticated reporting of survey results might, indeed, be most desirable in looking at Russian media audiences, it would be unrealistic to hold expectations for Soviet surveys that are hardly typical for the modal type of American survey.

In sum, by careful and rigorous piecing together and comparing of the Soviet surveys produced within the past ten to 15 years by reputable sociologists in the Academy of Sciences network, we obtain a rare look at Russian public opinion. By restricting our study to those surveys that impose upon themselves serious methodological constraints, we may isolate patterns of media behavior and, more important, relate those patterns of behavior and attitudes to differences in certain characteristics of the population. In so doing, we will be able to uncover to some degree the sources of satisfaction and dissatisfaction, approval and criticism, and see what shapes opinion and why.

# NOTES

1. For a thorough discussion of the history of Soviet sociology and opinion research, see Elizabeth Ann Weinberg, *The Development of Sociology in the Soviet Union* (London: Routledge and Kegan Paul, 1974); Gayle Durham Hollander, *Soviet Political Indoctrination* (New York: Praeger, 1972).

2. V. I. Chuprov and V. P. Shchevin, "Nauchno-Metodicheskie i prakticheskie predposylki razvitia edinoi sistemy upravlenia, planirovania i koordinatsii sotsiologicheskikh issledovanii v strane," *Sotsiologicheskaya informatsia i prakticheskie voprosy koordinatsionnoi raboty v oblasti sotsiologii* (Moscow, 1977), p. 14.

3. V. E. Shlyapentokh, *Problemy representativnosti sotsiologicheskoi informatsii* (Moscow, 1976), pp. 158-59.

4. V. E. Shlyapentokh, *Sotsiologia dlya vsekh* (Moscow, 1970), p. 47.

5. *Sotsialnye issledovania: postroenie i sravnenie pokazatelei* (Moscow, 1978), footnote 2, p. 235.

6. Angus Campbell, Philip E. Converse, and Willard L. Rodgers, *The Quality of American Life* (New York: Russell Sage Foundation, 1976), p. 106.

7. Ibid., p. 103.

8. Ibid., p. 105.

9. Shlyapentokh, *Sotsiologia*, p. 235; V. E. Shlyapentokh, *Problemy dostovernosti statisticheskoi informatsii v sotsiologicheskikh issledovaniakh* (Moscow, 1973), pp. 70-131.

10. Some examples of important surveys based on national samples are the surveys conducted by the Institute of Social Research of the University of Michigan and the Russell Sage Foundation, as well as the national survey of television audiences conducted by Gary A. Steiner in 1963 (*The People Look at Television*, New York, Knopf) and the resurvey done by Robert T. Bower in 1973 (*Television and the Public*, New York, Holt, Rinehart and Winston).

11. Shlyapentokh, *Problemy representativnosti*. For a description of the methods employed in the nationwide opinion survey of *Pravda*'s readership, see the source cited in note 21.

12. George Comstock, *Television and Human Behavior: The Key Studies* (Santa Monica: Rand Corporation, 1975), pp. 16-17.

13. Shlyapentokh, *Problemy representativnosti;* Shlyapentokh, *Sotsiologia.*

14. Comstock, p. 17.

15. John P. Robinson, *How Americans Use Time* (New York: Praeger, 1977).

16. Comstock, p. 17.

17. Campbell et al., p. 15.

18. Ibid., p. 147.

19. F. E. Sheregi, "Analiz praktiki primenenia vyborochnogo metoda v sovetskoi sotsiologii," *Proektirovanie i organizatsia vyborochnogo sotsiologicheskogo issledovania* (Moscow, 1977), p. 116.

20. Shlyapentokh, *Problemy representativnosti*, p. 195.

21. I. B. Muchnik, E. S. Petrenko, Ye. E. Sinitsyn, V. E. Shlyapentokh, and T. M. Yaroshenko, "Problemy postroenia vsesoiuznoi territorialnoi vyborki dlya sotsiologicheskikh issledovanii spetsifika postroenia pervoi stupeni," *Proektirovanie i organizatsia vyborochnogo sotsiologicheskogo issledovania* (Moscow, 1977), p. 8.

22. See Bower.

23. For a general discussion of these probability samples, see H. Blalock, *Social Statistics*, rev. 2d ed. (New York: McGraw-Hill, 1979).

24. Sheregi, p. 121.

25. See, for example, the widely used multivolume set published by the American Newspaper Publishers Association, *News Research for Better Newspapers*, as well as Steiner and Bower.

# 2

---

# WATCHING TELEVISION
# IN RUSSIA

In the United States television captured the living room in the decade of the 1950s. During those ten years the number of homes with a television set went from 4 million to 46 million, and thereafter tapered off as virtual total saturation was achieved.[1] In the Soviet Union the authorities were slow to seize on television as a major communications agent, and it was not until the late 1960s and on into the 1970s that television gained a mass audience. In 1960 there were only 4.8 million sets in the Soviet Union, but by 1975 that number had climbed to over 55 million and over 6.5 million sets were being produced annually.[2] Nearly 1.5 million sets are color sets, about 6 percent of the total. Broadcasts are transmitted through telecenters, which operate at the national (Moscow) level, the republic level (there is a major one in each of the 14 non-Russian republics), 19 are in cities of a million people, and 90 are located in various provincial capitals. In addition to the one in Moscow, color telecenters are planned for each of the republics as well as in the cities of Leningrad, Novisibirsk, Sverdlovsk, and Gorky. By 1975 color programs, carried by the national channel 1, had risen to 60 hours a week. In the early days of Soviet television, programs were broadcast only three to four hours a day, but as the number of hours of programming increased, unsuspected dilemmas were created for the government. The surface lines of communication could provide a rather broad dispersion of signals for a single channel, less so for a second, and a third reached only the nearby city. Apparently this resulted in local telecenters' substituting their own programs for the central programs they were unable to receive or amplify. In this way central programming was interrupted for certain localities and, of great consequence for the authorities, Russian-language transmissions were replaced by programs in local languages. The obvious centrifugal pull of localism or nationalism, however tentative, was countered by the formation in 1970 of a more centralized direction of all television and radio transmissions in the Union-Republic State Committee for radio and television under the Council of Ministers of the USSR. By this time most viewers could receive the first channel from Moscow, broadcasting all "social-political and cultural events both inside the country and outside," while an additional channel, located in each republic, would add its broadcasts in both Russian and the local language. But the decisive step in the centralization of transmissions across this vast country was the development of communications satellites, which were able to transmit to telecenters as many as eight hours away, which is the time-zone difference between, say, Murmansk and Magadan. In 1976 the surface network of television and radio cables had reached more than 67,000 km, unevenly distributed over the country; the European part was densely covered with networks of lines, while Siberia and the East often lacked anything other than local lines. Satellites are clearly the best solution, and their signals are picked up by a cable system for retransmission locally.[3] The non-Russian areas pick up Russian-language broadcasts and add broadcasts in their local languages as well.

The USSR still has not matched the density of television ownership of the United States. In 1974 about 67 percent of the families in the Soviet Union owned a set, as compared to about 95.5 percent density in the United States.[4] However, the distribution of sets in the Soviet Union is uneven. Some three-quarters of the Soviet population live in "zones of secure reception," and here some 85 to 90 percent of the families have television sets.[5] City households are much more likely to have a set than are rural ones, mainly because income is higher. In cities, ownership of a television set is not significantly related to the socioeconomic status of the family, and density of set owning is about the same for all social classes.[6] But in the countryside that is not so. One survey showed that an average of 42.3 percent of the rural households had television sets, but that among subgroups, one finds such differences as an 84.6 percent figure for specialists with higher education, 68.4 percent for engineers, 22 percent for farm workers, and 9.1 percent for families where the head of the household is retired and living on a pension.[7] The main reason given by people without television sets in the home is that they do not have enough money to buy one. Fewer than 3 percent said they did not own a set because they had no interest in television. Soviet authorities figure that the demand for television sets is very high and that as incomes rise, near total saturation will be achieved.[8] Interestingly, the higher density of sets in urban areas does not mean that urban residents watch more television. In fact, the reverse is true. There are 1½ times *fewer* television sets in the countryside than in the city, but television-watching time in the countryside *exceeds* that in the city by 1 1/5 times.[9] There is no question that among the rural population in Russia, television is the most popular and widespread form of mass communication.[10]

How much time do Soviets watch television and what do they watch? Soviet television broadcasts fewer hours than does American television. Their first channel, on the average, broadcasts from eight o'clock in the morning to eleven or twelve o'clock at night. The second and fourth channels go from 7 p.m. to 11:15 or 11:30 p.m. The third channel, broadcasting seven hours of programs daily, is strictly instructional, and carries lessons for schoolchildren and adult-education courses. The viewer may take such courses for credit, and the programs are, on the whole, dry instruction in, say, mathematics or history, or foreign languages (French, English, Spanish, and German). However, recently, perhaps as a result of surveys showing very low interest in these programs, some of the courses are being dramatized, made more visual and engaging. Literature lessons, for example, show a famous actor recounting how he approaches a famous play; novels are dramatized. Art and music lessons are next on the list for refurbishing. The first channel is, as noted earlier, the most important nation-wide television resource. The fourth channel features such entertainment programs as feature films, variety shows, and plays. It broadcast, in 1978 alone, some 1,246 hours of music, ballet, and opera. The second channel is devoted to programs of more local interest and less ambitious features for people in the region.

The content of Soviet programs differs considerably from that of American programs and, as will be seen later when program preferences are discussed, tastes are also somewhat different. Programming is decided and administered centrally and must conform to Soviet doctrines and norms of what is permissible and desirable. All the shows, whether explicitly instructional or not, are educational—that is, they have a distinct didactic flavor and are used to help socialize the viewers. The quiz show, a popular item, is an example. One, called "Let's Go, Girls" ("A nu-ka, devushki"), is telecast once a month for an hour and a half. Everyone wins something, a small prize of flowers or books, and the object is not to get rich, but rather to popularize occupations and encourage good work. Recently, a group of policewomen performed on the show, marching and drilling to music, using their nightsticks. They were asked ("quizzed") how to improve traffic rules, and they offered such suggestions as redesigning traffic signs. Other game shows and competitions involve family sports activities and information on other socialist countries. There is a popular detective series, called "The Experts Investigate," said to be based on material from actual police archives. There is, however, little of the sex and violence that U.S. police stories have; rather, attention is paid to the social origins of criminal deviance. The experts are a trio of young detectives, two men and a woman. A very popular program is "Incredible but True," broadcast twice a month and hosted by the son of the famous physicist Peter Kapitsa. It examines subjects from the point of view of science and ranges broadly over such questions as lasers, craft techniques, why the Tower of Pisa leans, and Japanese solar batteries. The noted ballerina Maya Plisetskaya discussed "science and ballet." Then, too, there are programs where figures of high culture appear: Bella Akhmadulina reads her poetry; Richter plays the piano; plays are telecast in their entirety, as are other cultural events. Musical variety, or pop music shows, and feature films, many from socialist countries, are very popular, as will be seen later. Two foreign nonsocialist television productions that have enjoyed great success recently have been the BBC's "Forsyte Saga" and "Lassie."

The news program "Vremya" (Time) is telecast in a half-hour segment at 9:00 p.m. Domestic news takes up almost two-thirds of each telecast. The program opens with news of the government, then domestic (heavily economic or production oriented) news, and then important regional news. Finally, before the closing three or four minutes of sports and two minutes of weather, there is international news.[11] Added to this is now another news program, "Today in the World," an attempt at a more lively format and some, though still very limited, on-location reporting. The debut of this program followed with conspicuous rapidity Brezhnev's November 1978 address, in which he was highly critical of the stultifying and ineffective use of the media.[12]

Are Soviets as keen viewers as Americans are? The Nielsen reports, which give the number of hours a television set is on (and not who in the household, if anyone, is watching), found in 1974 that the average daily television-viewing time for an American household came to six hours and 15 minutes. Perhaps more satisfactory for making cross-national comparisons are the Roper data. Here, viewing is measured in terms of median hours of daily viewing per individual respondent. For 1976, the average American said he watched television some 2.53 hours a day. For college-educated Americans, who have been steadily increasing their television attention, the median daily viewing time was about 16 percent less than the national average.[13] In recent years, a number of people who analyze television's impact on society have tried to separate the time devoted to television as primary activity from the time during which the set may be on but attention is divided, and television is a mere background, or secondary to some other activity, such as cooking, cleaning, eating, or conversing. Surveys that calibrate more finely the time spent watching television suggest that the average number of hours spent daily on television as primary activity may be only as little as 1.5 hours, with perhaps another 35 minutes daily spent on television as secondary activity.[14]

All of these methods of calculation give a figure for television watching that exceeds the median number of hours per week for the urban Russian viewer. In 1975 men averaged some ten to 12 hours of viewing per week, while women averaged about six to seven hours a week.[15] The American weekly average would come to 17.29 hours, using the Roper method, or 14.35 hours weekly, using the diary method and adding primary and secondary activity viewing. But Russian viewing habits come much closer to American habits if one looks at the Russian rural population. Here it was found that, on the average, men watched some 13 hours and 18 minutes weekly, women, nine hours and 55 minutes, and children, 14 hours and 22 minutes. For the group most attuned to television, the rural worker, viewing on the average may consume over 19 hours a week, compared to ten hours for his urban counterpart. That this pattern is very different from the urban pattern is suggested by a Leningrad survey that found that only about 16.5 percent of the 9,916 respondents in the poll could be termed as "extremely enthusiastic" about television watching; that is, they watched between 15 and 27 hours a week. Another 15.5 percent were termed "enthusiastic," watching from ten to 15 hours weekly. Altogether, 69 percent of the entire sample of Leningraders watched ten or fewer hours a week, and of that group, slightly fewer than half watched under three hours a week.[16] As might be expected, the greatest amount of television watching occurs during "prime time"—there, as here—from about 7:30 to 11:00 in the evening.[17]

The pronounced difference in television-viewing habits between rural and urban Soviets is related primarily to the kinds of options each population has. Options for using leisure time that cost money are less accessible to rural farm workers. The income for these workers has climbed significantly from 1950, when it was only 41 percent of the nonfarm average income, but it still lags about 14 percent behind nonfarm income.* It is not surprising that there is a connection between lower income and more television viewing, since alternatives to television might well be more expensive; the same relationship may be seen in studies of the inner-city viewer in the United States.[18] Then, too, in rural Russia, there are fewer things to do than in the city. Traditionally, only three options were widely available in rural areas: going to the club (a rural social center equipped with reading materials and other leisure activities, and often the place where lectures and semi-official gatherings are held), going to the movies, or visiting friends and relatives. Movies are not as attractive an option in the countryside as they are in the cities because new films take several months to get there, and in many rural halls there are inferior projection facilities and uncomfortable seating. Rural inhabitants are much more the homebodies than their urban counterparts. In Russia a rural family spends an average of three-fifths of its leisure time at home.[19] Given the lack of alternatives, it is understandable why television made the spectacular progress it has in the Russian countryside and why it might be expected to continue toward saturation of the area.

There are also differences in the way in which people of different ages depend on television to fill their leisure time. It has been observed that changes in life-style associated with aging are related to the amount of television one watches.[20] As one gets older mobility is lessened, in some cases income diminishes, and doing things outside the home becomes distinctly less attractive. In the United States both men and women over 50 watch more television than do young men and women. Men over 50 watch some 3.9 hours a day, as compared to men between 18 and 49, who watch 3.1 hours a day; women over 50 watch 4.6 hours a day, compared to 4.1 hours for the younger women.[21] In Russia

---

*This figure includes estimated income from private agriculture (garden plots).

there is an increase in viewing time as age increases. People over 61 watch television more than any other age group, with the exception of children 11 to 15.[22] As in the United States, Russian youth over 16 watch television least of all, and probably for the same reasons: they are the most mobile age group and have the widest range of options for leisure-time use outside the home. Later, marriage and raising a family will drastically reduce this range of options, and still later, aging and infirmity will further constrict them. Russians over 30 were found to be twice as likely to spend leisure time at home than were people under 30.[23] Young children in Russia are now, most certainly, the "television generation." Rural children between the ages of five and 16 now watch 85 percent of everything that is broadcast and spend as much time in front of the set as at school.[24]

In the United States housewives are among the most avid consumers of television programming; they form the bulk of the daytime audiences.[25] The Russian housewife, like her American counterpart, is a devoted television viewer. In fact, Russian housewives spend more time watching television than any other group in the population except retired people. However, as a percentage of the female population, the Soviet housewife is in a group far smaller than her American counterpart. Only about 15 percent of the Soviet female population of able-bodied age neither works nor studies, and this 15 percent includes women who are unable to work because of health reasons, as well as mothers of exceptionally large families, especially in the Central Asian provinces. The working woman, both in the United States and in the Soviet Union, cannot find the time to spend on television that the housewife or the industrial worker does.[26] In the Soviet case, the well-known "double burden" of the working woman requires her to shoulder the additional burden of housework and shopping, scarcely shared by her husband and only fractionally relieved by household appliances and fast-food outlets. In 1970 the Ministry of Trade for the Soviet Union estimated that about 30 billion hours were lost annually simply in trying to buy things: waiting in endless lines and going to and from stores. It was estimated that this works out to an average loss of 170 hours, or seven full days and nights during the year, for each person 16 and over.[27] But this estimate fails to take into account the fact that in 75 percent of all families it is the woman who does the shopping; in only about 1 percent of Soviet families do husbands do the shopping independently.[28] This means that three-quarters of those 30 billion hours lost each year trying to buy things should be shifted entirely to the female population, most of whom will also be holding down full-time jobs. Similarly, and in virtually the same proportion of families, women do the housework, such as cooking, washing, and housecleaning, by themselves. These patterns, which the Soviets themselves regard as "vestiges of past inequality," are changing. In the more developed urban areas of Russia, household duties are coming to be shared by husbands, though not without considerable social strain and domestic conflict as the transition takes place. One survey in a Moscow suburb found that the more the husband took on household tasks, the greater were the number of quarrels with his wife.[29]

Working women would undoubtedly have more free time if they were assisted by appliances at home and public catering services (or fast-food chains) in town. This situation, though currently difficult for women, is changing. Politburo member Mikhail Suslov recently announced that according to the 1970 census, about 50 percent of the families in the Soviet Union had washing machines and about a third had refrigerators, a tremendous improvement over the previous decade.[30] As might be expected, the more highly educated the working woman, and therefore the more skilled her job, the more likely she is to have appliances at home, to be able to afford them and to value their utility. Even in such a modern city as greater Moscow, a survey among working women with little education and repetitive, unskilled jobs found that only 25 percent had washing machines, 42 percent had refrigerators, and 20 percent had vacuum cleaners.[31] As to the possibility of buying food to go, it appears that here, too, Russian women working in high-skill jobs were more than ten times as likely to use these services than poorer, less well-educated women. But, in general, women are reluctant to use commercial cleaners and food operations even if they were more widely available. Surveys have found that the very high level of dissatisfaction of customers is based on the quality of service, the long waiting time and disorganization, and the "rudeness of the people one deals with."[32]

But one should not draw simple conclusions about the immediate freedom and increased leisure time that owning household appliances might seem automatically to produce. In the United States, where such appliances are more widely available, it has been found that housewives were actually spending more time on chores in 1965 than they did in 1954. Whereas there had been significant decreases in time spent on food preparation and ironing, there had been greater increases in the time spent shopping and in travel, particularly travelling to accomplish household errands and ferrying children. The suburban life-style and multiple car ownership created a situation for the nonworking American wife in which "the net effect is that greater amounts of time are being spent on home management." However, ten years later, the situation had changed dramatically. From 1965 to 1975 a 20 percent drop had taken place in time spent on family care—time taken away from household cleaning and upkeep. It is television that has soaked up that newly created leisure time. "The increasing pervasiveness of television in the expanding world of leisure is probably the most significant contrast between the everyday life in 1965 and that of a decade later.[33]

Then, too, differences among women in time spent in front of the television set are related to family questions. In general, men and women with families spend more time than do unmarried people of both sexes watching television, and mothers of youngsters watch less than their husbands.[34]

Education is one of the most important factors influencing television watching in Russia. In the United States, the lower the level of education, the more television time is consumed. However, if we look just at programming during weekends and on evenings, we find that, although education makes quite a difference in attitudes toward programs, it makes very little difference in total amount of time consumed.[35]

In Russia the college graduate will watch between 25 percent and 33 percent less television than the average viewer. College students watch less than half the television that the average urban Russian does, and scientists, among the most highly educated in the country, spend even less time than that in front of the set, making them the single group least likely to consume television time.[36] There is a virtually linear relationship between watching time and level of education, and there is near complete congruence between the extreme groups, defined in terms of education and television consumption. In rural Russia the same relationship obtains: workers with elementary education watch most often, and the intelligentsia and high-school-educated workers both watch less.[37]

A peculiar paradox will emerge when we look at the reactions or preferences exhibited by various groups with respect to particular categories of programs on Soviet television. In spite of the fact that those with the least education are by far the greatest consumers of television time, this group often seems to have the lowest level of interest in particular programs. In one survey such viewers, when asked about preferred programs, were hard put to come up with names of shows they had watched. The conclusion reached by the researchers was that these less well-educated viewers had the set on a great deal of the time, but often did not understand the material presented by programs or were inattentive to the content. Not surprisingly, Russians have found that 93 percent of the rural viewers with fourth grade education or less simply do not understand programs on political and social subjects. In tables representing percentage of respondents watching specific programs, this educational group is often severely underrepresented.[38]

Perhaps the clearest analysis of this phenomenon was given by Lidia de Rita in her brilliant study of the impact of television on the lives of southern Italian peasants. She found that for those who have the lowest levels of education, who do not read newspapers or magazines, the news programs are unquestionably the least interesting and least comprehensible, because even a very clear and simple discourse "inevitably presupposes the presence of certain cognitive structures in which to place the various news, statements, and arguments," without which the program is not understood. Even, for example, among the young and the more attentive, a particular, immediate meaning may be clear, but it will soon be forgotten precisely because of the absence of "schemes of cognitive referents in which the substantive elements may be ordered." Without such hooks on which to hang the associations, the program might be recalled as interesting, but the respondent would be unable to say very clearly what it was about.[39]

## PATTERNS OF VIEWING

Surveys find that responses to program categories of types have been rather stable. A large survey of Moscow viewers asked respondents to name which of 34 representative programs they watched. The most popular, those in the top seven, claimed more than 60 percent of the respondents, and these were clearly entertainment programs: movies and musical variety shows. Sports broadcasts, garnering an audience of 69.5 percent of the people polled, were in eighth place. For these most popular programs, age or level of education did not affect the results.[40] At the other end of the scale, the least popular programs were those that were in places 26 to 34 and were watched by fewer than 20 percent of the people surveyed. Three kinds of programs made up this group: educational programs on industrial production, "high culture" programs (such as poetry readings and broadcasts of symphonic music), and certain children's programs. The very last two spots were assigned by the respondents to adult education (instruction) programs, which are tuned in by 5 percent of the viewers, and programs reporting on economic production, which appeal to a mere 3.7 percent. A look at the audiences for feature films and sports and for the news broadcast "Time" reveals that differences are slight in the film audience, although scientific personnel are least interested. People in the armed forces are most interested in sports (and are undoubtedly encouraged in that interest, since a significant part of the amateur athletes who compete successfully in international events are drawn from armed forces sports clubs), and people with very little education are least interested. There is less interest in watching news programs, especially among the young and the less educated.

Although broadcasts of symphony concerts have relatively little appeal for Muscovites—only 9.5 percent watched them—other classical music programs are far more popular, such as opera and ballet, which appeal to almost 21 percent. If these types of "high culture" programs are examined in terms of the level of education of the viewers, then sharp differences become apparent. Whereas only 1 percent of the respondents with elementary school education watch poetry readings, 15 percent of the liberal arts college graduates do. And while about 6 percent of the less well educated watch operas and ballets, some 28 percent of the college graduates watch these programs.

A similar relationship between education and program choice is seen in the percentage of respondents who say they watch the political program "Unmasked Rulers," a program of exposés of "capitalist monopolists." In overall popularity rating, this program occupies fourteenth place and attracts an average of 42.2 percent of the respondents. However, in that audience is only 12.5 percent of the group with fourth grade or less education, 40 percent with high school education, 47.7 percent with college education in the humanities, and 47.7 percent with college education in technical and scientific fields. But the group with the highest levels of education, the scientists, are termed "least satisfied with existing programs" and, when asked about their patterns of viewing, display "the least interest in a significant portion of the broadcasts."

In contrast, industrial workers, many of whom are young, spend most of their television time watching musical entertainment and youth programs. "High culture" offerings—poetry, opera, ballet, theater classics, symphonies—enjoy very little popularity among this group.

Age makes some difference in patterns of viewing. Interest in political programs rises with age, peaking at about 55, and declining thereafter. Broadcasts of symphony orchestra concerts appeal less to younger audiences (4.7 percent of the age group under 11, 10.8 percent of the age group 36-40, up to 19.5 percent over age 60), and the reverse is true of pop music shows. Sex differences result in somewhat different patterns of viewing, and the patterns are curiously stereotypical: men watch sports programs more and women watch more about the arts, including plays. As both Moscow and Leningrad surveys have confirmed, women are significantly less attentive to sociopolitical programs. All programs are more popular with married people than with unmarried people. At a certain stage in the life cycle of the family, options are severely reduced and parents stay home, devoting more time to television and watching more varied kinds of programs. In the United States, sex differences in types of programs watched are minimal. Men might spend somewhat more time watching sports programs, and women watch a few percentage points more of the comedy-variety programs, but there are virtually no differences in news, information, and public affairs programs watching. Nor are there anything but miniscule differences in the proportion of time spent watching programs of light drama or music.[41]

One of the ways to look at demands of television viewers, without treating the question of dissatisfaction head-on in a threatening fashion, is to compare what people actually watch and what they would like to include in an ideal schedule of programs. Such a study was done in a major survey in Sverdlovsk. There are disparities between what people watch and what they would like to watch. The explanation for such disparities is not so simple. In part, they could be explained by a desire on the part of the respondent to put in his or her ideal schedule those categories of programs that appear to gain official and/or social approval. The very large disparities in programs involving "high culture," education, and sociopolitical themes might well be derived from this tendency to seek social and political approval. People say programs of this sort should be included in an ideal schedule far more frequently than they actually switch them on. But this hypothesis appears not to explain equally well all of the disparities. It may be that the demand for certain types of programs is accurately shown in the ideal schedule, and that it is dissatisfaction with the existing programs in the given category that accounts for lowered consumption. The greatest disparity in the survey results comes from the responses of the intelligentsia concerning scientific-educational programs. Here, twice as many people would include such programs in their ideal schedule than actually watch them regularly. These programs, it would seem, are particularly close to the interests and background of the intelligentsia, a college-educated, high socioeconomic status, and largely technically trained group. They show the highest demand for such programs along with the lowest rate of viewing of all groups in the survey. Similarly, they display the greatest demand for sociopolitical programs and, although they do not have the very lowest rate of regular viewing, they do show the greatest difference between demand and actual consumption. The pattern of dissatisfaction is a familiar one, as scientists have consistently shown the greatest degree of dissatisfaction with existing television fare and the least amount of time consumed in watching. In part, this behavior is related to their presumed greater range of options for utilizing their free time. But it must also be related to an overall dissatisfaction with the quality of programming in areas of interest to them.

Actually, the question of satisfaction and dissatisfaction with the political type of television program is a complex one. In all the polls, Russians consistently say, regardless of age, occupation, and education, that the most important function of television is to acquaint its audience with political events, both international and domestic. But people tend to use television primarily for entertainment and relaxation. This is not to say, however, that interest is not high in television news; on the average, almost two-thirds of the Russian respondents in a major survey watched the news. The reason that the category of sociopolitical broadcast is not very popular in the polls is because the news *analysis* program is not very popular and tends to bring down the averages for the popularity of the category as a whole. For the most part, the analysis program appeals to those with college education and the subgroup of party activists.[42] The comprehension of such programs depends to a large extent on cognitive skills and, therefore, on education. As the Moscow survey shows, there is a clear connection between level of attainment of education and interest in political programs. As levels of education continue to rise in the Soviet Union as a whole, one may imagine that there will be increased attention to this type of program. However, it is also true, as both the urban and rural surveys in Russia indicate, that levels of dissatisfaction also rise with increasing educational attainment. Those with higher education are most interested in the general area of politics and political analysis, but are far less satisfied than their less-educated fellow citizens with what they find on television.

Although the comparison is a loose one, Russian television programming has been compared to what Americans see on public television and, to some degree, Americans behave much as their Russian counterparts do in watching television. Of course, the numbers of Americans watching public television are far smaller than the numbers watching commercial television. For example, Luciano Pavarotti's recital attracted 3.6 percent of the households in New York owning a television set.[44] When Vladimir Horowitz played at the White House, the live broadcast gained a 3.8 rating (percent of households with television) in New York, and the star-studded American Ballet Theater extravaganza in May 1978 did better there, gaining a 5.8 rating. But, by far, the most popular programs on public television are those dealing with science, in particular the "National Geographic Specials," one of which in the spring of 1978 was seen by a whopping 11.7 percent of all American households owning television.[44] These ratings become meaningful when compared to the penetration or popularity of commercial television programs in the United States. During the last week in March 1979, the most popular program on commercial television gained a rating of 30.2 percent, and the fifteenth-ranked program received a rating of 22.7.[45] Thus, if one talks about the characteristics of the public television audience in the United States, one should bear in mind that, although growing, it is a small audience relative to that of the commercial networks and therefore has special characteristics.

One of those characteristics is educational attainment; education and public television viewing are related. But only 6 percent of the college-educated portion spend as many as five hours a week watching. The median amount of weekly public television for these viewers is one hour and 50 minutes. These amounts will vary with the educational level attained by audiences and, according to reports for spring 1978, college-educated viewers were reported to have watched a weekly average of slightly over three hours. Viewers with high school or less education averaged about two hours of public television consumption weekly. On American public television, most of the prime-time audiences, and most particularly the audience for public affairs programs, are usually skewed up-scale with respect to education and income. One example of a striking exception was "Live from the Grand Ole Opry," the audience for which was much more likely to have had high school than college education and slightly more likely to be blue collar than white collar. Although audience patterns change, public television programs that involve instruction in doing things like cooking, yoga, and efficient shopping are less likely to appeal to audiences so clearly dominated by the well educated.

In terms of satisfactions and dissatisfactions, in both the United States and Russia the better educated are less enthusiastic and more critical of television. American studies have shown that the better educated prefer other media for news, are less likely to enjoy the programs they do see on television, and state that they prefer different types of programs than those the average viewer prefers. The better educated want more informational and educational content instead of entertainment programs. Education, more than any other variable in American studies, explains the differences in attitudes toward television. However, curiously, the better-educated American's behavior—how he actually watches television— hardly differs from anyone else's: "The educated viewer distributed his time among program types—comedy, movies, action, information and public affairs, and so forth—in just about the same proportions as did those with less education, and even when he had a clear choice between an information program and some standard entertainment fare, he was just as apt as others to choose the latter."[46] And he watches about as much television on weekends and evenings as anyone else. Even when a special group was separated out—a group of people termed "high culture" (they went to concerts, read books frequently, played a musical instrument, went to meetings or lectures)—this group, although watching television somewhat less than others, tended to distribute their viewing time almost exactly as did those of medium to low culture. The only real difference between the two groups was that the high culture people watched 4 percent more news and 4 percent fewer sports programs.[47]

Some argue that the discrepancy in attitudes and actions might be related to the wish to conform to norms of prestige or "cultured" behavior. But it has also been argued, more convincingly, that the highly educated viewer has higher expectations and an enlarged conception of the potential of television, and that it is likely

> that the college man's expressions of attitude and preference derive, in part, from his notion of television's larger social role; a conception of what *might* be, translated into particular opinions about how television is currently performing and what it should be emphasizing. Much of higher education, after all, is devoted to the detached examination and evaluation of what would otherwise be considered normal and taken for granted; and we would expect of those who have undergone its regimen some ideals of performance, for television and for themselves, beyond the current norms.
>
> There is some evidence that the educated viewers are not at the moment finding in television the content they think should be provided for the public. When we asked about reasons for viewing, it was those with *less* education, not the college educated, who were apt to say they usually watched "because I think I can learn something". . . . It may be fair to say that television is not meeting the educated viewer's standards, and thus he is not expecting to find, and not seeking among its programs, the edification he thinks it should provide.[48]

The dilemma for the educated is more dramatic in Russia. The options for receiving information are significantly more limited; the thirst for acquiring it is, perhaps, greater. The salience of news, and most especially of any news of the international arena, is so strong among Russians that it cuts across social classes, levels of educational attainment, and media of communication. Unlike his American counterparts, however, the college-educated Russian does behave differently from the average Russian. Although he, too, turns to television primarily for entertainment and is, perhaps, embarrassed to say so, he stays away from much of the fare that attracts others. His demands are greater, and so are his alienation and frustration. He has not given up books and certainly not newspapers, as have others, and those who study the phenomenon are convinced that the educated will maintain this gap as, perhaps, in older days, when the top of the educational pyramid had little in common with the masses. This notion seems more credible when one realizes that the well educated of very different ethnic groups behave similarly with regard to television. In Moldavia, in Estonia, in Georgia, as well as in Russia, the indigenous intelligentsia watch less television, are more selective, and less satisfied than the workers and white-collar employees in their republics. However, other groups of differing ethnicity do not exhibit similar characteristics. Workers both on farms and in industry show clear differences from republic to republic in the way they regard television programming. There are similarities across the vast Soviet Union in the attitudes of the very well educated, but not among others. The intelligentsia, at least with respect to the powerful new medium of television, are more homogeneous than any other group.[49] On the other hand, television is still new, and perhaps the true television generation has not arrived yet in Russia. In time, the well educated may conform, not without guilt, to the pattern of the average.

## NOTES

1. Robert T. Bower, *Television and the Public* (New York: Holt, Rinehart and Winston, 1973), p. 3.

2. *Narodnoe Khozyaistvo v 1975* (Moscow, 1976), p. 491; L. N. Kogan, "Televidenie i dukhovnaya kultura sotsialisticheskogo obshchestva," *Televisionnaya auditoria: struktura, orientatsii, kulturnaya aktivnost* (Sverdlovsk, 1973), p. 127.

3. V. I. Zadorkin and A. V. Sosnovsky, "Perspektivy kommunikativnykh vozmozhnostei televidenia kak sredstva osveshchenia kulturnogo urovnya," *Issledovanie rosta kulturnogo urovnya trudyashchikhsya* (Moscow, 1977), pp. 90-101.

4. V. E. Shlyapentokh, "Rost urovnya obrazovania i otnoshenie k sredstvam massovoi informatsii," *Problemy sotsiologii i psikhologii chtenia* (Moscow, 1975), p. 92.

5. L. A. Gordon and E. B. Gruzdeva, "Rasprostranennost i intensivnost chtenia v gorodskoi rabochei srede." *Problemy sotsiologii i psikhologii chtenia* (Moscow, 1975), p. 60.

6. I. D. Fomicheva, *Zhurnalistika i auditoria* (Moscow, 1976), p. 57.

7. V. I. Volkov and G. A. Voitovetskaya, "Struktura, biudzhet vremeni i orientatsii teleauditorii," *Televisionnaya auditoria*, pp. 26-27.

8. Kogan, p. 128.

9. Volkov and Voitovetskaya, p. 34; E. P. Mikhailova and N. N. Mikhailov, "Selskaya televisionnaya auditoria," *Televisionnaya auditoria,* p. 102.

10. S. N. Soskin, "Preodolenie sotsialnykh raznits v sfere kultury: formirovanie sotsialnoi odnorodnosti selskogo naselenia," *Issledovanie rosta kulturnogo urovnya trudyashchikhsya*, pp. 49-50.

11. For an interesting critic's view, see Rita Cirio, "Chi beve Breznev campa cent'anni," in *L'Espresso*, Rome, January 29, 1978, pp. 74-81.

━ 12. Dan Fisher, "Change in the Air on Soviet TV," *Washington Post*, January 21, 1979, p. K2.

13. Roper Organization, Inc., *Changing Public Attitudes toward Television and Other Mass Media, 1959-1976* (New York, 1977).

14. John P. Robinson, *How Americans Use Time* (New York: Praeger, 1977).

15. Gordon and Gruzdeva, p. 61.

16. V. E. Shlyapentokh, *Sotsiologia dlya vsekh* (Moscow, 1970), p. 166.

17. Boris Firsov, *Puti razvitia sredstv massovoi kommunikatsii* (Leningrad, 1977), p. 121.

18. Bradley S. Greenberg and Brenda Dervin, "The Role of the Mass Media for Urban Poor Adults," in *Use of the Mass Media by the Urban Poor,* ed. Bradley S. Greenberg and Brenda Dervin (New York: Praeger, 1970), pp. 3-29.

19. Mikhailova and Mikhailov, p. 103.

20. See Bower.

21. *Social Indicators 1973* (Washington, D.C.: U.S. Department of Commerce), p. 228.

22. S. A. Iosifyan, *Televidenie i zritel'* (Moscow, 1975), p. 28.

23. Mikhailova and Mikhailov, p. 112.

24. Ibid., p. 113.

25. Bower, p. 19.

26. *Social Indicators*, p. 225.

27. I. Ia. Matiukha, *Statistika zhiznennogo urovnya naselenia* (Moscow, 1973), p. 116.

28. V. E. Shlyapentokh, *Kak segodnya izuchaiut zavtra* (Moscow, 1975), p. 125.

29. Z. A. Yankova and P. A. Protasova, "Sovremennaya struktura vnutrisemeinykh otnoshenii," *Problemy sotsiologicheskogo izuchenia semi* (Moscow, 1976), p. 38.

30. A. G. Kharchev and S. I. Golod, *Professionalnaya rabota zhenshchin i semya,* (Leningrad, 1971), p. 76; John P. Robinson, *Changes in Americans' Use of Time: 1965-1975* (Cleveland: Cleveland State University Communication Research Center, August 1977).

31. Z. A. Yankova, "Izmenenia struktury sotsialnykh rolei zhenshchiny v razvitom sotsialisticheskom obshchestve," *Izmenenie polozhenia zhenshchiny i semya* (Moscow, 1977), pp. 35-37.

32. Kharchev and Golod, p. 3.

33. John P. Robinson and Philip E. Converse, in "Social Change Reflected in the Use of Time," in *The Human Meaning of Social Change,* ed. Angus Campbell and Philip Converse (New York: Russell Sage Foundation, 1972), p. 49.

34. Volkov and Voitovetskaya, pp. 32-33.

35. Bower, p. 35.

36. Iosifyan, p. 30.

37. Mikhailova and Mikhailov, p. 104.

38. Iosifyan, p. 62.

39. Lidia de Rita, *I Contadini e la televisione* (Bologna: Il Mulino, 1974), pp. 143-44.

40. Iosifyan, pp. 58-59. The following information is drawn from Iosifyan, pp. 57-72.

41. Bower, p. 134.

42. Mikhailova and Mikhailov, pp. 142-45; Volkov and Voitovetskaya, pp. 54-56.

43. *New York Times,* February 14, 1978, p. 66.

44. My thanks to Ken Wirt, of the Public Broadcasting Service, for supplying this information.

45. *New York Times,* April 4, 1979, p. 26.

46. Bower, p. 179.

47. Ibid., pp. 138-39.

48. Ibid., p. 180.

49. Iu. V. Arutiunyan and L. M. Drobizheva, "Obshchee i osobennoe v sotsiolno-kulturnom oblike sovetskikh natsii," *Sblizhenie sotsialnoklassovoi struktury sovetskikh natsii i narodnostei* (Moscow, 1977), pp. 29-30.

# 3

# TELEVISION AND THE DISPLACEMENT OF TIME AND VALUES

What has television done to other activities? In Russia there have been distinct losers in the competition with television, and there have been activities that have suffered very little. The chief victims in the competition with television are radio, movies, lectures, and theater. Leisure time spent at home is less affected than are the activities for which one has to go out; the latter are reduced when television is introduced. Leisure spent alone is less affected by television than is social, or as the Soviets say, collective activity. However, radio listening, which has suffered most from competition with television, and newspaper reading, which has suffered least, are both individual activities that may be carried on at home. It seems that radio listening, the closest equivalent to television, has been most drastically reduced in both the United States and Russia. Similarly, in both countries it has been the newspaper that has proved most resistant to displacement by television. It is true that sometimes Russian viewers will say that as a result of watching something on television (for example, the BBC's "Forsyte Saga"), another type of activity was stimulated, in this case, the reading of the Galsworthy novels. However, it is sobering to note that in Russia, for every increase in books read or movies and theater presentations attended, there is a fivefold decrease due to television.

Different kinds of changes have been observed for different groups after television was introduced. Russian men in urban areas have been reading fewer books, but have engaged in more sports, meet friends more, and have not decreased their reading of newspapers. Russian urban women, however, have decreased their newspaper and magazine reading and sports activities; they have reduced time spent reading books, but not to the degree men have done. Women, much more than men, feel television has stimulated movie going and listening to the radio. For both men and women, the obligations involved in raising a family have led them to decrease their other activities, particularly going to the movies, and to substitute television watching. In a way, the situation of the aged is similar; they too are confined to their homes because, in many cases, of the infirmities of old age or the financial constraints of living on a pension. People on pensions in the Soviet Union showed the greatest reduction in the reading of newspapers, magazines, and books due to television. But even among people be-between 41 and 50, there were clear declines in the number of times they went to the movies, the theater, or the club. For young people (those between 21 and 25), television stimulated their own sports activities.[1]

The written media demand cognitive skills that the visual media do not, and one would expect, therefore, that there would be a connection between level of education and consumption of media other than television once television has been introduced. This has happened in Russia. The higher the level of education, the less significant the degree to which reading is curtailed. Among those with higher education, books were read more often after the television set was purchased.[2] It may be that the decrease in reading among older television viewers may in part relate to loss of concentration and physical difficulties, but also to the fact that the older population is less well educated.

Does television's impact wear off in time? Even though it is still fairly new to the Soviet Union, we do know that the reading time of urban viewers is most severely reduced during the first year they have the set. After the set has been in the home for up to five years, the diminishing reading pattern levels off and after five years, reading begins to increase, although it does not reach the pretelevision level.[3] Even after five years of having a set, other activities were still depressed: more than 25 percent of those surveyed were going to the movies and attending lectures and discussions less frequently, 20 to 30 percent were going to theaters or sports events less regularly, and only 4 to 6 percent found they were actually going more to sports events or visiting friends.[4] It would appear that even though there may be a very strong distortion of leisure-time activities when the television set is a wondrous plaything, and even though that initial impact might wear off, still, some five years after, a residual change is there.

This change is even being felt during working hours. Should television sets be placed in factories to relieve the boredom of repetitive low-skill jobs? Some Russians argue that television has a salutary effect in such cases; others argue that having the set on at work is distracting and annoying. Soviet officials, faced with a new source of conflict on the job, have suggested that factories set up regulatory procedures where such disagreements exist. In some cases, watching television while at work has resulted in near total neglect of responsibilities, as in the case of stranded Muscovites waiting for buses while the drivers were glued to sports programs at the garage. The game over, suddenly caravans of delinquent buses showed up at the crowded bus stops.[5]

The impact of the introduction of television is more strongly felt—much more strongly felt—in the rural areas than in the urban centers. For people living in the large cities in Russia, the principal reductions came in going to lectures, theater presentations, and sports events. A large spectrum of "losing" activities was given by people who lived in medium-sized cities: reductions in reading, radio listening, movie going, and socializing.[6] In rural areas, too, people also were more likely to curtail than to increase their leisure-time activities after they started watching television. Radio, in rural areas, is not the prime victim that it is for the average national viewer; it places third, after going to the movies and the club. The rural family is less mobile than its urban counterpart. More time is spent at home because of farming as occupation, weather and transportatin problems, and reduced options for entertainment. Rural females have much greater household demands—in part because of the traditional culture, and in part because of the lack of amenities and appliances—than do urban females, and radio listening can be combined with cooking, housework, and looking after children. Like their urban counterparts, though to a greater degree, leisure-time activities outside the home and those that take place in a social setting are reduced. And although television may stimulate some activities for some of the population, on the whole there is a far greater proportion of reduced activities as television enters daily life. Newspaper reading for urban viewers suffered least when television was introduced; this is not the case for rural viewers, but it is relatively little affected.

Although newspaper reading seems not, on balance, to be strongly affected by competition from television in rural areas, that is not so when one looks at subgroups in the population. The effect of television watching is radical for those with relatively little education. At the beginning of 1969, inhabitants of a rural community were surveyed about their reading habits. The community had not been able to receive television signals at the time of the first survey and was able to do so when the respondents were resurveyed in a panel study at the end of 1971. It was found that among people with a low level of education (up to fourth grade), reading of all kinds, including newspapers, had been severely curtailed, and virtually all information now was provided by television and radio. However, among those with high school education, the reduction of reading had been much slighter, and among those with higher education, reading habits remained virtually unchanged.[7] This was true not only of newspaper or current events reading, but also of fiction and purely entertainment reading. It was also found that reading habits, regardless of level of formal education, were of great importance. "Reading families" were defined as those families that had a library at home and where books are bought or borrowed. These households watch some six to seven hours a week less than do "nonreading" households. After the introduction of television, reading in these households had actually increased.[8] Reading habits, even independent of level of education, have displayed a stubborn tenacity in Russia. Whether such will be the case for the new television generation remains to be seen. At present, the influence of education is exceptionally strong and seems to prevent the rearrangement of leisure-time activities.

The debate about the effect of television on movie attendance is still going on in the United States, where television has saturated the country for over two decades. Like the United States, the Soviet Union has experienced sharp drops in movie attendance since television was introduced. Between 1960 and 1976, the average number of movie visits per urban inhabitant declined from 22 to 16.[9] A recent survey of movie going in Moscow found that as a result of competition from movies on television, each month Moscow movie houses lost about 1.2 million sales, or 18 million sales a year, which constitutes about 15 percent of the planned quota or norm. Although some, like the well-known Leningrad sociologist Boris Firsov, had roundly denied the possibility that this would happen and later amended that prediction to speak of only a temporary downswing, the fact remains that television has made significant inroads into movie attendance.[10] There is also evidence that television might have altered the composition of movie audiences. In an experiment, the same film was shown in one rural community on television and in the local social center at the same time. More than 90 percent of the youth preferred to go to the local center, while older people preferred to stay home.[11] In Moscow it was found that at least 20 percent of the people who do go out to some movies say they are deliberately missing other movies to see them on television.[12] There are differences in the degree to which television diminishes movie going. Young people prefer socializing to staying at home and are among the least interested in television; they will see the movie in the theater rather than on the television set. City people find their movie going less affected than rural inhabitants, and movie attendance has not suffered as much in urban as in rural areas. The reasons are not difficult to see: projection equipment, halls, and seating facilities are poorer in rural areas; movies are slower to arrive; weather and seasonal work are obstacles to going out at all; and transportation and roads present an even greater problem.

The case of radio is an interesting one. What seems to have happened, especially in rural areas where it has not suffered as greatly from the introduction of television as it has in cities, is that its function has changed for the rural listener. Radio still has a distinctive function that renders it less threatened and more relevant in rural than in urban areas. It tends to take on a utilitarian character, providing news, weather, and crop information for farmers. Radio also becomes a morning activity: almost 80 percent listen to it in the morning before going off to work, and only 2.3 percent listen in the evening when television programs are on. Daytime radio listening, cited by 21.7 percent of the respondents, is mainly for women at home, retired people, and schoolchildren.[13] It is radio that tells the farming community on its way to the fields what the weather and crop forecasts are, and keeps a relatively attentive audience, even after television has been introduced. In rural Bainy, even after the introduction of television, some 17.9 percent of the respondents specially turn on the radio to hear the weather, and over 22 percent do so to find out the time.[14]

American television viewers have always maintained that television is the leisure-time pursuit they would give up first. In that sense it is, as John Robinson states, "the most 'elastic' of all activities."[15] Russian audiences react the same way; it is television that is their most expendable activity—they say. This willingness to give it up does not seem to be related to a dissatisfaction with programming. Among Russians who are satisfied with television programs, 59.9 percent are willing to give it up, and among those dissatisfied, only somewhat more (67 percent) would replace television with some more interesting option.[16] Actually, it is very difficult to estimate the weight of such statements. People in the United States who consider the undesirable effects of television to have been vastly overstated, point out that television must not have had such a profound effect on U.S. society after all since it is obviously taken far less seriously than one would conclude simply by measuring the number of hours the set is on. If viewers would so easily give it up, then they cannot be so attached to it. On the other hand, it is not being given up by great numbers of people, and newspapers have detailed the trials of those "experimental" weeks or months in which individuals who decide to give up television go through agonizing symptoms, something like withdrawal. Blackouts and blizzards produce varying results—some go "stir crazy" without television, some reestablish conversation in a family setting—but when the power goes on again, no permanent change in leisure-time activities has taken place.

From the information available about Russian audiences, it is known that since the introduction of television some other leisure-time activities have undergone some changes, and that this is different for different age groups and levels of education. But there are also broader changes that the introduction of television seems to foster. One study maintains that in the cities the amount of time people watch television is greater than the amount of time by which they have reduced their reading. It is said that the bulk of viewing time does not come at the expense of other activities at all, but has been released by the shortening of what the Soviets call "nonactive rest," which means doing nothing or hanging around. For urban women, to a lesser extent, it has been drawn from time devoted to housework. This general trend, Soviet sociologists maintain, is quite healthy for society since the saturation by television of this unstructured, aimless free time, especially for youth, might lead to the reduction of delinquency and alcoholism.

But it is not just that television is thought to reduce undesirable or deviant behavior. Some Soviet observers of the social impact of television viewing suggest that the television set becomes a magnet, drawing the family together and strengthening family ties. This, in turn, gives the family a more powerful role in socializing the young and in exerting a positive influence—as opposed to the kind of random educating experiences the child learns on the street hanging around with peers. One study even showed that spouses of different social classes found their social differences narrowed by watching television together.[17]

But the integrating effect of television watching may be only temporary. What happens when more than one set is brought into the household? Americans have had more experience with multiple sets in a single household. In 1949 the prognostications were very favorable. As a result of television watching, there was a feeling of greater family solidarity and a narrowing of the generation gap as all joined together to watch. By the mid-1950s the picture was no longer as clear. Although more experiences and information were shared due to television watching, there was a decreasing amount of conversation and face-to-face interaction. A more recent study has found that the pattern of at least two television sets in the family has increased separation: "With extra television sets in the family, it would appear that more solitary watching takes place and that joint viewing tends to separate into smaller units; the children in one room and the parents in another."[18] Something of this sort is just beginning to happen in the Soviet Union, although the lag in the provision of television sets makes it less apparent. Soviet sociologists are beginning to revise their earlier optimistic opinion of television as integrator of the family. At present, 4.3 percent of the households in the Soviet Union report owning a second set. A process is beginning that is very much like what accompanied the ownership of several radio sets in a single family; in that situation, "collective family listening has given way to individual [listening]."[19]

There is another kind of integration in which television may be a very powerful force. Television is essentially a national medium, and it may help to forge a national consciousness, a national culture, a common mode of communication. The Soviet Union is a vast country with a large and dispersed rural population, many of whom have little education. There are literally scores of different ethnic groups, and some 120 different languages are spoken in the country. In the early days of Soviet television, an ethnic centrifugal pull was present before regional transmissions were fully controlled centrally. Television provides the opportunity for a standardized message; it helps to narrow the very real differences among regions, ethnic groups, and between rural and urban populations. Particularly for rural people, isolated as they are and relatively out of touch with modern life, television may present the only effective image of a dynamic, modernizing Soviet political culture.

But there are contradictory results. A Soviet sociologist puts it the following way—diplomatically opaque, but nonetheless clearly critical:

> Observing the radical influence of television on the intensification of cultural progress [and on] the spirtual life of rural workers, we are constrained to assert a definite deformation of value structure and psychology which television has caused among a part of the rural population in the area of cultural orientation [and] in the interrelationship between creative and consumer forms of leisure time use.[20]

The goal of the Soviet leadership has always been the molding of the creative individual who objectifies by making—man-the-worker (homo faber) in Marxist doctrine. This person should be an active contributor to society. Yet one of the undeniable results of the introduction of television on a mass scale in the Soviet Union is that the so-called creative activities have declined. Time previously spent on sports, hobbies, and tourism has now been given over to television. People have begun to watch sporting events more than they actually participate in sports; they watch music made by others and do it less themselves. Although the phenomenon is more visible among the rural population, it is hardly confined to that sector of society. The television viewer is very much the passive consumer, and the Soviet sociologists have had to coin a new word to describe this process of passive leisure: relaksatsia (relaxation).

Television watching also enlarges the private sphere of a person's life and reduces the social, or collective, sector. People are staying at home more, closed in one's own family. There is a decline in socially oriented, organized activities. This is the opposite of that collectivist social spirit so important to Soviet goals in character education. Going to the movies or social centers, even visiting friends and relatives, have all declined in both urban and rural areas since the onset of television viewing. This growing privatization of cultural consumption, without the socialization (and control) benefits of group activity, has given pause to some officials.

Television's greatest impact in Russia, in terms of how people reorient their time, has been produced on those at the bottom of the social scale. The urban poor and especially the rural poor have become the greatest consumers. These are people whose level of education is very low, whose cognitive skills are not highly developed, and whose occupational mobility is very limited. It may be argued that television has reached an audience previously isolated and outside the reach of the written media and brought it into the modern world. But some Soviet sociologists argue that it is television that has further impoverished the lives of these addicted viewers and has taken from them whatever motivation they might have had to read, upgrade their work skills, or engage in other officially valued activities. They find that class differences are now in danger of being exacerbated: "[Television has] *lowered* the amount and level of various forms of cultural activity among those inhabitants whose home leisure was spiritually poor (above all, people with a low level of general education)."[21] For the masses of rural viewers, the urban life they see portrayed on television throws into startling relief the tremendous disparities between town and country. It makes the hardships of rural life much harder to bear. In fact, since the introduction of television, the number of people who have become dissatisfied with rural life has doubled.[22]

We have no way of knowing whether the balance sheet of the future will show that the disintegrative impact of television is stronger than its integrative force. We can only say now that certain contradictory tendencies have accompanied the saturation of television sets in the Soviet Union. It is true that the decision to produce television sets and price them for mass consumption and household ownership was a critical choice that the Soviet leadership was not compelled to make. They could have placed television viewing firmly in a social setting by establishing the club or political meeting place as the locus of the set.[23] That they chose the route of private mass consumption was surely related to the benefits they felt would accrue to their society by increased exposure to the medium. Everywhere the impact of television has been powerful and fraught with ambivalent consequences. We are reminded again that there is no major policy anywhere, in any society, that is free of unintended consequences.

## NOTES

1. V. I. Volkov, "Vlianie televidenia na strukturu i intensivnost kulturnoi deyatel-nosti razlichnykh sloev naselenia," *Televisionnaya audotoria: struktura, orientatsii, kultur-naya aktivnost* (Sverdlovsk, 1973), pp. 79-80.

2. V. I. Volkov, "Vlianie televidenia na izmenenie intensivnosti chtenia," *Nauchnaya konferentsia posvyashchennaya problemam psikhologii chtenia i chitatelya* (Leningrad: Krupskaya Leningrad State Institute of Culture, 1971), p. 23.

3. Ibid., p. 24.

4. Volkov, "Vlianie televidenia na strukturu," p. 82.

5. *Literaturnaya Gazeta,* April 11, 1979, p. 13.

6. Volkov, "Vlianie televidenia na strukturu," p. 83.

7. L. N. Kogan, "Kniga i sovremennoe televidenie," *Problemy sotsiologii i psik-hologii chtenia* (Moscow, 1975), p. 112.

8. Volkov, "Vlianie televidenia na izmenenie," p. 24.

9. *Narodnoe khozyaistvo SSSR za 60 let* (Moscow, 1977), p. 610.

10. Boris Firsov, *Puti razvitia sredstv massovoi kommunikatsii* (Leningrad, 1977); Firsov quoted in S. A. Iosifyan, *Televidenie i zritel'* (Moscow, 1975), p. 39.

11. E. P. Mikhailova and N. N. Mikhailov, "Selskaya televisionnaya auditoria," *Televisionnaya auditoria,* p. 106.

12. Iosifyan, p. 96.

13. Mikhailova and Mikhailov, p. 107.

14. Ibid., p. 108.

15. John P. Robinson, *How Americans Use Time* (New York: Praeger, 1977), p. 173.

16. Iosifyan, p. 36.

17. Mikhailova and Mikhailov, p. 112.

18. Robert T. Bower, *Television and the Public* (New York: Holt, Rinehart and Winston, 1973), p. 149. Whether this development is the result of tendencies toward frag-mentation of the family, or the cause of it, cannot now be established.

19. Firsov, p. 110.

20. Mikhailova and Mikhailov, p. 126.

21. Ibid., p. 110 (italics mine).

22. I. D. Fomicheva, *Zhurnalistika i auditoria* (Moscow, 1976), p. 91.

23. In China, where there are as yet very few television sets (about 2 million for 900 million people), most people watch in groups in the neighborhood or at the place of work. (See "Chinese TV: Touch of the West," *New York Times,* August 28, 1979, p. 4.) Whether private home ownership will result from higher production levels and whether the social effects will parallel those in the Soviet Union and the United States remain to be seen.

# 4

# CHOOSING AMONG THE MEDIA

When a new medium of communication appears and becomes widely diffused, there are inevitably alterations in the kinds and amount of attention given the old media. Television has had such a displacing effect both in the United States and in the Soviet Union. People's notions of what to turn to a particular medium for, which medium is the most reliable, which is the most authoritative, which provides the most nearly complete coverage—these are all elements that enter into the popularity or penetration of one of the media in competition with the rest. In the United States, where television saturation was essentially completed at least two decades before the Soviet Union, the overall trend is for convergence on television as the medium judged "best" or "most" for an increasing number of criteria. In the Soviet Union this has not happened—or perhaps not yet happened—in large part because of the tenacity of reading habits, particularly reading of newspapers. But changes are taking place, and some old habits are weakening for certain groups in the population.

The primacy of newspapers over all other media in the allocation of leisure time turns up again and again in major Soviet surveys.[1] Soviet sociologists often point to the unbroken line of first-place for newspapers in audience preference from Strumilin's early time-use of studies of the 1920s to the present. However, underneath those global figures of preferences there are rather striking differences. For example, in a survey of Leningraders' choice of medium, it was found that college-educated people preferred the written media (newspapers, magazines, and books), while those who had only an elementary education had a clear preference for television among all the media. It also was found in this study that the most active users of all media sources tended to be males with a college

*41*

education who were members of the Communist Party. The only area in which women participated more than did men was in going to the theater.[2]

That education is related to greater overall media consumption and utilization of several media is suggested also by a study of industrial engineering and technical personnel in three major Soviet cities (Kharkov, Kuibyshev, and Novosibirsk). In virtually identical proportions in each city, a clear majority of the respondents (from 58 percent to 67 percent) said that having already received information from radio or television, they would still look for that information in the newspaper. Another third said they usually read in the newspaper about events previously aired on radio or television in order to understand them better. Most of the rest, a small number, skip in the newspaper what they have already learned from radio and television.[3]

Education is one factor that is related to the expansion of media use as newer visual media have been introduced: the higher the level of education, the greater the number of media sources used. On the other hand, lower levels of education are associated with lowered frequency of newspaper reading. This association does not appear to exist for radio or television consumption. Radio and television are far more accessible to the poorly educated, whose lack of cognitive skills makes newspaper reading a chore. In general, about 20 percent of the Russian population is thought to use only a single channel of information, and that channel is not likely to be the newspaper.[4] But it is not the only factor, and the relationship is by no means strictly linear.

Age is related to the choice one makes among the media of communication in the Soviet Union. The ages between 30 and 50 is the time of greatest attention to newspapers, although age makes little difference in attention to radio or television. Why newspaper reading is much lower among the oldest age groups may be attributed in part to the relationship between age and education. In a large urban survey in the Soviet Union, it found that 60 percent of the people who were 60 or over had had only fourth grade education or less; that percentage for the rural area was 93.[5] The preference for nonwritten media among older people might well be related to the difficulty they have in reading. However, quite apart from level of education, it seems that the old read fewer books and spend less time reading, perhaps because of the fatigue and diminished powers of concentration that old age brings.[6]

Place of residence is another factor that bears on one's choice of media. Certain aspects of rural life are well known; traditionally word-of-mouth has been perhaps the primary medium of communication, particularly with the distribution problems associated with newspaper consumption. Other factors also play a role. In rural areas, the seasonal nature of work results in reduced media consumption in the summer and increased consumption in the winter, when the demands of farming are least.[7] Women agricultural workers, who have perhaps the greatest burden of working time on the job and at home of any population group in the Soviet Union, do not read newspapers very much. In a survey of media attention, only one-third of this group said they read newspapers, while about half watched television, and about half listened to radio.[8] For women who are busy caring for large families and doing housework, the radio or television set can be on in the background as a secondary activity; newspaper reading demands primary attention. Even in cities it was found that 17 percent of the respondents reported that they mixed housework and radio listening, and 16 percent said they listened to the radio while on the job or during lunch break.[9]

Statistics about ownership of radio and television sets or about sales of newspapers do not tell the whole story. They underestimate the audience. Newspaper readership research shows that in one region, for 1,944 subscribers to the national newspaper *Literary Gazette,* there were 2,440 readers in the subscribers' families. However, a larger proportion of subscribers has, it is said, been found in the *Pravda* resurvey—about three-quarters of the total readership. Among people who subscribe to no newspaper at all, almost three-quarters regularly read the central press. Twenty-four percent of the people who do not own radios listen to the radio, and 66 percent of the people who do not own television sets watch television programs.[10] Since virtually any Soviet citizen who wants a radio probably has the means and opportunity to get one, it is likely that nonowners are essentially those who do not wish to listen. Television, on the other hand, while spreading rapidly in the last decade, is not yet available to all who wish to watch. Especially in the countryside, many have to go visiting to be able to watch their favorite programs, a pilgrimage reminiscent of the early days of television in America.

Which medium becomes the most popular or widely used depends in part on what interests the public, and in part on which medium is perceived as best suited to illuminate those interests. In a major study of urban residents' preferences, the respondents were asked: "Which themes, or problems written about in newspapers and broadcast on radio and television, interest you, in general?" There is an overwhelming interest in international news, given by over 80 percent of the respondents, followed by human interest materia.', cited by 68 percent. The subject called "activities of state organs"—that is, news and reports about the functioning of government and administration— was cited as salient by only one-third of the respondents. Only about one-fourth of the respondents said they were interested in the activities of the Communist Party, the trade unions, the Communist Youth League, and other public organizations.[11]

As might be expected, there are certain differences in salience for different types of people. Men and women have different interests. Men are far more likely to be interested in sports and industrial questions and tend not to share women's interest in family themes. Youth could scarcely be expected to share their parents' interest in family life issues, and only a quarter of the 18 and 19-year-olds did so, while 70 percent of the age group 30 to 39 found these questions extremely important.[12] Differences in level of education seem to be associated with broadness or narrowness of interest. People with little education find fewer themes of interest in all media and have a narrower range of attention than do the better educated.

It is one thing to ask respondents what they find most salient; it is quite another to ask them what they actually read, listen to, or watch in the media. Answers to the second question reveal, according to the Soviet pollsters, that "the spectrum of real interests is narrower" than ideal preferences. The only really stable result, the theme that is high both in preference and in consumption, occurs in the subject matter category of "international themes," where the same very high interest is exhibited, although distributed unevenly over the different media, with the national newspaper as the chief source. Questions of international politics can be explored in the Soviet Union only in the mass media. There is virtually no other source, and certainly nothing at the local level that is not merely a delayed transmission from the central sources. This exclusive domination of a matter of great interest by the mass media might play a part in the very high actual consumption and is consistent with the ideal preferences. But what accounts for the tremendous disparity between high interest and much lower actual consumption for all other categories, such as sports, literature and art, family problems, science and technology, and crime? The structure of preferences may be roughly accurate, but the media do not satisfy those preferences and therefore there are depressed rates of consumption. The stability of the international interest might, as suggested above, result from the monopoly on material of this kind in the central media, whereas interest in the other subject matter categories could be satisfied outside the official media—by word-of-mouth, daily experience—or simply remain unsatisfied. As one Soviet social scientist concluded: "The impression is created that the interests of the public remain unrealized to a significant degree. That is why the popularity of themes set forth in connection with individual channels [of communication] is lower than those put forth in connection with mass information as a whole."[13]

At present in Russia, no single medium is perceived as the best or most satisfactory source for all subjects. For the urban viewer, the central newspaper is the single most popular source for all questions of international events. Radio and television have a very small role in these matters, but the person who seeks news of international events is an avid consumer of all media at all levels. Another very popular subject for the Russian urban public is the story on morals— this may be defined as a story that treats ethical or moral choices in everyday life, or dilemmas of behavior in the microcosm of human relations. People follow these stories primarily in the central newspaper. Related issues—daily family life, educational issues, problems of youth—are all most popular in the central press, though radio plays a secondary role. Television is the primary source of entertainment and is *the* meduim for following sports. Local media, particularly the local newspaper, are most popular for subjects connected with the economy. This preference seems to derive from the fact that the urban public sees economics as issues involving the satisfaction of daily needs in everyday life. The thirst for news of crime, court cases, and maintenance of public order makes stories on these topics popular, both in the central press—where they are treated as abstract questions of legal norms and philosophy—and in the local press—where they are covered as news, although the coverage of these issues is extremely limited as compared to the Western press. The articulation of dissatisfaction with the individual media reveals a good deal about the reasons why people choose a particular medium. On the whole, the Russian public is far more critical of the press than of either television or radio, and the range of subjects criticized is far broader. Three-quarters of the people who find any deficiencies in television programming complain about films, concerts, or entertainment programs.[14]

People turn to a particular medium in part because the type of message is best suited to it; films or sporting events are best presented visually. But people will also turn to a particular medium because of what they perceive to be the reliability or authoritativeness of the medium, because they trust it most. Even in the Soviet Union, where the media are all organized under the central control of the government and the Communist Party, citizens have very clear and differentiated approaches to the media. Recently urban residents were asked two questions: (1) Where are events most fully and thoroughly illuminated—in the pages of the newspaper or in radio and television broadcasts? (2) Where are events illuminated most objectively and reliably? The public found that the newspaper provided both most complete and most objective coverage. At first glance it might appear that these urban assessments of the various media prove, once again, the tremendous prestige of the newspaper in the Soviet Union; it is perceived as the medium that most fully and most objectively and reliably transmits information. However, the public cited television as a close runner-up in most objective coverage, though far below the newspaper on the completeness dimension. Television has reached a mass audience in Russia only very recently; it is clearly a newcomer in the ratings competition. Saturation has not yet been achieved, although in cities it largely has been. Second, the Russian public turns to television primarily for entertainment and escapist fare. Television is not thought of primarily as a purveyor of information—that is a secondary or even tertiary function for the television public. Yet in a comparatively short time television has become remarkably competitive with newspapers as a prestigious source of information. It is not distant from newspapers in its believability or objectivity. This is a remarkable leap in a society in which the newspaper is virtually sanctified by ideological doctrine in general and the words of Lenin in particular, and where television was not taken seriously by the authorities until a short time ago. On the completeness dimension, the leading role of the newspaper is, naturally, more pronounced.

Because there is not yet a trend line or multiple surveys of this sort, we cannot really judge the dynamics of television's credibility in competition with newspapers. But we do have ample evidence from American society that television makes dramatic inroads on the traditional authority of the press. "Seeing is believing" is proverbial, apparently, because it is true. Visual transmissions are inherently less suspect and more trusted than are written words or printed pictures. The notion that the editing of these visual images affects the product is as yet only dimly perceived. In the United States between 1960 and 1970, television outdistanced all other media on several dimensions. In 1960 when people were asked to compare media (television, magazines, newspapers, and radio) on a variety of dimensions, it was found that each of the media (except magazines) had received a decisive plurality of responses on at least one of the dimensions. Television might be the most entertaining, but newspapers provided the most complete news coverage and did most for the public, while radio brought the news most quickly. There was a certain dispersion of trust over all the media. But ten years later in a resurvey, the dispersion had given way to a high degree of concentration of trust in and approval of television. Television had emerged as ahead of all other media on all positive items. In 1959 when Americans were asked where they got "most of their news," the answer was 57 percent for newspapers and only 51 percent for television. By 1971 television received 60 percent of the responses and the choices for newspapers had shrunk to only 48 percent. A 1966 survey found that Americans placed television ahead of both newspapers and radio on such qualities as accuracy, completeness, trust-worthiness, and open-mindedness.[15]

Those who watch the growing importance of television, particularly as a source of news and information, find that what may be happening is actually a mobilizing of a hitherto isolated stratum of the population. Whereas news-paper readers are generally the more affluent and better educated in society, the television news audience is not differentiated that way. In fact, it is virtually undifferentiated; it cuts fairly equally across different economic and social groups. This might well mean that a new audience has been attracted to news, an audience previously unreachable by the written media or certainly less involved in public affairs, and there is some evidence to show that this has happened and has had an impact on the new assessments of the media.[16]

Whether the reported television dominance of news communication is supported by actual viewing behavior is, however, by no means certain.[17] We do not really have comparable categories of analysis. We do know that some viewing figures are inflated because of poor memory or bias (a problem in any survey), and that the Nielsen figures tell us about the television set rather than its audience. The diary method might help to reduce the error. But we do not have comparable materials for newspaper reading and news viewing. News-papers contain a good deal of material that is not news, and reading, like viewing, varies. Methods have not yet been devised that evaluate in terms of perceptions and receptivity the time spent watching television and the time spent reading newspapers. Although these issues await resolution as further studies are con-ducted, there is no question that, at present, attitudes toward newspapers and television have undergone a radical change, as the latter has come to replace the former as the leading medium on virtually all positive attributes.

The current picture of the motivations that prompt the Russian citizen to turn to one particular medium reveals that television is the leading source of entertainment and relaxation, and among survey respondents agreement on this function is very high. For functions relating to sensitive political and social issues, a clear superiority is accorded the central newspaper. Such reasons as "reflects opinion of broad strata of the population on various questions"; "gives objective, reliable information about events"; "actively struggles with deficiencies in social life"; "covers events fully, thoroughly"; and "discusses problems with different points of view," turn people primarily to the central newspaper. This seems paradoxical. The central newspaper tends to treat issues in their abstract form, rather than as concrete instances of local, everyday life (which is what the local paper should do), yet public opinion is said to be better portrayed in the central press. The central newspaper provides information primarily about events that readers have no independent knowledge or experience (international relations, macroeconomic questions, national leadership and political policy, et cetera), yet the information purveyed by the central press is judged reliable— far more reliable than is the information coming from the local press, which covers local events known to the public. Similarly, the central press is accorded the advantage of more complete coverage of events than is any other medium. But how does the public judge the completeness of the coverage without any widespread access to alternative sources of information for those issues? Are these paradoxes simply the result of the traditional primacy of the press in the Soviet system? After all, it is the central newspaper that is cited more than any other medium as the habitual source of information. But the other media do score higher on other dimensions, such as the provision of instructional materials, or interesting, entertaining items, or cultural materials. Thus on what may be called the nonpolitical dimensions (those that have little bearing on judgments about the social and political system), the other media are often judged superior to the central press.

In part, the primacy of the central newspaper on the political dimensions might well result from its historic prestige and authority, although television is rising as a contender. But also in part, the relative respect and trust accorded the central press might result from the failure of the local media to be very convincing and persuasive when viewers or readers or listeners can compare official versions to what they have seen or heard themselves. The very lack of alternative information sources has inflated the prestige of the central press, and the policy of information restriction has been to this extent successful. This is a question that will be treated at greater length in the next chapter.

Because in the Soviet Union there is such a clear distinction between central and local media, the satisfactions and dissatisfactions of the public are illuminated by their choices not only of particular media, but also of level of medium. Certain of the media scarcely exist at the local level. For example, the Rostov television studio at the province level (oblast) transmits only four hours a day in segments inserted into the regular central television-programming schedule. Rostov provincial radio has two hours a day of programming, of which 17 percent is devoted to agricultural information. At a still more local level, city radio broadcasts some 90 to 100 minutes a week. Thus when one speaks of choices between local and national media, it is really only the local press that is competitive. In six months, the staff of the Grodno television studios received a total of 62 letters from adults. Of these, 36 were requests to perform a musical piece or show a film. During the same period, the regional newspaper received about 8,000 letters. When residents of the city of Taganrog were asked whether or not they listened to programs from the city radio station, 15 percent of the radio listeners said they did not. Mainly, these were people from the upper social and occupational levels and included about a fifth of the engineers, city and economic administration bureaucrats, and intelligentsia not on the production line. Other surveys have shown that radio listeners often cannot tell what is local about local programs, and among their favorite local programs they cited coverage of international events, clearly transmissions from the central network. These respondents found they could not remember a single fact about local events transmitted on city radio.

This is precisely the problem. Alienation from local media seems not to result from lack of interest in things local, but rather from dissatisfaction with the failure of the local media to provide truly local coverage. When asked if there are defects in the various media, the local ones—newspapers, radio, and television—always score as more deficient than their national counterparts. An interesting issue arose in connection with the proposal to construct a city television studio in Taganrog. Although residents of the city had, in a survey, made known their opinion that the provincial radio and television transmissions paid too little attention to events in their city, they were by no means agreed that therefore a city television studio would be an improvement. Almost half of those surveyed opposed the construction of such a studio. Most thought there was already enough information from other sources.

But those who cited the irrationality of expenditures on a studio also pointed to the critical need for housing construction and improvement in public services in the city. Those who said that the programs probably would not be interesting were likely to be those viewers who thought the television at the province level was boring because it showed few films and a good deal of agricultural programming and broadcasts about industry. Those who did not want any more time taken away from central television transmissions said the province-level television studios showed few films and devoted too much time to programs on economic production. The feeling of many of the respondents could be summed up by the comment of one of them: "Really, if there are hardly any interesting programs coming from the province studio, what can you expect from the city!" Radio listeners also are dissatisfied that city radio programs feature such large numbers of programs relating to specific production problems in industry, very little information about what actually goes on in the city, and virtually no purely entertainment programs. Of the people who are dissatisfied with local programs, 45 percent say there are too many programs on industrial production.[18]

Those who supported the construction of a local television studio did so primarily because they wished to have more "many-sided" information about the "life of the city." The failure of the local media to be truly local, although it results in dissatisfaction, does avoid another negative result. Insofar as the local media are truly local, they are covering events and issues of which the public has immediate, first-hand experience or word-of-mouth information. Divergence in media coverage and personal knowledge would involve serious problems of trust and authority in official media. However, it is now argued by the Soviets themselves that noncoverage of important issues does not cause those issues to disappear, but rather sends the public to unofficial sources of information. This is considered particularly damaging to the public's trust in the credibility of the official media: "The absence of an operational propagandistic [that is, officially formulated in keeping with the explanations provided by the political doctrine] version can turn out to be highly significant; it is known that it is easier to *create* an orientation to an event by explaining it first, than to *break* [one] that has already been established (our ideological adversaries are also oriented to this, as revealed by the way they operationalize coverage of events)."[19]

Official thinking on the role of local media seems to be caught between two negative outcomes. If the public's desire for local coverage is to be satisfied, the media run the risk of offering reports that, due to the requirement of ideological conformity, cannot stand up under the standards of independent verification imposed by the public itself. On the other hand, if local events about which the public seeks information simply go unreported, unofficial sources provide the information. It would appear that whichever of the two strategies is adopted at any given time, the result has been a loss of confidence, trust, and credibility for the local media as a whole. This, in turn, has made much more difficult the work of the local propaganda network—the agitators and propagandists—which faces a public skeptical of and alienated from the local sources of information. As a Soviet social scientist noted recently:

> . . . for local sources of information the problem of trust, satisfaction with their activity, authority and prestige (true of all the sources of mass information) is sharper than for the central [sources]. It is not only that the qualitative level of central information is actually often higher, and its range of subjects more diverse. Perceptions of local mass information are formed under conditions of strict control [verification] of the personal experience of the public, and also of other accessible sources.[20]

Finally, in choosing among the media and evaluating the strengths and weaknesses of each, the Soviet public tends to include among the criteria the potential of each medium to root out deficiencies in the system. Since the 1917 Revolution, it has been part of the official doctrine that the media must provide an outlet for the complaints and frustrations of their audience—as safety valve, as probe of public opinion, as information gatherer for official intervention. This practice, called samokritika (self-criticism), is by no means as muckraking and freewheeling as might appear from the theory. It has been limited, in effect, to certain kinds of criticisms, primarily at the local level, which do not call into question the basic policies, leading personnel, or legitimacy of the political system. When people were asked "Who most successfully presses for the taking of measures [and] tangible results as a result of your communication: editors of newspapers, radio, or television?" they singled out newspapers as most efficacious of all media: some 47 percent of the respondents cited newspapers, while 5 percent cited radio and 15 percent cited television. Twenty-six percent said all three media, to different degrees, were significant forces for improvement, and 2 percent said that none of them was.[21] But even by this criterion of public activism, the role of television is rapidly expanding. Although the medium for entertainment, it is also the medium that, as the Soviet sociologists remark, has the advantage of visual clarity. By simply showing something that is wrong it creates a powerful visual impact. Soviet media officialdom does not, for the present, actively support this potential of television, and this medium has not been brought decisively into the campaign for self-criticism and social activism. That dominance has been maintained, as has been traditional, by the press.

## NOTES

1. V. E. Shlyapentokh, *Sotsiologia dlya vsekh* (Moscow, 1970), pp. 159-65.

2. Ibid., p. 166.

3. B. V. Evladov, "Metodologicheskie problemy izuchenia chitatelskoi auditorii gazety," *Problemy sotsiologii i psikhologii chtenia* (Moscow, 1975), p. 125.

4. I. D. Fomicheva, *Zhurnalistika i auditoria* (Moscow, 1976), pp. 53, 58.

5. Ibid., p. 54.

6. L. A. Gordon and E. B. Gruzdeva, "Rasprostranennost i intensivnost chtenia v gorodskoi rabochei srede," *Problemy sotsiologii i psikhologii chtenia* (Moscow, 1975), p. 56.

7. I. T. Livykin and O. V. Kharitonova, "Poznavatelnye interesy sovremennogo kolkhoznogo krestyanstva i chtenie," *Problemy sotsiologii,* p. 70.

8. Ibid.

9. Fomicheva, p. 65.

10. Ibid., pp. 46-50.

11. Ibid., pp. 38-39.

12. Ibid., p. 39.

13. Ibid., p. 44.

14. Ibid., pp. 80-93.

15. Robert T. Bower, *Television and the Public* (New York: Holt, Rinehart and Winston, 1973), pp. 100-1.

16. Ibid., p. 122.

17. In a close analysis of diaries of 6,000 Americans, Robert L. Stevenson and Kathryn P. White raised serious questions about the actual numbers of people watching the evening network news. They maintained that those numbers are overestimated in polls that do not rely on the diary method. "The Cumulative Audience of Network TV News," *Journalism Quarterly* (1980).

18. Fomicheva, pp. 106-13, 147.

19. Ibid., p. 114 (italics in the original).

20. Ibid., pp. 116-17 (italics in the original).

21. Ibid., p. 71.

# 5

# READING NEWSPAPERS
# IN RUSSIA

Newspaper reading has occupied a special place in the priorities of the Soviet leadership. From Lenin's earliest writing, it was clear that the role of the newspaper, particularly the central newspaper, was not to be merely that of entertainer or even, entirely, of information disseminator. Rather, the newspaper had a much more complex and socially critical function: to organize and mobilize the population for defined tasks. In addition to these functions, the newspaper would be a major source for the probing of public opinion and also for channeling grievances, frustrations, and criticism. These last would be the province of the letters to the editor section.[1] All recent surveys of media consumption, over the course of the past decade or so, have shown that in the aggregate the greatest amount of leisure time is spent reading newspapers. Newspaper reading, of all leisure-time activities, has been least affected by the introduction of television.

The newspapers in the Soviet Union are, unlike those in the United States, organized in strata. At the top is the central press, called All-Union newspapers. The most important of the national newspapers (all of them in the Russian language) have impressively large circulation figures: *Pravda* (organ of the Communist Party of the Soviet Union)—circulation in 1976 of over 10.5 million copies annually; *Izvestia* (organ of the government)—circulation of 8 million copies; *Komsomolskaya Pravda* (organ of the youth organization)—circulation of almost 10 million copies; and *Trud* (organ of the trade unions)—circulation of almost 8.5 million copies. Below the national-level newspapers are those at the republic level, province, city, district, and, in individual factories or on collective and state farms, there are in-house papers. There are, nationwide, almost 8,000 different newspapers of all kinds published in a total of almost 170 million copies annually. More papers are published in the Russian Republic than in any of the others: all the national newspapers (published in Moscow) plus more than 150 papers at the province level, about 2,000 papers at the city and precinct level, and slightly fewer than 2,500 at the lowest level.[2] One might compare figures for American daily papers. There are, at present, more than 1,756 of them with a circulation of almost 62 million. In addition, there are some 7,673 weekly papers with a total circulation of 40.2 million.[3]

TASS (Telegraph Agency of the Soviet Union), which operates under the aegis of the Council of Ministers of the Soviet government, is responsible for the collection and distribution of news both within the Soviet Union and abroad. It provides news information not only to the central press in Moscow, but also to the other media networks. Reporters and editors also come under central supervision. Newspaper writers belong to the Union of Journalists, a centralized organization operating under guidelines set by the party leadership; officers of the union are party members. Editorial posts are usually allocated and authorized by the appropriate level of party organization. For example, filling an editor-in-chief slot of one of the national newspapers would be a matter for the central political leadership to decide. Training in journalism and editorial professions is the province of the schools of journalism attached to institutions of higher education and to the special schools that the party runs to train its professional elite. The most prestigious and influential of all the training grounds for media journalists is the School of Journalism of Moscow University. Here are prepared not only newspaper journalists, but also television and radio reporters, photojournalists, and the literary editors who will work with publishers. There are 110 graduate students and 1,078 full-time undergraduates. The school also trains some 577 evening students and another 977 correspondence student. In the student body are some 134 foreign students from 38 countries. There are eight departments within the school: theory and practice of the Party-Soviet press, history of the Party-Soviet press, television and radio broadcasting, moviemaking and editorial-publishing work, foreign press and literature, Russian journalism and literature, stylistics of the Russian language, and techniques of newspaper work and information media.[4] It is estimated that there are now about 100,000 journalists in the country.[5]

Although the Soviet Union is a vast country, the 25 national newspapers published in Moscow reach much of the country on the day of publication. Through telexing of newspaper stories, *Pravda* and *Izvestia* are received by many cities of the Soviet Far East, Central Asia, and other regions. *Pravda* is published in 43 different locations throughout the country, and in 21 of these places the newspaper columns are telexed from Moscow.[6] As a rule, the cities of European Soviet Union and the Caucasus receive *Pravda* on the day of publication. In Central Asia, considerably more distant from Moscow, this is not necessarily the case. In Uzbekistan, almost all the cities get *Pravda* on the day of publication, but that is true for only 40 percent of the cities in Tadzhikistan, and only 36.8 percent in Turkmenia.[7]  The job is made easier by the very small size of Soviet newspapers, as compared to American ones.  In the United States, the following is the median size of a daily newspaper with a given circulation:

| Circulation | Size |
|---|---|
| 50,000 | 23.7 pages |
| 50,001-250,000 | 40.2 pages |
| Over 250,000 | 65.4 pages |

A newspaper of 25 or fewer pages is considered small by American standards.[8]  In the Soviet Union the central newspapers, which are the newspapers with the largest circulation in the country, have, on the average, four to six pages per issue.  *Literary Gazette* is a weekly paper published under the auspices of the Writers' Union.  It has 16 pages, and although it also carries some of the political and economic stories found in the other national newspapers, it provides a good deal of material about writers, the visual arts, and performers, as well as examples of poetry, parody, and caricature.  It is, perhaps, the liveliest and most interesting of the national papers.

Most of the space in a typical national newspaper is devoted to domestic news or features.  A survey of subjects covered by *Pravda* in 1965 found that 70 percent of the total column inches in the paper were given to domestic items and 30 percent to international items.  The relative weight of the international had, moreover, been declining over the course of the previous decade.  Within the international coverage, about a quarter of the space was devoted to stories about Europe and NATO and another 19 percent to stories about the United States, adding up to 44 percent for the United States and its European allies.  This represented quite a bit more space than that given to stories about foreign communist countries (31 percent of the international stories).  Within the domestic coverage, editorials about politics and economics made up about 4 percent of the column inches.[9]  Most of the stories are written at some distance in time from the event; only about 15 percent of the paper reports events, domestic or foreign, that had occurred the day before.[10]

Many kinds of stories covered by the Western press are considered inappropriate for the Soviet press.  News of disasters and accidents is reported in the tersest fashion.  Crime and sensationalism generally go unreported.  Celebrity and socialite doings are not covered, nor is the host of entertainment features such as astrology, fashion, living, horoscope, travel tips, and advice to the lovelorn.  Advertising is absent.  There are human interest stories in the Soviet press, but they are designed to spur examination of social mores and the problems of choosing a correct path in life.  The most important function of the Soviet press is the socialization or education of its citizens.  To this end it seeks not to bring out base impulses or to cater to corrupting weaknesses, as it sees it, but rather to point out roles and models for imitation or avoidance.  That something happened is not sufficient cause for reporting; hence, the relatively little space devoted to fast-breaking news. Then, too, in keeping with the Soviet doctrine of permitting only one "scientific" theory (Marxism-Leninism) to be taught, opposing points of view or multiple explanations of a phenomenon will not be found in the press, except within a very narrow range of opinions about relatively trivial issues. There is a list of topics the editor must not cover. According to one American journalist who claims to have seen part of the list, it includes information about crime, drugs, accidents, natural disasters, occupational injuries, official organs of censorship, security intelligence, schedules of travel for the political leadership, income and purchasing power structure at home and abroad, arms sales abroad, crime or morale problems in the armed forces, hostile actions against Soviet citizens abroad, and special payment and education of athletes.[11]

In a newspaper such as *Pravda*, page one is devoted to an editorial, official news from the leadership, short news stories (domestic and foreign), and something about the economy stressing production. Page two features stories on the Communist Party. Page three carries domestic news, letters to the editor, and the results of investigative reporting. Page four will have stories continued from page one, as well as some foreign, particularly communist, developments. Page five is the place for foreign news and reporting from foreign capitals. The back page has all the rest: sports, human interest, humor, media schedules, practical information about medicine, and other matters. Photographs are few and not particularly eye-catching.

## READERSHIP

Who reads newspapers in Russia? Do some occupations or social classes read more than others? Who is unlikely to read the newspaper? Until the massive readership studies begun in 1964, the Soviet communications experts themselves did not know. Editorial boards had always assumed that the authors of letters to the editor were more or less representative of the readership. As will be seen later, they were drastically mistaken in that assumption. The recent surveys do produce a picture of the Russian reader. And it is the readership in Russia that forms the bulk of the entire Soviet readership of the central newspapers. It was found that 80 percent of the readers of *Pravda* speak Russian and that 67 percent of the subscribers live in the Russian Republic.[12] The reader of the national newspaper is very much better educated than is the population at large. Whereas in 1970, roughly 6.4 percent of the Soviet population over 20 had incomplete or complete college education, that percentage for the *Pravda* readership was 39 percent; for the *Izvestia* readership it was 47 percent, and for the *Trud* readership 25 percent. The well educated have the smallest overrepresentation in *Trud*, the trade union newspaper oriented to the industrial worker. The highest degree of overrepresentation of the well educated is in the readership of *Literary Gazette,* the organ of the Union of Writers that carries more information about culture than any other newspaper. In 1967 the well educated accounted for some 73 percent of the readership of this paper.[13] A resurvey in 1977 found that the college educated had dropped to 64 percent of the readership, still very high.[14] As the readership of the central press has enlarged, a more nearly "normal" distribution by education has resulted.

The proportion of young readers of *Literary Gazette* has also diminished from 46 percent in 1967 to 23 percent in 1977.[15] As is usually the case, the younger age groups tend to be better educated than the older ones, and as the readership structure shifts to the older groups, it shifts automatically to the less well educated. The drop in young readers brings *Literary Gazette* closer to the average; *Pravda*'s readers under 30 constitute 20 percent of the readership, *Izvestia*'s 22 percent, and *Trud*'s 20 percent.[16] In the population as a whole, the under-30 age group makes up some 50.8 percent, but the 15 to 29 age group is 21.9 percent, virtually identical to the weight of youthful newspaper readers.

As might be expected, the occupational spread in the readership of the national newspapers is by no means even. There is a high percentage of white-collar employees, and of a subcategory, the intelligentsia, which in Soviet usage denotes those with higher education in jobs requiring higher education. Engineers and technical specialists are the largest occupational group of *Izvestia* readers (24 percent), the second largest of *Trud* readers (20 percent), and the third largest of *Literary Gazette* readers (16 percent). Scientists and personnel working in higher education are also heavily represented among the readers of *Izvestia* (11 percent) and *Literary Gazette* (17 percent), where they are the largest single occupational group in the readership. Retired people account for 16 percent of the *Izvestia* readership and not more than 6 or 7 percent of the readers of the other national newspapers. Industrial workers are a very large part of the readers of the trade union newspaper, *Trud,* where they form about a third of the readership, but 12 percent of the readers of *Izvestia*.[17] Farmers and other members of the agricultural labor force are severely underrepresented. Even though about 42 percent of the Soviet population is rural, less than a third of the national magazine and journal circulation comes from the countryside. Only a quarter of *Pravda*'s readers live in the countryside.[18] In Leningrad and Moscow, 1,500 magazines and newspapers were purchased for every 1,000 persons in 1967; that figure for the rural areas was 820 per 1,000.[19]

Typical profiles of the occupations from which each national newspaper draws most of its readers might be described as follows:

*Literary Gazette*: scientists and university personnel, engineers and technical specialists, university and secondary school students, writers, journalists, people in the arts, and free-lance professionals.

*Trud*: industrial workers, engineers and technical specialists, people employed in public service and food delivery systems, and professionals in the trade unions.

*Izvestia*: engineers and technical specialists, scientists and university personnel, public health personnel, and personnel in education and cultural services.

*Pravda* and *Trud* appear to have a particularly important occupational orientation. About a quarter of the *Trud* readers claim that they read the paper because it provides them with information they need in their work.[20]

If one looks not at the national newspapers, but at newspapers at lower, more local levels, one finds a strikingly different picture of the readership. A district (or precinct) newspaper in Western Siberia was studied recently. Here it was found that only 13 percent of the readers were under 30 and only 18 percent had higher education. The readers were older and had much less education than the readers of the national papers. Their occupations were heavily rural, as is the region where the newspaper is published. Well over a third were in some agricultural occupation and another 15 percent were industrial workers—quite different from the skewed white-collar readership of the national papers. It would appear that the more local the newspaper the more the readership resembles the population of the area. A separate survey of collective farmers found that well over 75 percent of them read the local district newspaper, but only slightly over half read "their" national newspaper, *Rural Life,* directed to the farm audience.[21]

Even in such a sophisticated city as Leningrad, similar differences were found. A recent survey looked at readership patterns among young people (under 30) who worked in blue- and white-collar occupations in 15 factories in the city. These young people are not college students, and they are considerably less interested in central newspapers than in local ones. The less well educated and older (late twenties) workers in the sample were more attuned to the local paper; about half of them read the Leningrad city paper. However, most of the youths who were polled prefer radio and television as sources for information. Quite a different pattern is seen among young political activists. They get their information not from the electronic media, but primarily from newspapers and magazines. Communist Youth Organization leaders turned mainly to the national newspaper of that organization, *Komsomolskaya Pravda.* Young political activists in other places show a similar disposition to be heavy readers of the national youth organization press. In five major cities of the Ukraine, youth organization leaders were found to be exceptionally heavy consumers of *Komsomolskaya Pravda,* which 95.9 percent of them read. Not so for *Izvestia* and *Pravda,* which only about half of them read systematically. As for the local Communist Party press, fewer than half read it systematically. Rather, they prefer to turn to the local youth paper, which some 88.8 percent read.[22] As will be seen below, the patterns of satisfaction and dissatisfaction with the newspaper and the demands it should satisfy are also correspondingly different at the national and local levels.

From American surveys one knows that even though the percentage base of the well educated is much larger in this country than in the Soviet Union,[23] the same relationship obtains with regard to newspaper reading: "As education goes up, so does the reading of the daily newspaper."[24] Eighty-eight percent of the college graduates had read a newspaper the day before a major national survey, but only 70 percent of those who had not gone beyond eighth grade. In the United States, the younger the adult, the less likely that adult is to read a newspaper. It was found that somewhat under 70 percent of those in the age group 18 to 34 read the paper, as compared to 85 percent in the age bracket 50 and over.[25] At the two extremes of the age spectrum one finds the lowest levels of readership: the over-65 audience and the 18- to 19-year-olds.[26]

The skewing of readership toward the more urbanized and developed areas of society is also a familiar phenomenon. A 1970 survey in the United States found that newspaper penetration was lowest in the South.[27] A far more striking North/South or developed/less-developed spectrum of readership may be seen in a major national survey conducted in Italy in 1974. Nonreaders constituted only 15 percent of the sample in the industrial Northwest and 63 percent in the rural southern region of the Basilicata. Here, too, the crucial variable of education accounts for attention to newspapers. Among people who do not read the paper, fully 95 percent had not gone beyond elementary school (such people made up 68 percent of the sample). As in the American studies, one finds that the over-65 group is underrepresented among newspaper readers; they made up some 15 percent of the Italian sample, but some 26 percent of those who do not read newspapers.[28]

A kind of profile of American nonreaders might be as follows: low in the occupational scale, low in income, and low in education. They tend to describe themselves as working class rather than middle class. The nonreaders are more likely to be rural residents than city residents, and if a city resident, to live in the smaller rather than the larger city. They tend not to participate in social or political life, belonging to few, if any, organizations, no political parties, and they do not vote in elections.[29] The Italian nonreader tends to be uninvolved with social and political life, out of step with the times, indifferent, and, if female, "exiled in domestic duties" and "without aspirations."[30] Newspaper reading becomes a kind of indicator of the degree to which the individual is integrated into society and is part of the social fabric. The world of the rural inhabitant everywhere tends to be more isolated and more circumscribed than that of the city dweller. Newspaper reading, which requires certain cognitive skills and, therefore, certain levels of educational attainment, is less popular among rural inhabitants because, quite apart from access to papers, reading is more difficult for those with less education. It will be seen in a later chapter that the same pattern of isolation and detachment from society may be found in Russia among the less well-educated rural inhabitants who migrate to the city and who are not assimilated into urban life. These people, too, form pockets of nonreaders in the cities, and in their life-styles look much like the American and Italian nonreaders described above.

Sex differences in newspaper readership are not especially marked in the United States; men are only slightly more likely to have read the newspaper (79 percent as against 76 percent for women).[31] It is said that among subscribers to

*Pravda* women are about 30 percent, though they are 40 percent of the readers of the newspaper. There is some evidence that Russian women are much less likely to be systematic readers of newspapers. A survey of over 2,000 blue- and white-collar workers in Leningrad chemical factories found that over 85 percent of the men read newspapers regularly and systematically, but only 61 percent of the women did. Nearly equal proportions were nonreaders (about 3 percent), but the women were much more likely to be off-and-on readers (more than a third of the respondents) than were men (a little more than a tenth of the re-spondents).[32] It is likely that the difference in the Soviet case arises from the relative lack of free time that women may devote to newspaper reading. It is an activity that cannot be performed while doing something else, unlike watching television—or, more precisely, leaving the set on while cooking or cleaning.

## WHAT PEOPLE READ

How much of a newspaper do people read? Soviet newspapers have enor-mous circulation figures and very few pages. Should we assume that the paper is read cover to cover? The surveys say that Russians read, on the average, no more than half and often no more than a third of a single issue of a national or local paper.[33] In the United States about one-quarter of all items in a newspaper are read by the average reader.[34] Even if one subtracts advertising space from the American newspaper, one still finds that Americans, consuming only a fourth of newspapers well over 25 pages, are reading more column inches of news-print than Russians reading a third to a half of papers containing four to six pages.

Preference for particular kinds of newspaper stories has been remarkably stable and consistent. There are three readership surveys—of two national and one regional paper—in which respondents were asked what they turn to first in the paper. Readers of all three turn first to international news. Articles dealing with international events and light human interest or humor pieces are consistently the most widely read. Not only are these two types of newspaper story the leaders, but also there is a sharp drop-off in attention between the top two and all the rest. The numbers of respondents who read in their entirety articles on economics, science, and technology are far smaller than those who prefer inter-national news and light stories.

The interest in international news is one that cuts across all age groups, all levels of educational attainment, and all occupations. The intensity of the thirst for international news is such that respondents, when asked in what area they would like more information, say international news. This is true even of the readership of the trade union daily, *Trud*, which has a relatively small proportion of college-educated readers.[35] Level of education does make a difference in taste for other kinds of newspaper stories. The *Trud* survey found that readers with higher education preferred articles about art, literature, and history, while the "reader-worker" favored articles on technology. The very popular human interest stories, called articles on morals, are most popular in all the papers among high school graduates. These articles that give daily life lessons and discuss ethical choice as human interest have least appeal to the college graduate, who finds the level of discourse too primitive, and to the reader with elementary or less education, who finds the reading too heavy going.[36] In the *Literary Gazette* survey it was found that as education increases, so does attention to stories on science, sociology, and economics, but interest in stories on literature and art declines. The pattern of reading is related to the pattern of satisfaction with the way the story is presented, and education has a powerful effect on how likely readers are to be satisfied with what they read.

Men are much more likely to be systematic newspaper readers than are women, and the spectrum of newspaper stories they read is correspondingly broader. They are more interested in more types of newspaper stories than are women readers.[37]

The discussion materials, the liveliest, most topical stories in *Literary Gazette*, appeal differently to people with different levels of education. Readers with no more than sixth grade education find most interesting the stories on crime and legal proceedings, but this topic was in eighth place (of 15 places) for those with graduate education and seventh place for college graduates. Discussion articles on ecology are in last place for the poorly educated and first place for people with college and graduate education. The other subject that registers substantial differences by level of education of the reader is theoretical questions of science, which is cited by only 7.2 percent with elementary education, 22 percent of those with graduate education, and 16.7 percent with college education.[38]

Where the reader lives makes a difference as well. Discussion materials in *Literary Gazette* about recreation and leisure-time pursuits appeal much more to the small-town reader than to the metropolitan reader. Curiously, problems relating to conservation and ecology are much more likely to be cited by the metropolitan reader (for reasons of nostalgia?) and the rural reader (for practical considerations?) than by the reader in a small town. Rural readers show more interest in crime than their big-city counterparts, as well as in questions that deal with the rural economy and way of life.

Young people (under 25) prefer stories on literature and art to those on economics, sociology, or moral and ethical issues. The kind of story they prefer second to literature and art is the one on ecology. In terms of occupation, the discussion materials interest the apparatchiki most—those professionals who staff the Communist Party organization—and scholars in both the humanities and the sciences. The least interest in these materials in evinced by engineers and technicians, industrial workers, white-collar employees, secondary and primary school teachers, and university students. As might be expected, people find most interesting the subject matter that most closely approaches their occupation:

| Subject Matter | Occupation |
|---|---|
| Socialization, education, and teaching | Teachers and Communist Party professionals |
| Economics | Administrators, Communist Party professionals, journalists |
| Crime | Legal professionals |
| Art and aesthetics | Scholars in the humanities and professionals in cultural administration |
| Literature | Writers, journalists, scholars (humanities), teachers (humanities), professionals in cultural administration |
| Science | Scholars (humanities and sciences) |
| Technology | Engineers and technicians |
| Medicine | Physicians |

In some ways, readership patterns for local newspapers are not so very different. At the level of a province (in this case, an autonomous republic), it was found that men, more than women, read stories on politics, ideology, agriculture, industry, Communist Party affairs, and sports. Women favor more the items on everyday life, human interest stories, and fiction. This sex difference, given the depressed level of interest of women in newspapers and their lack of interest in political programs on television, has caused some concern among officials. Women, as a group, may be relatively out of touch of political communications; they have less free time and more household duties than do men. Most people read the paper after work, but this is the time when women, after a day at work, have to prepare meals, do housework, and look after children.[39] Newspaper reading claims virtually full attention and cannot be done as a secondary activity. It has been suggested officially that perhaps increased personal talks and conferences will have to fill the lacunae so evidently left by the lack of attention of women to political issues in the media.[40] It might be argued that even if women have less time to read the paper, the result may be diminished total consumption of newsprint, but it should not affect the structure of interests. Perhaps careworn fatigue, coupled with generally lower levels of education, tend to favor consumption of light, escapist fare. One striking exception to the low priority given political reading by women is their strong interest, equal to that of men, in news of foreign countries.

The fascination with international news appears also at the province, or republic, level. All readers except those in the Communist Party turn first to news of events outside the Soviet Union. Then, in order of preference, to local news, sports, science and culture, economics, and, last, party news. The member of the Communist Party, however, turns first to articles about the party before turning to the international news. There is no difference between men and women in the high priority given international news stories. People who are most interested in stories about Communist Party themes and economics are high-school-educated readers.[41]

The city newspaper is the most local paper for which there is a major readership study. At this level, some surprising paradoxes emerge, paradoxes that raise some fundamental questions about the Russian citizen's confidence in the reliability of the press. At the city level, it is again international news that is most popular, even though 80 percent of the respondents have also read the province- or national-level newspapers as well. Since international news has already appeared in the national papers and certainly on radio and television quite a long time before it reaches the city paper, the continued primacy of international news must be almost inexplicable, especially when more than half of the respondents say they have already read these stories in the central papers, and that would have been a week earlier.[42] Of least interest to the readership of the city paper is news about the city itself: stories on political and economic administration, such as information on industry, the activity of the Communist Party organs, and opinions of administrators, both political and economic. Instead, readers look for stories about human interest or moral questions, sights of the town, information on sports events, letters to the editor, and observations of city residents critical of what is happening in public life in the city. They are more interested in local materials that relate to problems of immediate importance in their everyday life as they perceive it, and to moral and ethical questions than to the more abstract stories on politics and economic administration. They tend to identify rather with the flow of information coming up from the population to the administration than with the information coming down "from the organs of administration of the city to the publication."[43]

Before turning to questions of the credibility of newspaper stories and the patterns of satisfaction and dissatisfaction of the Russian readership, it might be useful to glance briefly at American readers' tastes. It should be remembered that the multilevel, hierarchical organization of newspapers from central to local has no counterpart in the United States. Turning first to sex differences, of the five most popular categories of newspaper stories for men, two are also among the five most popular with women: stories about accidents and disasters, which is first for both sexes, and letters to the editor. Missing from the top five list for women, and second in popularity for men, are stories about government and military questions. Nowhere in the top five for women are there stories about national or international political or economic issues. In fact, women place political columns, business news and commerce, cultural events, and reviews in the list of five least widely read topics. Nowhere in the least widely read five of men do stories on politics and economics appear.[44] Although there is no particular difference in the proportions of men and women reading the newspaper, or even in the percentage of the newspaper actually read (about a quarter for each), the choice of story or topic does differ substantially. It is difficult to compare American and Soviet patterns since stories on accidents, disasters, and natural phenomena, which place first for both men and women in the United States, are almost entirely absent in the Soviet press, and when reported, are presented in terse, concise, unemotional form without photos. However, in spite of the great structural differences in the availability of different types of stories, the absence of women (except, in the Russian case, for international news, which women follow as avidly as do men) from the readership of political and economic stories, both of which are heavily reported in the American and Soviet papers at all levels, is a striking similarity in the American and Russian readership.

For the American readership, education makes a difference in which stories are read. At the lower educational levels (readers who have not graduated from high school), crime and human interest stories are among the most widely read. For the college graduate, these are not among the most popular; such issues as international and national news and public health and welfare command the greatest attention.[45] The strong effect of lower levels of education on interest in crime stories is seen in both the Russian and American readership studies. But in the United States, the only category that all levels of education of the readership find equally interesting is a category that has no counterpart in the Soviet press: accidents, disasters, and natural phenomena. In Soviet readership studies, the single category of story that cuts across all levels of education is international events.

## HOW SATISFIED ARE READERS?

The answer to this sensitive question involves using several different, though related, approaches. The simplest method is to ask readers to say what satisfies them most among the kinds of stories they read in the papers. All surveys of the Russian readership show that the articles readers find most satisfying are those on international topics. These are positively evaluated by one-half to two-thirds of all readers. Second are materials on economics, which one-third of the readers find satisfying, and third are articles on morals and social relations, which about one-third of the readers say they find satisfying.[46] Looking at the question another way, one might ask about satisfaction scores for different kinds of articles. When this was done for *Literary Gazette*, it was found that less than one-quarter of the stories in the newspaper were termed "almost always satisfying," and 34 percent were called "frequently satisfying." As expected, there is a statistically significant relationship between what people choose to read in papers and what satisfies them.[47] The articles that most often fail to satisfy the reader of *Literary Gazette* are precisely the specialty of that newspaper: literature and culture.

A related question might be put in the following way: To what extent do readers find in the paper what they would like to read? By comparing newspaper column inches devoted to various topics with the popularity those topics command, one might see to what degree reader demand is met. Such a study was done for four months of issues of *Trud*. During this time, up to one-quarter of the newspaper space was regularly devoted to official communications from the governmental news agency TASS. These messages are accorded from 3,000 to 8,000 lines monthly. Of least importance in terms of newspaper space are articles on humor, entertainment, and leisure time, each of which received fewer than 1,000 lines for a four-month period, and there was one month in the period under review when the subjects were not covered at all. Among the least covered topics (given fewer than 100 lines of newsprint monthly) were: light human interest articles called feuilletons, stories on medicine, events in Asia, Africa, and Latin America (not including TASS communiques), and international feuilletons. Among the subjects that fall into the least covered category most but not all of the time, are legal questions and international surveys. On the other hand, the subjects that always received maximum space (3,000 to 8,000 lines of newsprint monthly) were: industrial questions, foreign information from TASS, sports, literature and art, production in advanced work groups in industry, and professional information.[48]

If one compares a rank order of newspaper space by topic and a rank order of the top ten most popular topics for the reader, only two of the topics that were given prime attention by the editors reappear among the top ten readers' preferences: sports and the work of trade union organs. Human interest stories, crime, information about capitalist countries—all these are high in popularity and missing from the topics that take up most newspaper space. Soviet communications officials would reject out of hand the notion that reader demand should dictate editorial policy, but the lack of fit between demand and availability is extreme, and if readers were asked about their interests in subjects that do not appear anywhere in the Soviet press, the lack of congruence might well be much greater.

A word should be said about a category called "critical materials." These stories are the closest the Soviet paper gets to investigative reporting. They are stories that uncover deficiencies and wrongdoing and raise questions of policy, but always in a circumscribed and controlled way, never attacking or questioning the legitimacy of major political figures, policies, or the structure and norms of Soviet society. These articles are among the ten most popular for the average reader of *Trud,* but they occupied, in the four months the paper was analyzed, only 2.3 percent of the total newspaper space. In traditional Bolshevik theory, it was precisely this kind of story that would propel society forward, rooting out injustice and inefficiency, and giving to the newspaper its special function in Soviet society—a function that is, moreover, a popular one. But editorial policy has chosen a far less provocative route, and the demand here, too, is largely unsatisfied.

Still another attempt to plumb reader demand is to ask what kinds of articles should be improved in the newspaper. The human interest story is among the most popular topics in the newspaper. Unlike the very popular human interest story in American newspapers, the Soviet version stresses the ethical or moral choices and lessons to be learned from everyday life. These stories, as all others in the Soviet media, are essentially didactic, but they are the closest the Soviet press comes to gossip and sensationalism (muted though they be). These articles are read systematically by 75 percent of the readers of *Izvestia,* 67 percent of *Trud* readers, 62 percent of *Literary Gazette* readers, and 57 percent of *Pravda* readers. The obverse of this tremendous popularity is the finding that only one-third of the readers are satisfied with these articles; it is this kind of story that was named most often as among the subjects in need of improvement. It is this kind of story that elicits the highest degree of unfavorable criticism. Of the subjects said by readers to be in need of improvement, second were stories on science. International events placed third, even though quite a high percentage of the readers (almost two-thirds) generally approved of them.[49]

Education has an important effect on satisfaction and dissatisfaction with newspaper stories, and college graduates most often disagree with the editorial point of view. The more education readers have, the less likely they are to read articles on literature and art in their entirety, and the more likely they are to be dissatisfied with those articles. On the other hand, the more educated readers are, the more they read and the more satisfaction they derive from articles on science, sociology, and economics. Although all groups are interested in articles on international events, the percentage of readers satisfied with those articles declines with rising levels of education.[50]

With increasing age, disagreement slacks. People over 55 are twice as few in the category of those with lack of trust and confidence in the paper than is the average reader. The highest rate of dissatisfaction with articles on international news, economics, and broad questions of Soviet literature is in the 31 to 40 age group.[51]

Professionals are more likely to complain about the newspaper's coverage of their profession than is the average reader. For example, trade union officials read about trade union activities in *Trud* much more attentively than does the average reader. Only a third of the total readership read these articles in their entirety, while among trade union officials, 80 percent read them fully. But 25 percent of the trade union officials express disagreement and dissatisfaction with these articles, as compared to only 13 percent of the readership. Again, only 13 percent of the *Trud* readers complain about the failure of the newspaper to uncover problems or inefficiencies, but 36 percent of *Trud*'s own journalists complain about it.[52] *Literary Gazette* provokes the greatest amount of dissatisfaction from writers, people in the arts, and journalists. Other kinds of readers of *Literary Gazette*—government employees, cultural administrators, journalists, and natural scientists—are also dissatisfied with articles, but largely because they find them ineffective in practical terms; that is, some of the elites vitally involved in the functioning of the social system find inadequate guidance and information in the paper.[53]

What causes dissatisfaction and criticism is a complex issue. In the United States, where there is a real choice among newspapers, highly dissatisfied readers would probably stop reading a paper they do not like. The general level of agreement with newspapers is rather high for American readers. About three-fourths of the papers termed "usually" read are bought by readers who usually or sometimes agree with editorial positions. Agreement with the point of view of the paper is very much greater than is disagreement. There are, however, some relationships that are similar to those found in the Russian readership studies, although it should be emphasized that these relationships are much weaker than in the Russian case. In the United States the college-educated reader is somewhat more critical of the paper than is the average reader, and the young, 18 to 24, are more likely to express their disagreement with the editorial point of view. A further finding from the American study is particularly important. In spite of the general trend of agreement on the part of the American readership, there is a tendency for disagreement to increase as the story comes closer to the personal experience of the reader: 55 percent of the American readers agree with the position of their newspapers on local politics, 62 percent on national issues, and, highest percentage of support, 67 percent on international events.[54] Stories on international events, so distant from the lives of average readers, cannot be independently assessed or verified, and because possible dissonance is reduced by lack of information, agreement is greater. For the Russian reader, this was seen with the high rate of satisfaction with international stories, in spite of the demand that more should be published on this subject. Dissatisfaction increased as the story approached either the professional competence of the reader or human interest concerns of the average citizen. At the local level, the effect of cognitive dissonance is particularly strong.

A recent survey of the readership of a city newspaper found that about 19 percent of the readers did not read any articles on subjects that they said were of great interest to them. Another 37 percent read no more than a third of the articles on subjects in which they were interested. These two groups apparently find little to satisfy their demands in the local press. Only 24 percent of the readers read from one-third to two-thirds of the articles on subjects of interest.[55] When asked what was wrong with their city paper, they most often said that too little attention was given to questions of city planning, amenities, retail trade and daily services, and the protection of public order. These are the functions that are within the jurisdiction, at least in large part, of the city and district administration and government, but interest in materials emanating from official agencies is very low. What is printed in the local paper does not strike the average reader as accurate and reliable, given a personal knowledge of the events reported. Only 3 percent of the readers of a district newspaper in a city said that the newspaper rarely distorts the events it describes. As a Soviet communications expert remarked, the problem with the local newspaper is that readers are closer to the truth than they are with a central newspaper, and what is communicated may be verified by life.[56] The more local the medium of communication, the more critical the audience.

The readers of the district newspaper also said that the record of the newspaper in correcting errors it printed was not very good. Forty percent of the readers who said the district newspaper let mistakes be printed also said the newspaper refused to acknowledge or correct them. A comparison might be made with American readers, who, when asked "When your newspaper makes mistakes does it print corrections?" answered overwhelmingly (70 percent) yes or most of the time. Only 2 percent said no and 12 percent said not often enough.[57]

When Russian readers were asked about questions of newspaper format, the readers of the district paper had some complaints, and the complainers were differentiated by social class. The readers with relatively low socioeconomic status—blue-collar workers, for example—complained about bad illustrations and layout. The average reader found the photographs (often of people he knows) in the local paper to be standardized and repetitive—always the same pose, the same gesture, the same picture composition. The effect is chilling; readers are turned off by the unnatural, frozen version of the life they know. One reader said that "here [in the newspaper] it's not like in life."[58] The readers with higher status (engineers, administrators, teachers, doctors) were fairly indifferent to these questions and complained little. Their expectations might well be different; they know the rules of the game and in their largely careerist orientation use the local paper for professional information and instruction.

The pervasiveness of alienation from the local media, particularly the press—the most highly developed local medium of official communication—is of considerable concern to Soviet policymakers. That alienation is related not only to the dissonance created by official interpretations of local events, but also to the heavy dominance of official news (often about national or international news) and the short shrift given to local events and local concerns. Local readers want to find out about local things: hospitals and health programs, sports, cultural events, retail trade, and shopping. Youths in the 18 to 24 age group want more on recreation. Most people want practical, utilitarian information. Almost half of the readers of the city paper voice these demands for improvement, but only 8 percent of the readers of the central press do. By far, the single most important reason why people subscribe to the local district newspaper is because it will "illuminate local life."[59]

Why people cancel subscriptions also shows a good deal about reader satisfaction and dissatisfaction. Such a study of the flow of subscribers was undertaken for the central newspaper, *Izvestia*. The ebb and flow of subscribers for a single year was put at "several million." In Moscow alone, the turnover of subscribers was more than one-third the total number of subscribers. The chief reason why people stopped subscribing to *Izvestia* was dissatisfaction with the content of the newspaper. Forty-one percent gave this reason. Only 20 percent cited personal reasons (cost of paper, moving away) and 2 percent cited delivery problems. When people who had cancelled their subscriptions were asked what kinds of changes would induce them to resubscribe, they mentioned, first, improving the human interest articles; second, improving articles on international events; third, improving the critical articles; and fourth, publishing more stories expressing "differing points of view."[60] These are precisely those areas in which people have the greatest interest and in which they are least satisfied.

The contrast with American newspaper readers is particularly marked. A study of why Americans cancelled subscriptions to their newspapers found that problems of delivery and moving were given by half the respondents. If all of the categories that might indicate dissatisfaction with the news-editorial content of the paper are combined, only 3.4 percent of all those queried cite this reason—far from the overwhelmingly primary reason for the Soviet respondents. The critical stance of the Russian reader and the unfulfilled demand for both broader and more sophisticated coverage of issues of crucial interest to the readership seem not to be paralleled on the American side. It is likely that because of the greater choice of newspapers and points of view that Americans have, dissatisfaction with a single paper is diffused.

## LETTERS TO THE EDITOR

The letters-to-the-editor sections of the Soviet newspaper at every level perform that highly important function of samokritika—self-criticism. Lenin's works are full of prescriptions for curing the ills of society and lubricating the mechanism of governance by spontaneous, popular discussion, through letters to the editor, of shortcomings in the work of public officials and their agencies. These letters would also serve as the most important component of feedback for the new revolutionary regime, which had then, as now, rather few channels for extracting public opinion information. As time went on, the kind of policies, agencies, and personnel that could be criticized became severely circumscribed. A complicated process of selection determines which letters are actually printed in the paper. A large national newspaper like *Izvestia* prints a little over a quarter of the letters it receives. There are topics that go too far in revealing problems in the system, but it is not known what exactly are the guidelines. One American journalist reports that a deputy editor of *Pravda*'s letter department, referring to letters complaining about the behavior of local policemen, said, "It's not convenient to publish such letters. . . ." Another editor admitted that some letters were created by the paper's own correspondents.[61] Nonetheless, a large number of letters are published, and the process is taken very seriously by Soviet newspaper staffs. At *Pravda* alone, 45 people work in the letter department. The letters to be printed are selected at a daily staff meeting. These large newspapers may also have a special center for the receipt of letters or a telephone line for advice on various subjects and for receiving complaints or information.[62] The volume of letters received by the central newspapers is certainly impressive by any standards. In 1967 *Izvestia* received some 487,000 letters to the editor. This is almost ten times the number of letters received by the *New York Times.* Even when one controls for circulation figures, *Izvestia* still receives twice the number of letters as the *New York Times,* and the rates of letters to Soviet papers are increasing.[63]

Given this extraordinary volume of letters received by newspapers, it is not surprising that before the advent of the scientific polls discussed here, editors were confident that the letter writers represented the readership. As is now known, they do not. First, they are much older than most of the readers: 44 percent are over 65 and a total of 76 percent are over 55. Only 7.5 percent are 30 and younger, as compared to the readership figure for *Izvestia* of 22 percent under 30 and 16 percent over 60. The occupational spread of letter writers is also quite different from that of the readership. Almost a third of the letter writers are industrial manual workers and peasants, at least three times greater than they are represented in the readership. On the other hand, the contingent of scientists and scholars, a substantial portion of the *Izvestia* readership, is severely underrepresented among authors of letters. Engineers and technical and agricultural specialists, the single largest component of the *Izvestia* readership, account for less than 10 percent of authors of letters.[64] Editors who estimate readership from the mail they receive might well conclude that their readers are primarily older people, relatively few of whom are scientists, professors, engineers, or university students. They would underestimate, as well, the kinds of criticism and dissatisfaction that are produced, since the older readers are more likely to agree with the editorial point of view.

## THE NEWSPAPER AS MOBILIZER

Lenin, the theorist of the ideological function of the newspaper, also insisted that newspapers have the job of organizing and mobilizing the population. Though the revolution is long past, the function remains—no longer to make revolution, but to implement the directives and policies of the central government.

One way for the newspaper to mobilize the population is through campaigns to implement central policy. The initiative for these campaigns clearly comes from the central party officials.[65] It would be difficult to measure the effectiveness of these campaigns since there are so many factors that enter into the success of a broad social policy. However, the way in which the newspaper campaigns are managed suggests that sustained and unambiguous results are hardly likely. One study examined the way in which the central press helped to implement a June 1972 decree of the party's Central Committee combatting alcoholism in the USSR. The study involved measuring the space in the central press given to four kinds of coverage relating to the directives: descriptions of drunkenness and alcoholism; descriptions of consequences of drunkenness and alcoholism; indications or reasons why such phenomena exist in society; and measures for dealing with the problem. It was found that the pattern could be described as a single-burst publicity blitz. The frequency of these elements in the press was very high at the moment of the publication of the decree, but soon thereafter the blitz abruptly ended and the newspaper shifted to other subjects. As a program of public education and organization, the method was judged ineffective.[66]

How do Russian citizens judge their papers as combatants in the arena of social amelioration? To them the paper is the leading and most efficacious advocate of citizen demands. When asked what are the most efficient and desirable forms in which public opinion influences local organs of administration, the newspaper came in first. More precisely, it was the role of the newspaper in "the publication of requests, remarks, suggestions and demands of the population." Near the bottom of the respondents' list is the party organization; the public's perception is that talking to party officials yields scant results, and writing to them, even less. The advocacy role of the newspaper, controlled and circumscribed as samokritika is, is seen to be far greater for Russian citizens than is any other agency or activity to which they may turn. What makes this finding even more interesting is the fact that newspapers often turn over the letters they receive to the agencies or personnel who have been criticized, to the discomfort of the letter writer.

This does not mean, however, that the public is necessarily satisfied that the newspaper is an efficacious and satisfactory force for correcting society's problems. Readers of a largely rural newspaper at the district level were asked if the "newspaper helps to combat" a variety of antisocial acts. Between one-half and two-thirds said no or not very well, and this included a judgment of the newspaper's efficiency in exposing lawbreaking by officials. Respondents are more positive on the other issues of newspaper efficacy—issues that involve government and party responsibilities. However, although they are less likely to respond negatively, the no-answer category is much larger on these three issues, far larger than in any of the questions cited so far. The record of the newspaper on these sensitive issues is much more negative, for the public, than is its record in helping to improve industrial and agricultural production. Almost half of the respondents are positive and another 16.5 percent say the newspaper does do well with these questions, though not always.[67]

However attenuated the activist role of the Soviet newspaper, however distant from the Woodwards and Bernsteins, the fact remains that, in Russian eyes, it is the best they have of all official or legal channels for the expression of their opinions and demands. They prefer to turn to their newspaper rather than to their duly elected representatives (single slate), or to Communist Party officials, or to the agencies of administration in their locality. They turn least of all to the mass civic, or public, organizations that, in the eyes of the citizens, do not even do what they are formally empowered to do. Perhaps the tremendous reserve of attention and salience that the newspaper enjoys in the Soviet Union is more nearly an indicator of the limitations and frustrations of the citizen than of the positive role it plays. But reserve there is, and it is doubtful, no matter how popular, diverting, and even hypnotically attractive television may become, that it will supersede the newspaper as advocate of public demands.

## NOTES

1. See V. I. Lenin, *What Is To Be Done?* (New York: International Publishers, 1969).

2. *Mnogonatsianolnaya sovetskaya zhurnalistika* (Moscow, 1975), p. 50.

3. Deidre Carmody, "Newspaper Publishers Cite Gains," *New York Times,* April 24, 1979, p. D14.

4. *MGU: Fakultet Zhurnalistiki* (Moscow, 1972).

5. V. A. Medvedev, "Voprosy propagandy sotsialisticheskogo obraza zhizni," *Sotsialistichesky obraz zhizni i voprosy ideologicheskoi raboty* (Moscow, 1977), p. 87.

6. *Mnogonatsionalnaya,* p. 50.

7. V. A. Shpiliuk, *Mezhrespublikanskaya migratsia i sblizhenie natsii v SSSR* (Lvov, 1975), p. 54.

8. "News and Editorial Content and Readership of the Daily Newspaper," *News Research for Better Newspapers,* vol. 7, ed. Galen Rarick (Washington, D.C.: ANPA Foundation, 1975), pp. 14, 20.

9. These figures are based on a survey of news coverage in Gayle Durham Hollander, *Soviet Political Indoctrination* (New York: Praeger, 1972), p. 43.

10. Robert G. Kaiser, *Russia: The People and the Power* (New York: Pocket Books, 1976), p. 236.

11. Ibid., pp. 243-44.

12. E. S. Petrenko, "Territorialnaya vyborka dlya sravnitelnogo sotsiologicheskogo issledovania," *Proektirovanie i organizatsia vyborochnogo sotsiologicheskogo issledovania* (Moscow, 1977), p. 42.

13. V. E. Shlyapentokh, *Sotsiologia dlya vsekh* (Moscow, 1970), p. 169.

14. V. E. Shlyapentokh, "Problemy svoi i chuzhie," *Literaturnaya Gazeta,* November 30, 1977, p. 12.

15. Ibid.

16. Shlyapentokh, *Sotsiologia,* p. 169.

17. Ibid., p. 167.

18. B. V. Evladov, A. Pokrovsky and V. E. Shlyapentokh, "Chetyre tysyachi i odno interviu," *Zhurnalist* 10 (October 1969), p. 36.

19. Mark Hopkins, *Mass Media in the Soviet Union* (New York: Pegasus, 1970), p. 336.

20. Shlyapentokh, *Sotsiologia,* pp. 160, 167.

21. I. T. Livykin and O. V. Kharitonova, "Poznavatelnye interesy sovremennogo kolkhoznogo krestyanstva i chtenie," *Problemy sotsiologii i psikhologii chtenia* (Moscow, 1975), p. 70.

22. G. I. Khmara, "Pechat v sisteme massovykh kommunikatsii," *Problemy sotsiologii pechati,* vol. 1 (Novosibirsk, 1969), pp. 203-4.

23. U.S. Bureau of the Census, "Educational Attainment: March 1973 and 1974," *Current Population Reports,* Series P-20, no. 274, December 1974, p. 15. About 23 percent of the population over 25 and 42.5 percent of the age group 22 to 24 have had at least one year of college education. About 17 percent of the age group 22 to 24 has completed at least four years of college.

24. "News and Editorial Content," p. 12.

25. Ibid.

26. Ibid., p. 13.

27. "Media Exposure: Differences between Blacks and Whites," *News Research for Better Newspapers,* vol. 7, p. 3.

28. Alfio Colussi, "Radiografia dell'Italia che legge," *Corriere della Sera,* June 26, 1974, p. 4.

29. Bruce H. Westley and Werner J. Severin, "A Profile of the Daily Newspaper Non-Reader," *Journalism Quarterly* 41 (Winter 1963), pp. 45-50, 156; Jeanne Penrose, David H. Weaver, Richard R. Cole, and Donald Lewis Shaw, "The Newspaper Nonreader 10 Years Later: A Partial Replication of Westley-Severin," *Journalism Quarterly* 51 (Winter 1974), pp. 631-38.

30. Colussi, p. 4.

31. "News and Editorial Content," p. 12.

32. Khmara, p. 197.

33. Shlyapentokh, *Sotsiologia,* p. 168; E. O. Dobolova and D. D. Lubsanov, "Chitatelskie interesy i otsenki," *Iz opyta konkretno-sotsiologicheskikh issledovanii* (Ulan-Ude, 1972), p. 98.

34. "News and Editorial Content," p. 34.

35. V. E. Shlyapentokh, "K voprosu ob izuchenii esteticheskikh vkusov chitatelya gazety," *Problemy sotsiologii pechati* vol. 2 (Novosibirsk, 1970), p. 61.

36. Shlyapentokh, *Sotsiologia,* p. 172.

37. Khmara, p. 197.

38. These findings and the data supporting the following points are drawn from "Literaturnaya Gazeta i ee chitatel," *Problemy sotsiologii pechati,* vol. 2, pp. 131-35.

39. Dobolova and Lubsanov, p. 98.

40. D. D. Lubsanov, G. K. Balkhanov, E. A. Golubev, and E. O. Dobolova, "Nekotorye problemy izuchenia effektivnosti sredstv massovoi propagandy v Buryatii," *Iz opyta konkretno-sotsiologicheskikh issledovanii* pp. 53-55.

41. Dobolova and Lubsanov, pp. 96-97.

42. G. Strukov, "Gazeta, chitatel, zhizn," *Gazeta, chitatel, zhizn* (Voronezh, 1971), p. 124; Fomicheva, p. 144.

43. A. V. Zhavoronikov, "Potreblenie materialov gorodskoi gazety," *Sotsiologicheskie problemy obshchestvennogo mnenia i deyatelnosti sredstv massovoi informatsii* (Moscow, 1976), pp. 56-57.

44. "News and Editorial Content," pp. 24-25.

45. Ibid.

46. Shlyapentokh, *Sotsiologia,* p. 170.

47. Ellen Mickiewicz, "Policy Applications of Public Opinion Research in the Soviet Union," *Public Opinion Quarterly* (Winter 1972-73).

48. B. Z. Kogan and Iu. I. Skvortsov, "Stroki, temy, zhanry," *Problemy sotsiologii pechati,* vol. 2, (Novosibirsk, 1970), pp. 43-49.

49. Shlyapentokh, *Sotsiologia,* pp. 230-31.

50. Mickiewicz, p. 571.

51. "Literaturnaya Gazeta i ee chitatel," p. 127.

52. Shlyapentokh, *Sotsiologia,* p. 231.

53. Mickiewicz, p. 572.

54. "News and Editorial Content," p. 30.

55. Zhavoronikov, p. 60.

56. I. D. Fomicheva, *Zhurnalistika i auditoria* (Moscow, 1976), pp. 110-15, 132.

57. "How Skeptical Are Readers and Why?" *News Research for Better Newspapers,* vol. 5 (New York, 1971), p. 79.

58. Fomicheva, p. 116.

59. Ibid., pp. 137-48.

60. Shlyapentokh, *Sotsiologia*, p. 171.

61. Kaiser, pp. 242-43.

62. Mark S. Rhodes, "Letters to the Editor in the U.S.S.R.: A Study of Letters, Authors, and Potential Uses" (Ph. D. dissertation, Michigan State University, East Lansing, 1977).

63. *Handbood of Soviet Social Science Data,* ed. Ellen Mickiewicz (New York: Free Press, 1973), p. 171; and Rhodes. The volume of letters to *Pravda* increased from 300,000 in 1967 to 464,766 in 1976. S. I. Igoshin, "Pisma chitatelei kak vyrazhenie sovetskoi demo-kratii," *Problemy zhurnalistiki,* vol. 9 (Leningrad, 1977), p. 56.

64. V. T. Davydchenkov, "Organizatsia sotsiologicheskogo obsledovania i vnedrenie poluchennykh resultatov v tsentralnoi gazete," *Problemy sotsiologii pechati,* vol. 2, p. 148.

65. Craig R. Whitney, "Soviet Reports Investigate, too, but only within Limits Set at Top," *New York Times,* March 27, 1978, pp. 1, 3.

66. V. I. Kazantsev, "Opyt issledovania antialkogolnoi temy na stranitsakh gazety," *Metodologicheskie i metodicheskie problemy kontent-analiza,* no. 2 (Moscow-Leningrad), pp. 68-69.

67. E. O. Dobolova and S. G. Komissarova, "Raionnaya gazeta v otsenke svoikh chitatelei," *Iz opyta konkretno-sotsiologicheskikh issledovanii,* p. 90.

# 6

# THE AUDIENCES FOR MOVIES, THEATER, AND MUSIC

## THE MOVIE AUDIENCE

The Soviet film industry has had a long and distinguished history. In the immediate postrevolutionary period it produced some of the most interesting and innovative movies in the world. Dziga Vertov's *Man With a Movie Camera* had already utilized the multiple split-screen technique in 1929; Eisenstein, Pudovkin, and Dovzhenko were stars in the early Soviet cinematic galaxy. The importance of a medium that did not depend for its effect on literacy was recognized by the revolutionary Soviet regime from the start, and it seized upon a medium that would carry the regime's message over the highly differentiated regions and peoples of a vast country.

At present the Soviet film industry is centralized under the authority of the State Cinematography Committee of the Council of Ministers; it is also subject to the control of the party's Central Committee through the Film Section of its Department of Culture. Until 1976 the production of feature films by Soviet movie studios had increased steadily, up to 248 during 1976. During the next year, however, the number of new films produced had declined to 1975 numbers (241), including some made for television. Until the late 1960s there had been a steady and impressive increase in movie attendance, but by the 1970s a clear per capita decline had become visible. The decline was registered first in cities (where television appeared first). Nationwide, the per capita urban movie attendance rate fell from 21 in 1970 to 16 in 1978. In the Russian Republic the decline was identical. Per capita rural attendance continued to increase, or at least remain stationary, up to 1975 and then began to decline in several republics

(Russia, Uzbekistan, Kazakhstan, and Tadzhikistan). Between 1975 and 1978 a per capita increase in the rural movie audience was registered only in Georgia and Azerbaidzhan. In rural areas of the USSR as a whole, per capita movie attendance fell from 17 in 1975 to 16 in 1978, and in the Russian Republic it fell from 23 to 20.[1] As television becomes increasingly widespread in the countryside, the decline may become more dramatic.

In the Soviet Union there is a vast rental system, a kind of inventory of films, from which the individual theaters book films. The movies in the inventory are of varying ages. The store of movies is constantly changing, as new movies replace some older ones. There is detailed information available about what the film inventory contained in October 1970. At this time, over 1,200 movies in the inventory were Soviet made, about 400 were produced in other socialist countries, and about 150 came from capitalist, or Western, countries. The rest were imported from Arab, Indian, and other third-world countries. By far the single largest category or type of movie in the inventory is movies with a contemporary setting. These make up about a third of the total; most were produced not earlier than the 1960s. In terms of sales, they are the least popular movies (see Table 1). Average sales for movies about current problems are near or at the bottom consistently. Adventure, comedy, and musical films, though there are many fewer of them, outgross serious movies with contemporary settings by over 200 percent.[2]

An example of an extremely successful movie with a contemporary setting is *The Journalist,* about a 30-year-old newspaper reporter whose job is checking allegations sent in to the letters-to-the-editor section. In its second part, it follows the hero, on assignment with a delegation of Soviet journalists, to Paris and Geneva. The almost 28 million attendance figure is high for a movie with a contemporary theme, since these average between 9.5 and 12.5 million sales per movie. About a quarter of the imports from socialist countries are about contemporary issues, and they are even less successful than their Soviet counterparts. Films of this sort produced from 1965 to 1969 brought in, on the average, about 8 million sales per film. In speculating why these films consistently do so poorly compared to other kinds of movies, Soviet critics suggest that although contemporary life may be used as a kind of backdrop, the actual here-and-now problems and conflicts are superficially passed over and never actually grappled with; they remain empty and ultimately unsatisfying exercises. We shall return to this question later, when we discuss what audiences think of some individual movies.

Movies about World War II make up about 12 percent of the movie inventory; half were made in the 1960s. Historical-revolutionary movies, about 150 of which are in the inventory, tend to be fairly old. Only a third of this type of movie had been made in the four or five years preceding analysis of the inventory. Another 12 percent of the Soviet-produced films in the inventory are screen versions of novels and plays, 9 percent of them of foreign works (*Hamlet* and *King Lear* were major productions). Of native works, those most often brought to the screen are the plays of Ostrovsky, followed by works of Gogol,

**TABLE 1: Average Number of Sales for Type of Film, 1967-69**

| Year of Film Production | Film Type (million sales) | | | | | | | |
|---|---|---|---|---|---|---|---|---|
| | Contemporary | Historical-Revolutionary | World War II | Historical-Biographical | Literary | Adventure | Comedy | Musical |
| 1967 | 11.3 | 13.6 | 19.3 | 13.1 | 18.8 | 23.6 | 32.9 | 13.6 |
| 1968 | 9.4 | 14.3 | 15.4 | 10.3 | 14.1 | 34.9 | 12.6* | |
| 1969 | 12.8 | 15.7 | 16.2 | 8.9 | 14.5 | 25.5 | 30.5* | |

*Figures combined for comedy and musical.

*Source:* Adapted from B. Dolynin, "O Strukture deistvuyushchego filmofonda," *Trudy vsesoyuznogo nauchno-issledovatelskogo kinofotoinstituta,* vol. 66 (Moscow, 1973), p. 118.

Chekhov, and Tolstoy. Gorky is the most frequently filmed Soviet author, by a wide margin. Screen versions of literary works, though they tend to be expensive and important productions, make up a small part of total annual movie production, about 10 percent.

The historical movies in the inventory are old. Most of them were produced between 1920 and 1950, and their total proportion of the inventory is just under 7 percent. Socialist imports of these kinds of movies are relatively unpopular, in striking contrast to the great box-office success that Western historical movies enjoy.

Most but not all films in the inventory are about these weighty subjects. Serious movies make up almost three-quarters of the total available for rental; light entertainment films make up 27 percent. In this category of light entertainment, which includes comedies, musicals, adventure stories, fantasies, and fairy tales, imports play a greater role. Almost 40 percent of all the movies from socialist countries and 30 percent of all the movies from capitalist countries are of this type. The adventure movie (mainly detective and spy stories) is a relative newcomer to the inventory. Only 11 of them (just under 13 percent of the genre) are over ten years old; most have been very recently produced. They enjoy tremendous popularity, with the 1968 movie, *Shield and Sword,* a spy story, reaching attendance figures of almost 70 million nationwide. Soviet comedies, though heavy-handed for American tastes, are certainly popular at home. A 1967 production, *Caucasian Captive,* a contemporary satire on the traditional theme of the stolen bride in the wheeling-dealing spirit of the caucasian nationalities, played to an audience of 76.5 million people in the year following its release.[3] The tremendous disparity between the demand for light entertainment movies and the number of such movies available in theaters suggests that the declining sales and the criticism of the movie repertoire, which we shall look at later, might be reversed by a policy of production more nearly congruent with audience demand.

Because the Soviet film industry concentrates most of its resources in heavyweight films, which are thought to be good for the audience, it is primarily the imported film that makes up the deficit of light entertainment movies. The implications are twofold: on the one hand, the foreign film is disproportionately associated with what satisfies audience demand; on the other hand, as Soviet observers note, the foreign movies might be good examples of the particular genre, but many of them represent a mass culture that, by Soviet standards, is far from ideal or not even quite healthy, and these movies often play to the largest audiences. The Soviet government has sole control of the importation of movies. The foreign movies they permit in the country meet their ideological criteria, but their reliance on imports to fill a need they do not wish to satisfy or, perhaps, to acknowledge, has had some subtle, unexpected, and, from their point of view, possibly dysfunctional effects. This problem will be looked at in detail when we consider how Soviet audiences evaluate individual movies.

**Evaluating Movies: Sources of Satisfaction and Dissatisfaction**

Most people in the Soviet Union, no matter how well educated, go to the movies to be entertained, to escape from everyday life, to relax.[4] A large survey of Moscow film audiences found that comedies were by a wide margin the single most popular type of movie for all age groups. After that, different types of movies appealed to different age groups. Second, for the under-25 audience, were science fiction movies, which are of rather little interest to all others. People over 40 placed historical-revolutionary movies second; these, in turn, were close to the bottom in the under-25 group's preferences. High for all age groups were adventure movies, musicals, and folk epics.[5] The same disparities across age groups in the cinema audience were revealed by a survey of Sverdlovsk audiences. Young people are relatively indifferent to movies about war and re-volution, including World War II. In this, they differ radically from older people in the movie audience. This finding is a very disquieting phenomenon for media officials in the Soviet Union. The themes and images of war and the perpetuation of the memory of invasion and patriotism are crucial components of the propaganda system. That the young are increasingly impervious to these themes may simply be a function of time, and first-hand knowledge of the events portrayed and the emotions associated with them may now be restricted to older age groups.[6] The artificial prolongation of the life of historical events through the media may well have a diminishing effect over time.

It is known what audiences prefer from various surveys, one of the most ambitious of which is a republicwide sampling of opinion in Estonia. For many reasons Estonia is not typical of the Soviet Union. It is probably the most Western, most highly developed, most urban of all Soviet federal republics. Estonians and Finns are ethnically related and special ties to Finland are main-tained; Finnish workers are employed in Estonia and Finnish television programs may be received. Not least, Estonia is different because it had been an indepen-dent country between the two world wars. In their movie diet, Estonians look much like other audiences; they prefer musicals, followed by psychological dramas, adventure films, and comedies. Then there is a sharp drop-off in level of popularity and the serious movies are listed: tragedies and historical-revolution-ary movies, then science fiction, popular science, animations, epics, fairy tales, and large-scale spectacles. Here, too, the young (15- to 16-year-olds) are five times more likely to prefer to go to adventure movies than are their over-60 elders, and comedies enjoy across-the-board popularity with all groups.[7] The pattern is the same as seen before. Even in this highly developed, highly educated region, there is a distinct preference for light entertainment movies and movies involved with domestic life situations and conflicts. War and history lag behind. But the picture may be different in some rural areas.

Surveys were taken in two rural provinces in Russia, one in the Ukraine, and one in the Central Asian republic of Uzbekistan. The Uzbeks reported preferences for domestic love and conflict films, comedy, and adventure movies. Movies about World War II ranked fifth. But in the Russian and Ukrainian rural areas, World War II movies were first.[8] The unusual salience of war movies is no doubt a result of a very different history: these provinces were occupied by Nazi forces during the war and were the scene of considerable violence. In addition, personal ties are much more meaningful in the countryside than in the cities; families are bound more closely together, and within such close units, the memories might well have remained more vivid and more profound.

What makes a movie popular for Soviet audiences may have little to do with criteria of quality or aesthetic standards. This is a fact that the audience itself recognizes. For example, in Estonia, people were asked to rate some 52 films. Eight of them were produced in Estonia. The respondents gave these very low ratings, but the same respondents who thought the films poor reported very high rates of attendance, irrespective of level of education. Similarly, light entertainment movies (comedies and adventure films) were not highly evaluated by the audience, but were among the most popular. What seems to be happening is that where demand is very high, even low-quality films achieve considerable success. This is particularly true of Estonian-produced, Estonian-language movies, which, virtually regardless of quality, are box-office smashes in the home republic.

Estonian moviegoers place foreign movies very high in their ratings of films, and the younger the audience, the more it is inclined to favor the less serious imports. Older moviegoers prefer the more serious films, whether domestic or foreign. Among moviegoers under 20, of the nine most highly rated, two were Western movies: *The Magnificent Seven* (USA) and *Marriage Italian-Style* (Italy), one was Polish (*Ashes and Diamonds*), and one was a Soviet-made Western classic (*Hamlet*). The 19-year-olds, the heaviest consumers of movies in Estonia, rate four movies highest: *Hamlet* (USSR), *Quiet Flows the Don* (USSR), *Marriage Italian-Style* (Italy), and *The Magnificent Seven* (USA). In the over-20 film audience, *Judgment at Nuremberg* (USA) joins the list of the most highly rated movies (and the Italian comedy drops off the list). The Soviet movies given highest marks are such classics as *The Idiot, Quiet Flows the Don, Chapaev* (this, for the over-60 audience), and (for many of the over-25 audience) and two movies by Grigory Chukhrai that enjoyed considerable popularity abroad, *Ballad of a Soldier* and *The Forty-First*, both very human portrayals of small-scale incidents in World War II and the Civil War, respectively. Another Soviet movie that was rated highly by the over-20 age groups was Mikhail Romm's *9 Days in One Year*, a movie about an atomic physicist and the intellectual and moral conflicts his professional life engenders. The only other Soviet movie that enjoyed high ratings among several age groups was *Father of a Soldier*, a powerful Georgian-made movie about an old Georgian peasant who goes to the front to visit his wounded son during World War II and is drawn into the fighting.[9]

The Moscow audience survey asked about two Soviet movies, *Silence* and *Family Blood*, both widely distributed major movies of the mid-1960s. At the time the survey was taken, over 37 million people had seen the films nationwide, and some 57 reviews had been published, all extremely favorable, praising them for their "exceptionally positive educational effect," and the celebration of "the noble feelings and selflessness of the character of the Soviet man." *Silence* is a movie about problems of postwar Soviet life, and *Family Blood* relates the story of Fedotov, a soldier returning from the war, his chance meeting with Sonya, their love, and the story of her children who must eventually choose between their real father and their heroic and caring stepfather. Given this solid climate of praise and support in the official sources, the dissatisfaction of the college educated goes against the official grain. Over 80 percent of the workers who saw these movies were satisfied, but only a third of the well educated were satisfied, most of whom thought the films slow, boring, irritating, and confusing. Only about half of the audience under 30 was satisfied, but almost three-fourths of the rest liked the movies. Young people were more than twice as likely as others to point to the slow pace of the movies and to complain of boredom and confusion. Men were more than twice as likely to be critical and dissatisfied than were women.[10] People with little education, manual workers, and women were more patient and more approving.

What accounts for satisfaction and dissatisfaction among audiences in Russia is particularly well detailed by the Sverdlovsk survey. There, two surveys were conducted. In one, the elites, referred to as "competent judges," were asked to rate the best films of the year. These were creative personnel in movie and television studios and also leading newspaper and television journalists, theater and movie critics, and professors of aesthetics at universities—altogether 107 people. At the same time, the mass survey, referred to before, was done. In the experts' list, the prominence of foreign films is again apparent. Of the 12 movies called best of the year (1965), four were Soviet made and eight were foreign imports. In the top half of that list were five foreign movies (listed in order of rating): *Judgment at Nuremberg,* (second was the Soviet movie, *The Chairman*), *Ashes and Diamonds* (Poland), *The Entertainer* (England), *The Four Days of Naples* (Italy), and *The Stones of Hiroshima* (Japan). The experts were also asked to list the 12 worst movies of the year, and here, too, foreign movies were heavily represented; five were foreign-made, but of a very different kind. Four of the five in this group were third-world movies, either Arab or Indian. Only one (*Scaramouche*) was American, and no other Western movies were on the list. Of the Arab and Indian movies, the survey researchers had this to say:

> It is not a secret that the majority of films of these countries which are shown in our theaters are not of a high artistic quality. The banality of the subject, the imitation of life's truths, the everyday down-to-earth quality, the melodramatic accent, the triteness in the use of expressive means to a greater or lesser degree, [these] are typical of most of the Indian and Arab pictures. And the evaluation of such films by moviegoers is a quite definite indicator of the level of their artistic taste, aesthetic demands [and] general culture.[11]

So speak the experts. The masses have quite a different opinion. The 16- to 25-year-old audience is not particularly drawn to the more serious movies. *Judgment at Nuremberg* and *Ashes and Diamonds* were rated as about average. But they do like *Scaramouche,* and list an Arab and an Indian movie (judged worst by the experts) among the best, and two Indian melodramas (in the worst list of the experts) increase in popularity with the age of the audience. Probably the very worst movie for the population at large was the Czech movie *Lemonade Joe,* a heavy-handed satire of American westerns, which lacked credibility and style.

Arab and Indian movies are preferred by many moviegoers with less than college education. All of the four placed by the experts in the bottom 12 were very popular with people who have up to four grades of schooling—far more popular, in fact, than the American movies *Judgment at Nuremberg* and *One Potato, Two Potato.* A Sverdlovsk survey, taken two years before, had asked people, "Which foreign movies do you like best?" Indian movies were preferred by over a third of those with elementary education, almost 50 percent of those with five to seven grades of education, but only 17 percent of those with college education. The tremendous popularity of these movies cannot be dismissed lightly, for it reveals the demands and tastes of large numbers of film-goers. The Indian *Flower in the Dust* was among the top ten movies in the mass survey and the fifth-worst movie of the year in the experts' poll. It treats, as do many Indian movies, daily life and family problems through the prisms of emotion and pathos. It is this category of movie—family and children—that respondents say is most lacking in movie theaters. The Indian movies treat these issues in a moving way, eliciting the compassion and empathy of the audience for the "insulted and injured" (so familiar in Russian literature). This affective commitment, coupled with the exoticism of the settings, makes these movies extremely popular among people in all subgroups of the movie audience. Two Indian movies placed in the best 12 in the 1965 mass survey. They were *Flower in the Dust* and *Ganga and Dzhamna.* Although they enjoyed across-the-board success with viewers, it is true that the less well educated were higher in their praise than were the college educated. What disturbs Soviet authorities is that these tremendously popular movies (which they call "craftsmanlike fakes") seem convincing in their portrayal of the underside of life and have great emotional power (that Soviet movies seem to lack), but display, from the Marxist-Leninist point of view, mere mimicry rather than social truth. "The real trouble," they say, "begins when the unreal fake is taken as the measure of truth and beauty in art, and then, perhaps, in life."

The commitment to these movies is strong, as may be seen from the reactions provoked when critics are harsh in their reviews. There are floods of letters from movie fans, some frank and illuminating, such as the following letter received by the magazine *Soviet Screen* after it had published a devastating review of *Flower in the Dust.*

> Our [Soviet] films studiously avoid eternal human problems, pretending that there are none in our country. Some people think that the "posturing" of the heroine in *Flower in the Dust* is funny. But I don't. The heroes of the movie have a noble purpose—to awaken in the audience compassion for the fate of the abandoned girl. And maybe the movie is sometimes sentimental and melodramatic. It's for simple people and these are the means which are most intelligible to them. Movies started with melodrama and so did theater, and there's nothing wrong with that.[12]

What has happened in the film industry, as has happened in other of the media, is that the failure of the government to provide for the satisfaction of audience demand has distorted that demand in a way that runs, unexpectedly, counter to government goals. In this case there is a huge demand from masses of people, many of whom have little education, for movies the Soviet movie industry refuses to produce or produces in very small numbers. As a critic observed, "a long time ago the genre of melodrama in our cinema was reduced from art to the situation of an 'old, worthless lady,' thanks to the efforts of zealous administrators and vulgar theoreticians. The balance between audience demand and their real satisfaction was destroyed. It was not long before the price had to be paid: The theme of everyday family life, which is the most accessible melodrama, was 'farmed out' to foreign films." In fact, the big box-office blockbusters in recent years have been just this type of movie: the Egyptian *Unknown Woman*, the American *Rhapsody*, and later, the Indian *Love in Simla*. It might well be that it is the foreign film that satisfies, to the extent possible, the most powerful audience demand, and thus comes to be associated (more than are domestic-made movies) with pleasure and catharsis.

Attendance figures for these foreign films are far higher in rural areas than for the more serious foreign films the experts rate as among the best. For example, some 52 percent of the rural residents in the survey went to see *Flower in the Dust*, and 33 percent went to see the Arab movie *Sunglasses*. But only 7 percent saw *Judgment at Nuremberg*, 4 percent saw *The Four Days of Naples*, 7 percent saw *The Stones of Hiroshima*, and 9 percent saw a Vittorio De Sica comedy. In rural areas, the success of the Indian and Arab movies was by no means confined to the less well educated or the older population, but cut across all age groups and levels of education and included the rural intelligentsia as well. The success of the third-world melodramas is not simply due to the fact that other movies might be less accessible. Even when Soviet movies with similar themes are shown much more widely in rural areas, it is still the third-world melodrama that is rated much more highly.[13]

The audience reaction to a recent war movie reveals sharp differences among generations in Russia. This movie of the early 1970s was called *Belorussia Station*, the name of a railroad station where the characters met at the conclusion of World War II. The narrative of the film is expressed through the reminiscences of older people who had been in the war. Now they have become a director of a factory, a bookkeeper, a journalist, a plumber, and a nurse. They tell about their earlier lives in wartime. The survey of reactions to this movie was carried out in the Russian province of Belgorod, among rural people over 14, in March 1971. The 270 respondents were chosen randomly from lists of residents. On the whole, positive reactions to the film increased with age; the young were least satisfied. The young (15 to 18 years old) were also much less likely to believe that the movie described real life or real events. Over 40 percent of this age group doubted the authenticity of the events and conditions portrayed in the movie. In general, young people were less enthusiastic about the movie than their elders, and they were considerably more critical of it. When the respondents were asked if the movie contained episodes that recalled to the audience their own experiences, almost 85 percent of the respondents between 15 and 18 said no, as contrasted with 8 percent who said yes. This is virtually the mirror image of the audience between 51 and 60, of whom 87 percent said yes and 8 percent said no. The sharp break in the pattern of reactions comes after the age of 40. Under 40, from 70 percent to 84 percent claim that nothing in the movie is meaningful in terms of their own experience. After 40, at least three-fourths of the audience find that the movie relates to their own lives.[14]

The discontinuities between the under-40 and over-40 generation suggest what authorities call a "fathers and sons" problem. The young have not lived through the war and do not share the memories of the old. Perhaps the major propaganda resource of the government—the lesson and impact of World War II—might simply have been exhausted. It just does not, apparently, produce the effect or touch the same chords it once might have done—at least not for the coming generations. These movies are far less popular with young people than are trivial comedies and detective stories, even in the countryside, where they are most successful. They do not reach new audiences and cannot be counted on for the automatic response they might once have produced.

It might be asked why is it that an Arab or Indian movie, with its exotic locale and stylized alien customs, more surely and powerfully reaches large numbers of the Russian audience than such a film as *Belorussia Station*, which describes an event in the shared recent past of unsurpassed importance in the history of the Soviet Union and in the history and suffering of individual families. In part, the Soviet audience has been oversaturated by war movies and war messages. But also it is apparent that Soviet movies do not convey the kind of sentimental or melodramatic emotionalism that the audiences perceive as genuine and therefore actually touching. There may be a time limit governing the durability of memories, even those that unite and integrate a society. The artificial perpetuation of a high emotional pitch is also subject to laws of entropy.

## Who Goes to the Movies and Who Stays Away

A survey of American moviegoers taken in July and August of 1979 found that three-quarters of the film audience was under 30. Almost half were from

12 to 20 years old. Fewer than a quarter of the tickets were bought by people aged 30 and older, although they are 61 percent of the population.[15] Moviegoers are young in the Soviet Union, too. Eighty percent of the Estonians under 30 report going to the movies twice a month or more, but only 48 percent over 30 go that often. Ten percent of the 19-year-olds go to the movies more often than twice a week.[16] In the Russian city of Sverdlovsk, where just under 8,000 people were polled, the young account for the single largest factor in movie audience composition. Seventy-nine percent in the 16 to 25 age group go to the movies at least once a week, as opposed to 17 percent in the over-60 age group. Over three-quarters of the regular (at least weekly) moviegoers are under 35.[17] Another survey in the Russian Republic, of 2,630 people in the city of Stavropol, found that as of 1977 young people under 30 made up about half of all movie audiences, and the most ardent moviegoers were elementary, high school, and college students.[18] In all of the Soviet surveys, older, less well-educated people go to the movies least often. Even before television began to compete for an audience, this was true.[19] Although somewhat different definitions are used, the overall conclusion is unmistakable: movies appeal to the young, both in America and in the Soviet Union. But that does not imply that movies are tailored to youthful tastes. Such would seem to be the result of the audience structure in the United States, but, as has been seen, the supply and demand for various kinds of movies are far from congruent in the Soviet Union. Then, too, it was only very recently that Soviet officials, confronting declining box-office receipts, began to ask questions about who goes to the movies.

Who does not go to movies, and why, tells a good deal about the effect and range of the medium. In the Estonian survey, it was found that some people went not at all, or rarely, to the movies. Rural people make up a large proportion of them. Over 40 percent of all of the collective farmers went to the movies not more often than once a month, but this includes 16 percent who do not go to the movies at all. About 40 percent of all of the administrative personnel and agricultural specialists are infrequent moviegoers, as are almost 43 percent of the farm mechanics, the elite of the agricultural labor force. The nonmovie-going population is also made up of housewives. Over 15 percent of the Estonian housewives never go to movies. There are differences among people in different occupations. The Estonian pollsters ranked 24 different occupational groups according to their frequency of movie attendance. The last two places were filled by collective farmers and housewives. Two other agricultural occupations filled two more of the last eight places. Retired people living on pensions occupy still another of the last eight places. Some of the reasons why these groups do not participate as actively as others in the communications world were given earlier. However, also listed among the least frequent moviegoers are doctors (who rank twenty-second on the scale), high school teachers (who rank eighteenth), and scientists and university professors (who rank seventeenth).[20]

What are the obstacles to movie going? The Estonian survey found that people most often cited the lack of good movies. Second, for men, was the conflicting commitment to evening study and, for women, the demands of housework. The demand for better films is more important for the better educated, who most frequently give this reason for staying away from movie theaters. People with elementary education and some high school education are more likely to give the reason of burdens of housework as the chief obstacle to going out to the movies. Overall, though, it is the dissatisfaction generated by the quality of the movies that is the primary reason why all age groups and people of all levels of education say they do not go to movies. External problems, such as lack of free time or income or geographical difficulties, are all exceeded by complaints about the films themselves.[21]

Two other major surveys, the Sverdlovsk survey and one taken in Moscow, confirm many of these findings. The Sverdlovsk study also found that the pressures of housework and care of small children limited the free time of many people who found it difficult to go out to movies. It found that older people, with reduced income and mobility, were inactive moviegoers; almost 70 percent of the over-60 age group went rarely or not at all to movies, as opposed to only 11 percent of the 16 to 25 age group. Industrial workers studying at night to raise their qualifications and wages are strapped for time and find it difficult to go to the movies, and this is especially true of the older workers (between 36 and 60) and those with up to seven grades of schooling.[22] In the Moscow study, too, although the high cost of tickets is the main reason for not going to the movies when educational levels are merged and the average taken, the picture is very different when disaggregated results are given. Dissatisfaction with movies is increasingly important as the respondent becomes more educated.[23]

Going to the movies in rural areas poses special problems and is particularly important, considering the very large proportion of Soviet citizens who live in the countryside. A separate survey was taken to tap attitudes of the rural movie audience. The survey was carried out in two large provinces in the Russian Republic (Belgorod and Saratov), and one each in the Ukraine (Poltava) and Uzbekistan (Samarkand). Part of the study, restricted to the two European regions in Russia and the Ukraine, found that almost half (47.3 percent) of the rural population over seven did not go to movies at all in Belgorod province, almost 40 percent in Saratov province, and over half (52.9 percent) in Poltava in the Ukraine. This added up to an estimated 1,133,000 rural people in these three provinces who never went to the movies. Two-thirds of the entire stay-at-home population are women, and even though women outnumber men in the rural population, they are far more heavily represented among people who never go to the movies (77 percent, as against 23 percent for men). At least three-quarters of the people who do not go to movies are over 40, and about two-thirds have only four or fewer grades of education. It is estimated that in these three provinces, about 16 percent of the people who are not moviegoers have never in their lives seen any movie at all; in this group are religious believers, as well as those who are incapacitated mentally, blind, or deaf. The authorities are not optimistic about mobilizing any part of this group.[24] The Sverdlovsk study found, too, that certain groups in rural areas contained large numbers who never go to movies. Such people made up almost 40 percent of the non-working population, almost 17 percent of agricultural laborers, 9 percent of rural specialist and nonspecialist white-collar employees, and 8.5 percent of the rural people who commute to cities to work. Almost a quarter of the rural people with elementary or less education never go to movies, and another quarter go very rarely. Among the population with high school education, those percentages drop to 0.7 percent and 5.9 percent. Every subgroup in the rural population, except for the rural intelligentsia and schoolchildren, has members who never go to movies.[25]

Enthusiasm for movies is fairly low in Belgorod and Saratov, even among people who go to them. When moviegoers were asked at the movie theater or club, where they had just seen a movie, if they thought they would lose much or little if movies were no longer to be shown there, about 20 percent in the two Russian provinces said they would not lose anything at all by not being able to go to movies. The great majority of the rural respondents were satisfied with the technical quality of the movies shown, but only between a quarter and two-fifths said they would go to the movies more often if more movies were shown. These judgments might be read as a kind of implied criticism of the movies themselves. Direct criticism of the movies they are shown was given by between 12 and 22 percent of the respondents as the main reason they do not go to movies more often.[26]

It would be impossible to speak of trends in movie going in the Soviet Union, or anywhere else, without taking into account the profound effects produced by the introduction of television. Without question, the audience for television is far more massive than is the audience for movies. Even as early as 1960 in the city of Sverdlovsk, the ratio of movie to television audience was 15 to 100. Six times more people would see an average television program in those early days of television than the much-touted films *The Cranes Are Flying* and *Clear Skies,* by the eminent director Chukhrai.[27]

On the other hand, it is the feature film that is the most popular television fare. To what extent does watching a movie on the home set keep people away from the movie theater? The Estonian survey found that some people prefer to go to the movies rather than to see the movie on the home screen, where it will appear in a matter of a few months. Only the college students and professionals in arts and culture are far more likely to go out to the movies than to watch a movie on television; no other groups in the republic are as committed to the movies as these two. As was noted earlier, age makes a big difference in whether a person will see a movie at home or in the theater. Young people aged 20 to 24 prefer going out by a wide margin, as do 19-year-olds and 25- to 29-year-olds. People with college education and advanced degrees would rather see a movie out.

Even though at the time of the Estonian study there was an overall preference expressed for watching a movie in the movie theater, it was clear that television was cutting into the movie audience, and the trend could only accelerate as more sets appeared in more households. The most avid moviegoers would be least affected. The habits of the highly educated and arts professionals would undoubtedly endure even into the mass television age. However, it appeared that the alternative offered by television sharpened the demand for better films, and an element of choice had been introduced, particularly in Estonia, where Finnish programs are received. Another aspect of the trend was seen to be purely economic and potentially very serious. As one Soviet communications specialist observed, "The competition between movies and television is manifest mainly in the economic plan and only with the intensive spread of television."[28]

For rural people, the introduction of television has been revolutionary. In the two Russian provinces and the Ukrainian province where a survey of the rural populations was done, it was found that up to 1968, movie attendance figures were increasing annually, but that beginning in 1969, the audience began to decline. From 1968 to 1969 almost a million fewer movie visits were recorded in Belgorod province, with per capita visits dropping from 17 to 16.3. On days when popular television programs were broadcast, movie receipts fell by 50 percent. Even more dramatic was what happened with the movie *Liberation*, the cycle of movies making up an epic about the exploits of the Soviet Army in World War II. Done on a mass scale, this movie was to be the answer to the "falsified results of the Second World War [given] by many foreign countries."[29] When the first two parts of this cycle were shown in a theater in Poltava province in the Ukraine, they grossed 3,552 rubles from a paid attendance figure of 12,052. However, shortly afterward in May 1972, these two parts appeared on television and the announcer stated that the remaining two parts would soon follow. When the last two installments arrived at the movie theater, attendance dropped to 5,502 and box-office receipts to 1,459 rubles.

The problem of attracting movie audiences is further complicated by the fact that most of the films in rural rental systems are old movies: 50 to 60 percent of the rural repertoire are not first-run movies. Beyond that, it is not at all unusual for a movie to reach the television screen before it gets to a rural movie theater or club. Movies take only six to 12 months to go from first booking in big cities to the television screen. New films are booked first into the widescreen urban circuit; then the prints are modified for second-circuit movie theaters without modern projection and film facilities. Before the reworking of the film has been completed for the rural audience, the film might well have already appeared on television. In March, April, and May of 1972, when a study was done, this had happened with a number of much-publicized pictures in Poltava province, and a second-circuit movie theater there reported that its planned movie receipts were realized by only 46.6 percent. Before 1960, when television sets were not yet in wide distribution in the countryside, second-circuit theaters in Poltava usually realized box office receipts above planned projections. Afterward, the degree of plan fulfillment began declining.[30]

It might be said that what television has done is actually to broaden the movie audience by activating a population that would not, in any case, have gone out to the movies; they now watch movies at home. It is estimated that television increased the rural audience for movies by 22.3 percent. On the other hand, when rural people were asked why they no longer went out to the movies, 24 percent said it was because they had television at home.[31] In Belgorod province in Russia, just on the central channel alone some 69 movies were broadcast in one month, and twice to three times as many people watched movies than watched news or other sociopolitical programs on television. It was also found that some people were staying home waiting for the movie to play on television. Such types accounted for over 15 percent of all the people served by Belgorod rural movie theaters, 14.2 percent for Saratov rural theaters, and almost 28 percent of the people served by Poltava rural theaters, where density of television sets was the highest. In these three provinces the effect of the pull of television programming in general, not just of the movies playing on television, reduces the potential movie audience by between a quarter and a third.

What draws rural audiences to their movie theaters and clubs is the social aspect of movie going: going out with friends. It is for this reason that the younger people would much rather go out to the movies than stay home with the family. They may be the single really enthusiastic group of rural moviegoers. For the rest, television is a free source of films in a setting more comfortable than the rural movie theater, where people complain about the bad sound, the insufficient heating in winter, the lack of ventilation in summer, the dirt, the disorderliness in the audience, and the uncomfortable seats. Staying at home, it is possible to see on the average over a two-month period some 400 hours of films broadcast over central television.[32]

## Movie Advertising

Almost all of the movie advertising in the Soviet Union is in the form of posters. The movie poster has been and continues to be the single most important channel for the dissemination of official information about movies. Over two-thirds of all expenditures on advertising (some 70 percent) is allocated to posters and only 12 percent is spent on advertising in the media.[33] The Sverdlovsk survey found that people are attentive to posters, which ranked first as the reason why people were prompted to go to a movie. In Estonia, the leading source of information about movies is the press. The Estonian case is likely to be the exception because of its very high rates of literacy and urbanization. Unofficial sources of information, word-of-mouth communications from friends and family are extremely important, given second place in both Estonia and Sverdlovsk; in Moscow, the opinions of one's friends were the chief factor guiding people over 25 to a particular film.[34] As might be expected, the task of advertising and disseminating information in rural areas is much more difficult than in the city. The survey of the rural provinces in Russia, the Ukraine, and Uzbekistan found that on the average only about half of the people polled knew what movies were playing or even that movies were playing. In the Russian provinces people were slightly more likely to have information (almost 63 percent in Belgorod and 60.5 percent in Saratov knew about movies in the area), but in Poltava and Samarkand only 51.3 percent and 50.5 percent, respectively, had been informed about local movies. The main source of information about films in the countryside is the poster, claiming the attention of between 80 and 90 percent of the respondents. Word-of-mouth from friends is a much more infrequent source of information, given by about 11 percent of the respondents, on the average (highest for Poltava: 18.8 percent and lowest for Saratov: 6.3 percent). Even if one adds to this responses citing advice of family members, the total word-of-mouth advertising is cited by a high of 28.7 percent in Poltava and a low of 9.8 percent in Saratov. However, if one looks at the effectiveness of the source of information rather than the reach of the channel of information, then unofficial communications play a much larger role. The advice of friends, family, and the projectionist far outweighs official announcements and advertising, but the single most effective source is still the poster. Friends' opinions are a close second.

Considering the importance of the poster as the main advertising channel in the countryside, it is surprising how little information it provides, rarely anything more than the date and time of showing and name of film. Usually, nothing is given about the subject of the movie or who made it, what actors are in it, or who directed it. From surveys, it is apparent that the overwhelming majority of the rural movie audience would prefer to know the subject of the movie rather than any other information about it. The advertising poster for rural audiences is hardly the slick commercial product one might expect. It is often handwritten, casually and ungrammatically, with smeared ink and careless format. Since a movie in a rural area will play only in one place rather than the several theaters often available to the urban audience, and only for a single day, the importance of advertising could scarcely be overestimated. Without the powerful word-of-mouth advertising, it would be impossible to inform the rural audience, even to the extent that it is informed, and odds are essentially even whether or not they will know anything at all about what is playing and where.[35]


## THE THEATER AUDIENCE

Theaters are an essential component of the communications system. They are given the task of socializing and educating the citizenry, as well as satisfying their aesthetic demands. Because the theaters are in trouble in most parts of the country, official attention and sociological research efforts have been focused on them, and many hitherto unknown aspects of their functioning have come to light. Comparing movie visits for 1976 (about 4.5 billion nationwide) and theater visits (about 117 million) shows how relatively small are the numbers of theatergoers.[36]

A tourist in Leningrad and, especially, in Moscow might not know that theaters are having a difficult time. It is virtually impossible to get into the most popular theaters. A ticket to the innovative Taganka theater in Moscow, directed by Iury Liubimov, is a great prize for the capital's intelligentsia, as well as for visiting theater buffs. The Taganka holds only 665 people, average by Soviet standards, and one has to wait months to get in. But Moscow is not Russia. In fact, theater attendance nationally is declining. If one takes theater attendance per 1,000 urban residents as a measure of the popularity of the theater, the national decline is steady: 790 visits per 1,000 in 1955, 766 in 1960, 716 in 1965, and 670 in 1970.[37] In the largest cities, where many of the theaters are located and where attendance, in part swelled by numbers of tourists, has been highest, theater attendance per 100 residents fell from 180 in 1959 to 130 in 1974. Nationally, average attendance at theaters is about 400 people per performance, and the average theater has 660 seats. The per capita decline in attendance does not reflect a growing population unable to get into theaters, but rather reduced interest in theater.[38] Even in Leningrad, where per capita theater attendance in 1960 was about twice the average for cities in the USSR, there has been a steady decline, with a decrease of 270 visits per 1,000 in the population between 1960 and 1970.[39]

The total number of theater visits had been rising slightly until 1975, but started dropping off in Russia and a few other republics. National numbers were down by 500,000 between 1975 and 1977.[40] Every September in the Russian Republic, the Ministry of Culture holds a review of the work of all the theaters in the republic, The repertoire of each theater is discussed; standards of operation come under scrutiny, and so does the budget. Some have stable balance sheets from year to year and are termed "prosperous," but there are many theaters in the republic that report at the beginning of the season that during the previous season they were unable to fill more than 40 or 50 percent of their theaters for a performance.[41] The theater may be much more closely tied to the traditions and cultural habits of the region than are other of the media. In this sense, it may not have attained the status of a "mass" medium, in spite of the centralization of the administration and the government's control over repertoires and funding.

The different republics exhibit rather different degrees of attachment to the theater. Theater is most popular in Estonia, where in 1970 there were 945 theater visits per 1,000 people. Latvia, another of the highly developed Baltic republics, followed with 887 visits per 1,000 population. The theater is more than twice as popular in these regions than in the USSR as a whole, where the average is 440 per 1,000. Very low are the Central Asian republics of Uzbekistan, with 277 per 1,000, and Kazakhstan, with 246 per 1,000.[42]

The theater's loss of vitality in most parts of the country has stimulated discussions at the highest levels of the culture bureaucracy. Sometimes arguments are made that the theaters never really recovered from the severe cuts made after World War II. In 1940 there were a total of 908 theaters in the country; 25 years later, there were only 501. Most of the reduction had been made in theaters of drama, comedy, and music; opera and ballet theaters and special children's theaters had been less affected. All told, the largest single component of the theater network had been slashed by more than a half. Why the tremendous reduction in the number of theaters took place in 1948 under Stalin is not altogether clear. The reason usually given refers to the tremendous job of postwar reconstruction, the dire straits into which the economy had been thrown, the destruction of many theaters, and the impossibility of allocating resources in a major way to the network of theaters. These are very good reasons and may have been the basic cause for the contraction in theaters. But it is also true that ideological reasons underlay this cultural policy. Many theaters that had not been destroyed were closed down because of "weakness in creative attitude." The culture specialists were convinced at the time that the relaxed standards of wartime had produced a serious situation in which the desired forms of socialization were not coming from the theaters. Defending the mass closings, they argued: "Why inculcate people with weak, low-quality productions, [and] spread rotten taste?" Thus at least part of the reason why the number of theaters nationally was halved after the war was a prophylactic one on the part of the politicocultural overseers, who feared contamination and were not able to assert ideological control at the time. Better to remove the source, even though the remaining theaters could not increase their work to make up for the loss. The actual result of the policy might have had unexpected long-term consequences. One Soviet sociologist estimates that by 1960 the potential theater audience under 35 (and this age group forms the bulk of the theater audience) had had very little opportunity to attend theater productions. World War II prevented it from 1941 to 1945, and by 1949 the number of theaters had been cut in half. Is it any wonder, he asked, that this generation, the future for the theater, was drawn instead to movies and television?[43]

Theaters are not primarily commercial operations in the Soviet Union, but educational ones. "The commercial activity of the theater is secondary to its social function, which serves as the fundamental existence of the theater."[44] Lowered attendance figures suggest diminished effectiveness as an instrument of education or socialization, but they also show up in the debit column of the theater's balance sheet, and this is no small matter. While financial considerations are certainly not paramount in the Soviet mass media system and, in fact, they have yet to work out measures of profitability, they are increasingly important. People at the top talk more and more about efficient allocation of resources and are looking more seriously at the subsidies on which the culture network runs. The majority of Soviet theaters have in the past operated and continue to operate in the red. Furthermore, the deficit is growing. Officials are now asking why most theaters have to be chronically run on a deficit, and some are suggesting that with the proper organization and management, theaters could become profitable enterprises. However, specialists doubt this will ever become possible. The Ministry of Culture of the Russian Republic, under whose direction all the theaters there function, found that only 30 percent of the state subsidy goes into the actual daily operation of the network of theaters. The rest goes into areas not involved with the running of the theaters and is independent of actual theatrical operations. It is the social function of the theater that fixes its unprofitable position. Ticket prices must be kept low, the repertoire must reflect ideological criteria, and attendance must be stimulated regardless of costs. Between 1945 and 1965 the number of plays produced annually almost doubled, but the average attendance for a production fell from 465 to 423. Elasticity of demand is not great enough to absorb higher ticket prices, and it is estimated that if ticket prices went up, attendance would be sharply reduced. The social mission of theater in the Soviet Union requires the widest possible attendance. The only answer is the state subsidy, which is rather simply determined: the size of next year's audience is estimated on the basis of the actual size of last year's audience, plus the amount by which it is possible to increase it in the next year. Box-office receipts are estimated for the planned number in the audience. Costs are estimated in conformity with the already existing norms and practices. The subsidy, then, is simply the difference between income and costs. There are no qualitative assessments of the theater's activity built into the subsidy model. In fact, some have advocated a single criterion for the success of a theater: minimization of the state subsidy.

If breaking even, or even making a profit, becomes the criterion of success in the Soviet theater world, then one comes back to the primacy of audience demand. Right now, such a single determinant of theatrical productions does not exist, but such questions are beginning to enter into official thinking. Weighting consumer demand more heavily in planning theatrical productions might well lead to a change in the structure of the offerings. An attempt to get at the question of demand underlay an analysis of the most widely produced plays in the Soviet Union. The All-Union Agency for Authors' Rights (VAAP) publishes lists of plays that have appeared in at least 300 theaters nationwide and the number of performances for each play. The top 50 plays in the list account for about 50,000 performances; the remaining 250 titles represent another 50,000 performances. These top 50 are clearly the national leaders for theater audiences, although at any one time the theaters in a given city might be featuring a different program. Leningrad, for example, had rather few productions by Anatoly Sofronov in 1960, by far the most produced playwright in the Soviet Union that year (10,662 performances in 329 theaters), but in 1969 and 1970 the Leningrad theater repertoire looked much more like the most popular list nationwide.

In the ten years from the 1959-60 season to the 1969-70 season, the vast majority of the most frequently produced plays were written after 1945, though the percentage of such plays was declining from over 90 to 79 by the end of the decade. Plays in the Russian language have been declining as a proportion of all plays. Plays in other Soviet languages were 10.5 percent in 1967, and by 1969 almost 30 percent.[45] It would appear that under the Brezhnev regime there is a clear attempt to increase the number of plays in languages of the ethnic minorities, and the dominance of Russian-language productions has diminished. Among the most widely produced plays of this decade of seasons, the leaders are comedies, entertainment (including detective stories and mysteries), and melodrama.[46]

Is consumer demand satisfied by the supply of plays and other theatrical productions? A rough notion of the gap, if any, comes from comparing the number of productions (or titles) among the national leaders and the total number of performances. If in a given category the percentage of titles exceeds the percentage of performances, one might conclude that there is more supply than demand; if the performances are a higher proportion than the titles, one might conclude that this type of play is more popular and demand exceeds supply. Table 2 gives the results of such a comparison. It should be borne in mind, however, that a difference of one percentage point is equal to about 500 performances. The greatest disparities are generated by the public's desire for more escapist fare and pure entertainment. They are clearly less attentive to message plays and explicitly ideological works than the authorities would like them to be. But they are also less interested in serious classics and intellectually demanding works.

A group of professional theater critics and professors in Leningrad found that for the decade of seasons discussed, only a maximum of two-thirds of the productions "are in conformity with general ideological-artistic directions of the Soviet theater of the contemporary period."[47] They found an average of only half the plays produced over the ten seasons "artistically satisfactory."[48] It was seen before that, on the whole, most people's tastes in movies and television run to entertainment, relaxation, and escapism, although the highly educated may differ. The problem for theaters, according to one Soviet sociologist, is that the audience has now become a mass audience. Before the development of networks of movie theaters and before the widespread private ownership of television, theaters related to a particular ambience, to their own publics. Competing artistic models were few. Now the public has become a mass public, keyed into the mass media and adopting those standards and values. The dilemma of the theater is expressed in the following terms:

> The fight for the mass audience, which today has been diverted away from the theater by television and the movies, spurs many theaters to look for ways and means of theatrical expression which are accessible to everyone. The formation of the repertoire promoting a well-known unscrupulousness is tied to this approach. It seems that plays which are deprived of deep social content and even now and then frankly vulgar are "convenient" to produce. In other words the conditions are created for the flowering of what can only be called literary consumers' goods. . . .[49]

Calling the audience consumers conveys the writer's distaste for demand as *the* criterion guiding theater productions. The educating and guiding role of the theater should not, in his opinion, be replaced by consumer and sales criteria. Yet the role of sales and precisely that consumer demand, at variance though it

TABLE 2: Supply and Demand for Soviet Plays, Average 1959-69 (percent)

| Type of Play | Percent Titles (supply) | Percent Performances (demand) |
|---|---|---|
| Disparities | | |
| Comedy (primarily) | 54.7 | 56.2 |
| Pure comedy | 25.6 | 29.0 |
| Melodrama (primarily) | 46.0 | 47.8 |
| Pure melodrama | 11.5 | 14.4 |
| Entertainment (primarily) | 47.9 | 49.9 |
| Pure entertainment | 16.8 | 18.5 |
| High artistic work | 53.2 | 49.1 |
| Socially significant work | 51.2 | 46.5 |
| Relative Congruencies | | |
| Contemporary plays | 85.0 | 84.9 |
| Prerevolutionary plays | 9.7 | 9.9 |
| Russian plays | 74.6 | 73.1 |
| Ethnic-minority plays | 13.5 | 14.4 |
| Foreign plays | 11.8 | 12.5 |
| Detective plays (primarily) | 24.9 | 25.1 |
| Pure detective plays | 5.5 | 6.2 |

*Source*: Adapted from A. N. Alekseev and V. N. Dmitrievsky, "Teatralny repertuar kak obekt sotsiologicheskogo analiza," *Teatr i zritel* (Moscow, 1973), pp. 113-14.

be with the indoctrinating role of the theater, is increasingly at issue. The balance is ever more tenuous between "audience demand and the interests of the state."[50] The organs of governmental administration of culture have told theaters to look to "the reduction of state subsidies and the conversion of theaters to self-sufficiency."[51]

Economists are being drawn into the planning process for theater subsidies in order to devise models that are more sophisticated than the simple identity between costs and ticket sales. Perhaps to forestall the implementation of oversimplified models, they have attempted to draw up models that treat the socialization-versus-demand conflict in a more complex way. A first stab at the problem was a model that takes into account the type (genre) of the play, the number of productions in the given genre, the number of performances of each production, the time of year during which it is given, the average ticket price, the costs for a given production, and the amount of the state subsidy. Such a formula tells the theater administration and the funding agency it approaches the optimal proportion of certain genres in the repertoire and the number of performances. This optimal size is then subject to the "interests of the state" in limiting the number of plays of a particular genre (comedies, for example) and the number of performances in the genre. Even though the final structuring of the schedule for the theater is based on indoctrination goals, in this model, nonetheless, the whole model is derived from the "level, size, and structure of audience demand," without which it would be impossible to determine the scope of governmental activity.[52] Even when state interests in molding the audience are accorded primacy, it is a primacy that can only work in conjunction with known audience demand. The most basic notions of efficiency—avoiding growing deficits and reaching the population—require attention to the consumer, as the failing theaters have realized.

Another element in the complex and difficult financial circumstances of theaters outside Leningrad and Moscow is the stability of the theater public they serve. In Moscow and Leningrad, where tourists from both the Soviet Union and other countries swell the ranks of ticket buyers, geographical reach of the theater and the size of the population served are large. Theaters in these cities put on only from two to four new productions a year, and they are performed from 50 to 100 times each. However, provincial theaters, with their smaller and more stable public, are constrained to add more new productions to attract the audience. Theaters in regional capitals mount from six to eight new productions a year, and city theaters from nine to ten a year, with number of performances averaging from 20 to 30 for each new production.[53] Thus these smaller and less popular theaters, which have more modest resources than do the famous theaters of the capital, are required to invest in more new productions and strain their budgets even more severely.

## Composition of the Theater Audience

Several surveys have been done of theater audiences in different parts of the Soviet Union. In drawing conclusions about what kinds of people are theatergoers and who stays home, one should bear in mind that the habit of going to the theater is much stronger in Estonia and Latvia than elsewhere, and that cities such as Moscow and Leningrad are not typical. There are surveys of audiences available for theaters in the republic of Estonia, for 16 regional theaters in the Russian Republic, and for theaters in Moscow, Leningrad, and the Urals cities of Nizhne Tagil and Sverdlovsk. All the surveys show that the theater audience is predominantly female. As a rule, women make up about two-thirds of the entire theater audience. The lowest proportion of women recorded by the surveys was the average for the eight theaters in Leningrad, which was 55 percent.[54] This report of the Leningrad survey shows an average of 40 percent of the audience is male.[55]

The theater audience is also young. In the Russian Republic and in Estonia, about 72 percent of the theater audience is under 40; in Moscow 69 percent are under 40, and in Leningrad this figure is 65 percent.[56] Some theaters, such as the Vanemuine in the Estonian university city of Tartu, are filled with students. Over half the audience is, on the average, under 30, but for some productions, such as modern ballet, the under-30 audience makes up two-thirds of the audience. The classic *Gypsy Baron* draws only 45 percent under 30. Leonid Andreev's *He Who Gets Slapped* attracted an audience three-quarters of which was under 30.[57] Throughout Estonia the young are attracted to theater, and almost half the audience republicwide is under 30.[58] The average age of the theater-goer in the Russian Republic is also young: 32. However, the audiences in Moscow and Leningrad are older. There the average age is 35.[59] It may be considerably more difficult for students to go to the theater in these cities; it is more difficult to find tickets and more expensive to buy them. In Moscow's famous Theater of Satire, only one-third of the audience was under 25, and this proportion has not changed over the years. In Leningrad students make up somewhat more than a quarter of theater audiences, and in the Russian Republic generally about 12 percent.[60] The Leningrad audience is a fairly stable one. Long-time residents make up the vast majority of Leningrad theater audiences; an average of 68 percent have lived in the city for ten or more years.[61]

The theater attracts the more highly educated. In the Russian Republic, people with some college education make up about only 6 percent of the population, but they are 50 percent of the audience in theaters. At the other end of the spectrum, people who have had up to ten grades of education are 73 percent of the general population, but only 18 percent of theater audiences.[62] In Estonia, although there is a significant overrepresentation of the college educated in the theater audience, the proportion of people with some college education in the audience is much less than in Russia: about 33 percent. People who are low on the social-occupational ladder, such as blue-collar workers, are much more likely to go to the theater in Estonia (where they make up about 13 percent of the audience) than in Leningrad, where they are between only 1 and 3 percent of the theater audience.[63] But Leningrad is not typical; in theaters in the Urals, workers make up somewhat over a quarter of the audience.[64] In the Russian Republic theaters, the average proportion of workers in theater audiences is 11 percent.[65] With the exception of the most popular and sought-after theaters of Moscow and Leningrad, it would appear that blue-collar industrial workers do go to the theater in sizable numbers. True, they are underrepresented in terms of population proportion, but they are by no means closed out by the prosperous and educated. Some kinds of productions appeal particularly to those with little education; folk and popular comedies in Tartu play to audiences where over half have not gone beyond elementary school.[66] In general, workers prefer their own ethnic productions, and especially comedies about daily life situations. The intelligentsia there, however, by far prefer to go to see dramas. Less than a quarter of this social stratum likes operettas, and less than 10 percent go to musical variety shows.

A new survey prepared for the League of New York Theaters and Producers attempted recently to profile the Broadway audience. Broadway, like Moscow and Leningrad, is not typical of the theaters of the country and certainly not of their audiences. However, the findings of this new survey show that the New York audience is very well educated: about two-thirds have had some college education, not unlike the imbalance in the theater audiences of Russia. The New York audience is young: 57 percent are under 35. Women form the majority of theatergoers, just over half the audience (51 percent), which is lower than the proportion of women in the audiences of provincial theaters in Russia, but not very different from their proportion of the audience of the Leningrad theaters.[67]

In the Soviet Union children are encouraged to go to the theater. There are puppet theaters, which are attended by 843 per 1,000 children aged five to nine. There are youth theaters, for ages ten to 15, where attendance is 288 per 1,000 in that age group.[68] But theater is far from the most popular art form for children. A survey of about 11,500 schoolchildren in grades one to ten in 36 schools of 17 large cities in the Soviet Union found that theater was probably the least popular art form: one in two likes literature; one in three, movies; one in five, music; and only one in ten, the theater.[69] Encouraging children to make going to the theater a part of life, a habit, would provide for future generations of theatergoers and ease the plight of theaters.

## THE AUDIENCE FOR MUSIC

Russians listen to various kinds of music, from light, popular fare to serious classical works. Although certain musical forms, such as those that exhibit extreme modernist and formalist complexity, are considered ideologically deviant, what is left runs the gamut from mindless entertainment and escapism to "good" (classical) music. This does not mean, however, that all kinds of music, officially allowed music that is, are considered equally worthy and valuable. There is an explicit official hierarchy of values in which classical music is placed at the top and pop music, even Soviet-style, is at the bottom. Soviet officials are concerned about the tastes of Soviet citizens not only because of planning and financial considerations, but also because they hope that over time people will become educated in the appreciation for and love of classical European music (particularly nineteenth century), the highest musical value and the tradition to which the "best" examples of contemporary Soviet music are said to belong.

A large research project in the Urals cities of Sverdlovsk and Cheliabinsk between 1967 and 1970 produced results that were sobering. Most people like pop music and vastly prefer it to serious music. Melodia records reported to the survey analysts that their sales in the region were overwhelmingly dominated by light music: 90.4 percent of all record sales were of pop music and only 3.1 percent were of classical music. Between 1963 and 1968, sales of classical music increased about 1.5 times, but sales of popular music records increased 7.5 times.[70] Even live performances by symphony orchestras are increasingly devoted to pop music. In 1955 the Sverdlovsk Philharmonic's program for the year had only a very small portion devoted to the standard symphonic repertoire (5.5 percent) and another small part devoted to chamber music (4.9 percent). The rest was show tunes and other forms of popular music. Some ten years later, chamber and symphonic music together accounted for a mere 3.7 percent of the entire annual program. Again, the rest is light music. The Omsk Philharmonic devoted some 87.7 percent of its entire repertoire for 1968 to pop music offerings.

Is this typical? Are not opportunities significantly greater elsewhere? One might expect the Baltic republics, with their higher levels of urbanization, education, and Westernization, to have different patterns of performance and attendance. Latvia, which together with Estonia exhibits these high levels of development, shows a mirror image of the Urals audience pattern. In Latvia, 86 percent of all concerts were devoted to classical music, while only 14 percent were devoted to popular music. But for the Soviet Union as a whole the Latvian case is untypical. It was estimated that in 1967, across the entire nation, almost 60 percent of all programs of all symphony orchestras were devoted to popular music, and this was described as a significant improvement over previous years, when popular music had taken up a larger portion of the repertoire. In addition, attendance at concerts of popular music is very much higher nationally than at concerts of serious music. Probably the pop music audience is underestimated. Serious music is usually performed only by symphony orchestras; pop music is performed by all sorts of ensembles, in addition to taking up large parts of the symphonic repertoire. Radio stations increasingly drop classical music broadcasts in favor of pop music. They do it because the audience is there, just as Melodia markets pop music more energetically than classical music because the sales (and therefore fulfillment of the plan) are there.[71]

Just for the sake of comparison, one might observe that in the United States, popular records outsell classical records by 20 to 1. Traditionally, classical music has accounted for about only 5 percent of the total sales of the U.S. record industry.[72]

The Soviet pollsters developed profiles of types in the music audience. One type, said to represent small numbers of people, has no interest in music at all. This type is not confined to a particular social class or age group. The second, much more common, type is the pop music devotee. People in this group are not interested in any other kind of music. Here are found most of the elementary and high school students, as well as most workers and white-collar employees who have had from five to nine grades of education, and many engineers and technical specialists and college students in technical institutes. The third type in the music audience includes older workers and white-collar employees who are over 45 and do not have a great deal of education. These people prefer light or pop music, but not exclusively; they will also listen to some more complex musical forms. The last type, the classical music audience proper, is almost entirely made up of liberal arts college students and liberal arts college graduates who work in related fields. These people usually have had some formal training in music or music theory; it is said they possess a "high level of musical culture." It is clear they are not very numerous when compared to most of the other types of listeners in Russia.

Competition from television was directly cited by 20 percent to 33 percent of all people surveyed as the reason they do not go out to performances of live music. Workers, housewives, and retired people are particularly heavily represented in this group. It might be argued, as it has been argued about the news and movie audiences, that for these people, there would not be any consumption of serious music if it were not broadcast by television—that television has not kept these people away from concerts, but rather activated a hitherto isolated population, a population that will, in time, be attracted to live concerts as well. One has no way of judging the validity of this idea, but it is known that the tastes of this type of television viewer do not run to classical music. To some extent television has also depressed concert going among the more sophisticated listeners. Television presents the best performances and forces local ensembles and performers into an unequal competition. Outside the great cities, experienced concertgoers are shifting their attention away from live music locally performed to the televised music of national figures.

Opportunities are available to those who are gifted and who wish to specialize in music, but the opportunities are unevenly distributed. In 1964 the city of Sverdlovsk had a population of about a million people, and the greater Sverdlovsk region had about 4.5 million people. But in the city the seven elementary schools that specialized in music admitted, all told, about 300 children a year. Outside the city of Sverdlovsk, but in the greater Sverdlovsk province, 40 more such special schools could be found. The quality of the teaching varies; the urban schools employ much more highly qualified teachers. A total of 660 teachers are employed in the network of these special elementary schools in the Sverdlovsk region, but only 41 of them have finished college, and 30 of these teachers work in the city of Sverdlovsk. Of the total number of teachers in the Sverdlovsk special music education system, 492 have specialized secondary education in music, and 127 have no special training in music at all. Most of this last group of teachers work in the smaller cities and towns.[73] Music high schools are even harder to enter. There are only three in the entire greater Sverdlovsk region. One of them is the Tchaikovsky music high school. A look at the class composition of its students shows that just under 1 percent are children of collective farmers, slightly less than a third are children of blue-collar workers, and fully two-thirds are children of white-collar employees. Are musical gifts distributed along class lines this way, wonders the Soviet pollster? Probably not, but certainly the value orientation and greater financial means of the white-collar class are advantages—advantages the culturally isolated peasantry do not enjoy.[74]

Music is not the most popular of the arts, though it is second, after literature, for college students in the humanities, and third (after literature and theater) for specialists in liberal arts fields. Generally, music is a less popular pastime for workers and white-collar employees than are movies, vaudeville or variety shows, theater, and reading. The "humanistic intelligentsia" are held up by Soviet officialdom as the model of taste. They attend concerts more often and listen more attentively to music because, it is claimed, they are to a greater degree free from the "hypnosis of mass communications," which results in a growing insensitivity or numbness to music. This picture of the mindless radio and television audience swaying to the beat of repetitive patterns at high volume is at odds with that hoped-for new audience made aware of classical music through the media. A survey of young industrial workers in Sverdlovsk found that music was outranked by the circus and music hall entertainment in their preference scheme.[75] In Orel in Western Russia, a survey of almost 1,200 young workers in three factories found that almost 90 percent had not gone to a single concert of classical music during the preceding year. Eighty-eight percent of the sample were most interested in movies; only 5 percent gave music as their first interest.[76] The preference of these young workers for entertainment and uncomplicated light forms of relaxation may be both a cause of and response to the predominance of such music around them, but it also reflects the average taste seen before. Escapism and entertainment—uncomplicated and undemanding—are what most people in the broad base of the population seek.

## NOTES

1. S. P. Goriunov, "Faktory, vliayushchie na poseshchaemost kinoteatrov," *Sotsiologicheskie issledovania*, no. 3 (1979): 133; *Narodnoe Khozyaistvo SSSR v 1978* (Moscow, 1979), pp. 494-95.

2. B. Dolynin, "O Strukture deistvuyushchego filmofonda," *Trudy vsesoyuznogo nauchno-issledovatelskogo kinofotoinstituta,* vol. 66 (Moscow, 1973), p. 118.

3. Ibid., pp. 115-26.

4. A. L. Vakhemetsa and S. N. Plotnikov, *Chelovek i iskusstvo* (Moscow, 1968), p. 130; Felice Gaer, "The Soviet Film Audience: A Confidential View," *Problems of Communism* (January-February 1974), p. 54.

5. Vakemetsa and Plotnikov, p. 132.

6. *Kino i zritel* (Moscow, 1968), p. 134.

7. K. Yanulaitis, "Zritel i zhanrovaya tematika kinematografii," *Trudy,* vol. 60 (Moscow, 1971), p. 86.

8. Z. G. Kutorga, "Voprosy funktsionirovania kinorepertuara na sele," *Trudy,* vol. 69 (Moscow, 1973), p. 61.

9. K. Yanulaitis and E. Zelentsov, "Otsenka filmov zritelem i ego khudozhestvenny vkus," *Trudy,* vol. 60, pp. 73-84.

10. Vakhemetsa and Plotnikov, p. 150.

11. *Kino i zritel,* p. 204.

12. Ibid., pp. 230-31.

13. Ibid., pp. 170-291.

14. G. Lifshits and I. Rachuk, "Vospriatie filma 'Belorusskii Vokzal' selskim zritelem," *Trudy,* vol. 66, p. 112.

15. Tom Buckley, "At the Movies," *New York Times,* November 23, 1979, p. 12.

16. G. Lifshits, "Poseshchaemost kino razlichnymi sotsialno-demograficheskimi gruppami zritelei," *Trudy,* vol. 60, p. 44. Grushin's earlier study of nationwide movie audiences agrees with the Estonian survey, with slight differences, for the under-25 age group, but claims a 20 percent larger audience for the 25 to 29 age group and a 10 percent larger audience for the over-60 group. The lower rate of attendance recorded in Estonia may well reflect the impact of television, particularly important in a prosperous republic like Estonia. Grushin's data have undoubtedly become dated. See B. Grushin, *Svobodnoe vremya* (Moscow, 1967).

17. *Kino i zritel,* p. 65.

18. Goriunov, pp. 133-34.

19. John David Rimberg, *The Motion Picture in the Soviet Union: 1918-1952* (New York: Arno Press, 1973), pp. 130-41.

20. Lifshits, pp. 49-50.

21. A. Ionkus, "Prepyatstvuiushchie i sposobstvuiushchie faktory," *Trudy,* vol. 60, pp. 53-56.

22. *Kino i zritel,* pp. 63-64, 67-69.

23. Vakhemetsa and Plotnikov, pp. 136-37.

24. M. I. Zhabsky, "Metodika i nekotorye rezultaty sotsiologicheskogo issledovania poseshchaemosti kino na sele," *Trudy,* vol. 69, pp. 38-41.

25. *Kino i zritel,* p. 275.

26. B. Dolynin, "Svobodnoe vremya selskogo zhitelya i kino," *Trudy,* vol. 69, pp. 52-56.

27. *Kino i zritel,* pp. 95-100.

28. Ionkus, p. 61.

29. *Istoria sovetskogo kino: 1917-1967,* vol. 4 (Moscow, 1968), p. 459.

30. M. I. Zhabsky, G. I. Kopalina, and L. D. Rondeli, "Vlianie televidenia na chastotu poseshchaemosti kino," *Trudy,* vol. 69, pp. 68-69.

31. Zhabsky, pp. 38-43.

32. Zhabsky, Kopalina, and Rondeli, pp. 69-76.

33. L. P. Devlikamova and K. Yanulaitis, "Effektivnost kinoreklamnoi informatsii," *Trudy,* vol. 66, p. 133.

34. Vakhemetsa and Plotnikov, p. 126.

35. L. P. Devlikamova, "Nekotorye problemy effektivnosti reklamy v selskoi kinoseti," *Trudy,* vol. 69, pp. 94-98.

36. *Narodnoe Khozyaistvo v SSSR v 1977* (Moscow, 1978), pp. 608, 611. It is estimated that in the Russian Republic about 7.5 percent of the urban population between 16 and 70 goes to the theater. V. Zhidkov, "Voprosy Upravlenia," *Teatr,* no. 12 (December 1973), p. 46.

37. G. G. Dadamyan, "Sotsiologicheskie i sotsialno-ekonomicheskie problemy issledovania teatra," *Teatr i zritel* (Moscow, 1973), pp. 160-61.

38. L. A. Gordon, E. V. Klopov, and L. A. Onikov, *Cherty sotsialisticheskogo obraza zhizni: Byt gorodskikh rabochikh vchera, segodnya, zavtra* (Moscow, 1977), pp. 58-62.

39. A. Alekseev, O. Bozhkov, and V. Dmitrievsky, "K izucheniu sotsialnykh problem funktsionirovania teatra v sovremennykh usloviakh," *Problemy sotsiologii teatra* (Moscow 1974), p. 161.

40. *Narodnoe Khozyaistvo v SSSR v 1977*, p. 516.

41. S. Vulfson, "Nekotorye voprosy organizatsii, ekonomiki i sotsiologii teatra i vserossiiskoe teatralnoe obshchestvo," *Teatr i zritel* (Moscow, 1973), p. 260. The decline in theater attendance and the increasingly visible phenomenon of the partially empty house has sparked a debate about the goal of anshlag (the sold-out performance). During 1977, five authors joined the debate in the pages of *Literaturnaya Gazeta*. Although the articles are rather more general than those of the model-builders we examine in this chapter, they are evidence that the discussion has gone beyond the circle of experts and administrators. See *Literaturnaya Gazeta*, 1977, nos. 25, 31, 38, 49, and 52. I thank Professor Alma Law of Columbia University for providing me with these sources.

42. Dadamyan, p. 161.

43. Ibid., pp. 183-86.

44. A. Rubinshtein and B. Rubinshtein, "Sotsialno-ikonomicheskie problemy funktsionirovania teatra," *Teatr i zritel* (Moscow, 1973), p. 227.

45. A. N. Alekseev and V. N. Dmitrievsky, "Opyt kachestvenno-kolichestvennogo analiza preobladaiushchikh tendentsii razvitia repertuara dramaticheskikh teatrov SSSR—sezony 1959/60-1969/70gg," *Aktualnye problemy organizatsii, ekonomiki, i sotsiologii teatra* (Moscow, 1972), pp. 36-37.

46. Alekseev, Bozhkov, and Dmitrievsky, p. 162.

47. A. N. Alekseev and V. N. Dmitrievsky, "Teatralny repertuar kak obekt sotsiologicheskogo analiza," *Teatr i zritel* (Moscow, 1973), p. 116.

48. Alekseev and Dmitrievsky, "Opyt kachestvenno-kolichestvennogo analiza," p. 38. This is in spite of the fact that two-thirds of all the administrators of theaters in the Russian Republic are members or candidate members of the Communist Party. Zhidkov, p. 49.

49. Alekseev and Dmitrievsky, "Teatralny repertuar kak obekt," p. 115.

50. A. Ia. Rubinshtein, "K voprosu sotsialno-ekonomicheskogo obosnovania repertuarnoi politiki teatra," *Aktualnye problemy organizatsii, ekonomiki, i sotsiologii teatra* (Moscow, 1972), p. 91.

51. V. S. Zhidkov, "Nekotorye voprosy upravlenia teatrami," *Aktualnye problemy organizatsii, elonomiki, i sotsiologii teatra* (Moscow, 1972), p. 97.

52. A. Ia. Rubinshtein, pp. 92-93. Data collection for a computer-based plan of greater complixity has already begun in the Kiev Opera and Ballet Theater. For a description, see V. Gonchar and Iu. Kogan, "Sistemny podkhod v upravlenii teatrom," *Teatr*, no. 6 (June 1975), pp. 102-8.

53. G. Dadamyan, "Problemy auditorii teatrov," *Problemy sotsiologii teatra* (Moscow, 1974), p. 118.

54. V. Dmitrievsky, "Zritel v tablitsakh," *Teatr*, no. 10 (October 1968), p. 77.

55. Five percent of the respondents did not provide information about their sex. For comparable survey findings from other regions, see M. Ormaa and Ia. Khion, "O sostave zritelei teatra 'Vanemuine,' " *Aktualnye problemy organizatsii, ekonomiki, i sotsiologii teatra* (Moscow, 1972), p. 29. L. N. Kogan, "Publika teatra," *Teatr i zritel* (Moscow, 1973), pp. 52-53. K. Kask and L. Vellerand, "Struktura teatralnoi auditorii v Estonii," *Teatr i zritel* (Moscow, 1973), p. 121.

56. G. Dadamyan, "Sotsiologicheskie i sotsialno-ekonomicheskie problemy issledovania teatra," *Teatr i zritel* (Moscow, 1973), p. 163.

57. Ormaa and Khion, pp. 29-32; Dadamyan, "Sotsiologicheskie i sotsialno-ekonomicheskie problemy," p. 150.

58. Kask and Vellerand, p. 121.

59. Dadamyan, "Sotsiologicheskie i sotsialno-ekonomicheskie problemy," p. 163.

60. Ibid., p. 167.

61. Dmitrievsky, "Zritel v tablitsakh," p. 79.

62. Dadamyan, "Sotsiologicheskie i sotsialno-ekonomicheskie problemy," p. 165.

63. Kask and Vellerand, pp. 120-23.

64. Kogan, p. 47.

65. Dadamyan, "Sotsiologicheskie i sotsialno-ekonomicheskie problemy," p. 167.

66. Ormaa and Khion, p. 31. The Tartu theater, well before Estonia was incorporated into the USSR, had always encouraged and welcomed the attendance of workers. The proportion of workers in the audience had been, and continues to be, higher than average for the Soviet Union.

67. Richard F. Shepard, "A New Portrait of the Broadway Theatergoer," *New York Times,* March 16, 1980, section 2, pp. 1, 30.

68. B. I. Firsov, *Puti razvitia sredstv massovoi kommunikatsii* (Leningrad, 1977), pp. 136-37.

69. Iu. U. Babushkin, "Teatr v khudozhestvennom razvitii shkolnika," *Aktualnye problemy organizatsii, ekonomiki, i sotsiologii teatra* (Moscow, 1972), p. 22.

70. This information and the material that follow are drawn from the only major survey of taste in and exposure to music: V. Tsukerman, *Muzyka i slushatel* (Moscow, 1972).

71. In a recent report at the All-Union Conference on Concert Operations, Tikhon Khrennikov, head of the Composers' Union, brought up once again the "painful old subject of how philharmonic societies 'make' their financial plans with the help of hastily organized performances by variety-style singers and groups that are by no means of high quality." Reprinted in *Current Digest of the Soviet Press,* December 19, 1979, p. 7.

72. Peter G. Davis, "Classical Records: The Sounds of Crisis," *New York Times,* January 13, 1980, section 2, p. 22.

73. L. N. Kogan, *Khudozhestvenny vkus* (Moscow, 1966), p. 182.

74. Tsukerman, p. 169.

75. Ibid., p. 48.

76. V. V. Shmatov, "Esteticheskie interesy molodykh rabochikh," *Uchenye zapiski,* vol. 75 (Kursk: Kursk State Pedagogical Institute, 1971), p. 168.

# 7

## POCKET OF ISOLATION: MIGRANTS TO THE CITY

People in Russia respond to the media in different ways, depending on their education, life-style, age, and other factors. But there are two types of sub-groups in the population that are placed at the extremities of the media expo-sure scale. One subgroup, which will be examined in the next chapter, are mem-bers of the Communist Party, whose consumption of media messages is both more massive and more specialized than that of any other group. The other sub-group represents an extreme of isolation in the midst of urban life. They are people who are relatively cut off from official communications and culture. We may call them pre-urban migrants. In their way of life, their relatively deprived status in the urban world, and in their tenacious grip on their old, rural tradi-tions, they look very much like those people termed nonreaders in the United States and Italy.

Who is the pre-urban migrant? If one were simply to say "migrant," one would have to include huge numbers; Russian cities have grown enormously since the October Revolution and the movement from countryside to city has been phenomenal. In 1930 the rural population made up 82 percent of the total population of the Soviet Union. By 1970 that proportion had been reduced to 42 percent.[1] Between 1926 and 1959, the growth of the urban population, due to natural increase and migration to the city, was about 8.2 percent per annum.[2] Since 1959 that growth pattern has slowed, though people are still moving to the cities from the countryside, and every year the percentage of people living in rural areas declines. The fact that in four decades the proportion of the population in rural areas was halved has had serious social consequences.

The process of urbanization and modernization is a familiar one all over the world. In many cases the influx of people from the countryside produces strains on the cities to which they move, and the result is a shattered political order. The effects on city life are familiar. Rarely have housing, schooling, transportation, and living amenities been prepared in advance so that the migrant may find all the necessary facilities. In the absence of advance preparations, housing becomes overcrowded, and the predictable pattern of disruption, tension, and dislocation ensues. In many cities squatters set up makeshift quarters and illegally occupy public land without even the most rudimentary of public health and sanitation services. These extremes are not found in the Soviet Union. However, it is also not the case that the entry of the rural migrant into the city has been preceded by fully satisfactory advance preparations. The influx of rural migrants has indeed produced strains, both for themselves and for the city residents whose world they enter. These strains, both in adjustment of the migrant and in impact on the city environment, are not much different in kind from the strains that affect the social order of cities all over the world.

In nonsocialist systems, where unemployment and underemployment are more visible, the influx of migrants is clearly related to increasing numbers of the jobless. On the other hand, significant economic growth may result from the expansion of industrial production and the expansion of demands for goods and services without the strong upward pressure on wages that the resident urban working population might exert. As agriculture is mechanized and labor productivity increases, urban migration is more efficient than would be the resulting rural unemployment or underemployment in a less labor intensive and more highly developed agricultural sector. Quite apart from these effects on the economic system, there are immediate and painful difficulties for the migrants. For those involved in this population shift, the consequences may be serious. The migrants must leave their homes, their way of life, their culture. They must abandon the occupation they have been used to and in which they have experience. They must somehow, in the city, place themselves into a work situation in which there are new and different styles, systems, and rhythms of life and production. They must do all of this and assimilate the changes and adapt to the dislocations in the absence of the network of social controls that characterize the countryside. To add to the disorientation will be strains and problems within the family; there will be problems of authority—patriarchal preeminence will be chipped away, and it will be difficult, if not impossible, for the rural migrant to find models in the alien culture of the city for the socialization of the children.[3]

Since so much of the Russian urban population was originally rural, and since many of them have adjusted to urban life over the years, the term pre-urban migrant, the isolated subgroup referred to earlier, is smaller and has special characteristics. One cannot say precisely how many people fall into this category, but it is known that the question of the pre-urban migrant is a very important and thorny issue for both Soviet sociologists and the authorities. The pre-urban, or unassimilated, migrant forms a group whose numbers are officially given as "millions of people."[4] In these millions are those who cannot adapt to city life, living isolated in its midst on a permanent basis, as well as some who commute to cities to work. This latter group, called "pendulum migrants," is a relatively recent, though growing, phenomenon, estimated in 1976 to include at least 10 million people.[5] They may come to the city to work for the day, for the week, or, in some cases, for a period of several weeks or even months.[6] About 500,000 out-of-town commuters work in Moscow alone.

We do know where these marginal pre-urban migrants are most likely to be found. They live either in workers' dormitories or in more permanent substandard housing where they engage in urban agricultural work in their spare time. The dormitory residents are, for the most part, youthful migrants to the city, and their isolation and life-style differ to some extent from that of the second group. In general, young people make up a large part of the migration movement to the cities. Young rural inhabitants are generally regarded as the most likely to adapt to the changes in life and work involved in moving to the city; they are also the least likely to have forged the ties that would make moving difficult. Throughout the world, those most likely to move to cities have been the young.[7] That the migration of young people is an important component of total migration to cities in Russia has been shown in a recent study, in which it was found that youth aged 16 to 19 constituted some 30 percent of the migrants who left the countryside to go to the cities between 1957 and 1966. They were, for the most part, graduates of rural secondary schools or had had some secondary education; their job skills were not high.[8]

Where do these young migrants live when they reach the city? Many will live in substandard housing. In one city it was found that migrants who come to work in cities are more than twice as likely as workers from the city to live in dormitories, barracks, someone else's apartment, or in apartments without amenities. This type of living arrangement requires a large expenditure of time simply to provide basic requirements, such as getting water or tending a heating stove. Because such housing arrangements are seen as temporary, the migrant has little incentive to furnish them with television sets, libraries, or other sources of relaxation and culture.[9] The workers' dormitory is an important type of housing arrangement in the Soviet Union. In 1966 dormitories housed over 2.6 million workers, and by 1970 almost 3.5 million. The dormitory population is averaging an increase of about 200,000 people a year.[10] In large cities, some 17 percent of the females in the labor force and 7 percent of the males are dormitory residents.[11] Among migrants to the city, the young ones are most apt to go into dormitories. A very large survey of over 23,000 young workers in 105 industrial enterprises in 73 cities in the Russian Republic found that 22 percent of them were living in dormitories and another 20 percent were renting a room or part of a room in someone's apartment or house.[12] In a city such as Moscow, where living space is severely constricted, the proportion of dormitory residents among young workers is apt to be very much higher. In the large automobile factory there, of the 9,000 young workers employed, some 7,000 live in dormitories.[13]  Dormitory residents, then, are apt to be young (one survey of a number of large workers' dormitories in towns and cities near Moscow found that 80 percent were under 28) and the overwhelming majority of them have come in from the countryside.[14]

On the whole, these large groups of youth live a life of isolation on the cultural fringes of the cities to which they have come. Dormitory life is considered by the Soviet authorities themselves to be less than satisfactory; they rank life in dormitories and communal apartments as the least desirable of living conditions and clearly less than adequate.[15]  About 3 million of the dormitory residents in the Soviet Union are living in the obsolete type of dormitory (though it is said these will have to last at least "scores of years"), where beds are arranged in parallel rows in a single large room—a type of barracks structure. The new type of dormitory, as yet in limited use, is divided into small rooms, with three or four to the room.[16]  The dormitory is often out-of-bounds to casual visitors and official visiting hours are kept. In many dormitories the entrance is, as one observer noted, "guarded like a fortress," and even residents must show passes to enter.[17]  Not only are outsiders kept on the outside, but the young rural newcomers also stay on the inside. One survey found that although they had plenty of leisure time with their new city jobs, between 4.5 and 6.5 hours a day, most of it was spent inside the dormitory and spent "with astonishing passivity."[18] The conclusion is inescapable that far from helping to integrate the young migrant into the city life, the dormitory serves to insulate and isolate the newcomer.[19]

The dormitory is supposed to ease the transition of the new migrant, but is not notably successful in fulfilling its charge. Even access to television programs, which enables the rural population to be plugged in to official culture and norms, is lacking. Dormitory residents are the group that has the lowest proportion, or density, of television sets in the country. Very few of the residents own sets, and only one television set is actually required by law to be placed in the dormitory, which typically houses between 250 and 500 people. A superintendent, who does not live in the dormitory, is in charge of its order and activities, but social and counseling activities are in fact organized by the counselor (if the dormitory has a minimum of 250 residents). The social activities are marked by low attendance and lack of interest. One survey found that only 0.5 percent to 3 percent of the residents' leisure time was taken up in such activities.[20] Among the residents, "heavy drinking has become extremely widespread."[21] Dormitory counselors, mostly former schoolteachers, are little more than dormitory policemen, untrained in sociopsychological skills. A noted Soviet demographer observed recently that dormitory residents say that city life is dull, and it is for them because "migrants from rural areas have not developed the cultural requirements that city life could satisfy, while the city cannot satisfy the person's spiritual requirements. To want to go to an art museum, let's say, one must at least have an interest in painting; to go to a symphony concert, one must have developed a taste for music."[22]

The newcomer to the city must adapt to a different, and often difficult, housing arrangement, daily life away from the family, and a fund of leisure time unconstrained by the web of family and social relationships that had provided a strong measure of social control in the countryside. The city is seen to be—and is—very much more impersonal than the countryside. Anonymity is very difficult to find in rural life, but it is characteristic of the city. The result is often disorienting and alienating for the rural migrant. Unless the migrant possesses a strong internal compass, the absence of social control and the attendant strains of the move to the city may generate serious social problems. Soviet social scientists have found that many of these youthful migrants are indeed without the stable internal compass, the pattern of socialization that enables them to adapt to city life: "The limitation of [their] world view, the absence of any aspiration toward the widening of knowledge, indifference to art, lead to a primitive utilization of free time [and] filling the vacuum it creates with empty, even often also with pernicious forms of leisure."[23]

As might be expected, "pernicious forms of leisure" involve social deviance. For example, it was found by Soviet sociologists that there was an association between the frequency of illegitimate births and the rural migrants in the cities. Thus one-parent families were also more frequent among the rural migrants in the city.[24] Although, in the past, illegitimate births were related to the marked sex imbalance at the end of World War II and the desire of many women to have children even if there was little hope of marrying, it presently appears that the steepest rise in the rate of illegitimate births is among young girls, most of whom are migrants to the city. A major study of illegitimate births in the populous republic of Belorussia has found that in the cities throughout the republic there is a new kind of sex imbalance, produced by the preponderance of females among migrants from the countryside. The new sex imbalance in Soviet cities has occurred because girls move to the city earlier, often at 15, as soon as they finish eighth grade. Boys generally move later, after they have completed their military service. In addition, girls are more likely to be attracted to the city because there is such a narrow range of jobs for them in the countryside: milkmaid, farm worker, or, in large communities, service jobs. For men, the range of jobs available in the countryside is both more varied and more interesting.[25]

The new population disproportion is associated, apparently, with a host of what are referred to as "moral-ethical" problems. There are

> many thousands of young people (in Belorussia girls predominate among them) who lack a guardian, the advice and constant support of near ones, a family atmosphere. . . . Moving to the city (especially if it is a large city) on the one hand shakes the personality of the young migrant. [The migrant] is open to all "psychological winds,"

trusting in all forms of solidarity and participation including [those which are] lying and mercenary. On the other hand, the external social control over the behavior of youth, which is characteristic of the countryside, disappears. The anonymity of relations in large cities under conditions of low moral culture and insufficient up-bringing work can be perceived by a part of the youth as "permissiveness."

Abortion and contraception are obviously not as available or acceptable to these young rural women who come to the city from the country.[26] Where a relatively large stratum of migrants is present in a city, there is, it is said, a lowering of the "effectiveness of social norms as regulators of the behavior of youth," who are dislocated from their families and from their accustomed environment, and exposed to the anonymity of personal contacts in the city.[27]

In fact, the alienation and disorientation would be mitigated if the rural migrant had in the city a network of personal relationships and friendship groups. That this is extremely difficult to form in a large city is by now a truism. In a recent survey of 470 families living in a newer district of Moscow, it was found that more than 60 percent of the surveyed families had no contacts whatever with neighbors in the apartment building. Those families that did have such contacts, had them on a fairly impersonal basis, practically never discussing personal problems and rarely attaining a psychological closeness. "At present, in large cities [of the Soviet Union] neighborly relations of this particular type predominate."[28] Thus at home, whether in dormitories or apartments, it would appear that stable and satisfying patterns of social relationships integrated into city life do not await the rural newcomer. As the Soviet demographer Perevedentsev writes:

> It is characteristic of the typical village that everyone knows everything about everyone else, that they all know each other. Relationships are personal—that is, everyone relates to everyone else as a specific individual. . . . In the typical city, on the other hand, relationships between people are functional; . . . One does not know the overwhelming majority of persons one encounters, and one is indifferent to them; that is, they evoke no emotions. Correspondingly, one evokes no emotions in them. Hence there is a sense of coldness, or being lost, "alone in a crowd," something that yesterday's villager feels very keenly but a real urbanite does not feel at all. . . . [29]

Are friendship groups formed at the place of work rather than in the apartment complex? There is some evidence that rural migrants do experience difficulty in entering friendship groups composed of associates at work. A survey in the capital of the Georgian republic looked at the personal intera-actions in work groups in the factory and in informal, social groups of factory workers. It was found that rural migrants had fewer close friends than did their urban counterparts at work, and that the city-reared worker had, as a rule, already established a network of personal ties that were relatively impermeable to the inclusion of the new rural fellow workers. As a result, the rural migrant tended to seek personal ties among other marginal groups, such as nondominant nationality or ethnic groups.[30] Although caution should be used in generalizing from the results of this study, it is logical that rural migrants, so culturally distinct and often with inferior educational attainment, should experience some difficulties in entering friendship arrangements among urbanites, even when they work together.

Often isolated, removed from an understandable, familiar, and authoritative set of norms and judges, and exposed to a life of great and sudden change in a threatening or confusing environment, the rural migrant represents for any urban setting the possibility of a destabilizing or disrupting presence. Soviet sociologists speak of the "pernicious forms of leisure" adopted by the migrants, or their "haphazard and irresponsible decisions," but warn that it would be incorrect to stigmatize the rural migrants as a social group.[31] Obviously that condemnation of the intruding group, so familiar in cities around the world, exists also in the Soviet Union. One is told that

> It would not be correct to consider that rural youth, finding themselves in urban conditions, become potential destroyers of the norms of morality and law. That's not so. But changes in living circumstances [and] accustomed surroundings strengthen the role of external negative influences on the personality. And, on the contrary, stability of moral positions [and] a broad interest in culture promote the social development of the young person.[32]

As has been seen, the broad interest in culture does not, in general, characterize the rural newcomer to the city.

Dormitory residence is meant to be transitional, except for the steady stream of commuters, but it and other substandard arrangements last long enough to give the new migrant a taste of dismal living. For the first three years of life in the city, the majority of rural migrants (two-thirds of them) have no private living space at all. By the end of six years, only somewhat over half of them have moved into some private living space, even if only a private room. It would seem that it would take pretty nearly a decade of life in the city for the bulk of the young migrants to have at least a room of their own.[33] For the most part, they will either be crowded into someone else's apartment or living in the bleak surroundings of a dormitory.

Not all migrants come to the city and stay there. Some stay for a few months or even for a year, but appear not to be able to overcome the problems associated with the move and return to the countryside. Some live in the city for a very short time—not even enough time to register with the authorities and receive a permission to stay (which should be done within a month, but may, in fact, be delayed for several)—and then either go back to the countryside or move to another type of urban settlement, usually a smaller one. One major study found that 10 percent of the rural inhabitants who registered themselves in the city in 1960 and 20 percent of those who did so in 1965, left because of their inability to adapt to the urban way of life. The average annual rate of departure of the rural migrants who came to the city in 1960 was about 1 percent, but the rate for those who came in 1965 was about 5 percent.[34] Staying power has noticeably decreased; the process of adaptation is becoming more difficult. However, instead of returning home, they still opt for migration away from the countryside. The majority of those who cannot adjust to one city will try to find another in which to live, perhaps in another region, but the adjustment problems apparently continue. As one authoritative Soviet study declared, migrants to the city face significant difficulties "which lead to the arising of serious social problems." Sometimes they arrive without jobs. "In connection with this," the Soviet study continues, "they can experience material difficulties during the period of settling in a new place, which in unaccustomed conditions are more difficult to overcome."[35] Soviet experts, and rural migration experts all over the world, stress the importance of instituting measures to help the rural migrant adjust to the city.

The long-term upward mobility of these youthful rural migrants seems to depend on their improving their skills and rising to jobs for more highly qualified workers. It is often impossible to improve one's qualifications without the necessary education, and more specialized education, both secondary and higher, is frequently available only in cities. For example, in Novosibirsk province, all 13 institutions of higher education are located in the city of Novosibirsk itself, and 40 of the 53 technical and vocational high schools are in cities. Getting ahead in the Soviet system, as in all industrialized systems, depends on occupations that are increasingly specialized and that require increasingly higher levels of educational preparation. For many young people in the countryside, the decision to migrate is the result of the pull of educational opportunity for future occupational and social mobility. Youthful migrants who go to the city acquire technical skills much more frequently than do similar young migrants who leave one rural community for another.

The most highly mobile rural migrants are those who come to the city with between eight and ten years of schooling, are between 16 and 18 years of age, and who have chosen to migrate to the city in order to go to school there because they are dissatisfied with the career options available upon completion of education in the countryside. Those with least mobility in the long run are those who come to the city with an agricultural occupation already established, and who seek no further specialized education and do not wish to acquire more complex skills. These migrants wish only to live in a city and work there. As a rule, they are older than the first group, already have families, have no specialized job skills, and have experience only in agricultural occupations. These people are attracted to the city for the simple reason that the same or similar work commands higher wages in the city than in the countryside.[36] Actually, short-term gains are made by the majority of migrants to cities, whether or not they are in the process of improving their job qualifications. Immediate improvement in wages is the result not so much of getting a better job in the city, but rather of being in a city, where wages for the same work are higher than in the country-side.

## PRE-URBAN MIGRANT FAMILIES IN THE CITY: PROFILE OF ISOLATION

When rural newcomers are compared to their fellow factory workers, they appear to be far less involved in political or social activities and to be relatively cut off from the media. Pre-urban migrants are less likely to use a library; they read less, own fewer books, and do not take advantage of adult education op-portunities as much. Migrants are distinctive in their relative disinclination to have hobbies, participate in sports, or even attend sporting events. City-reared workers will devote some 2.1 hours a week to public civic tasks, but migrants spend only 1.6 hours on them. Migrants are, additionally, only half as likely as their urban counterparts to attend official meetings, conferences, and public gatherings. Going to the movies takes up slightly less than an hour a week on the average for migrants, but somewhat over two hours weekly for city workers.[37]

In part, the distinctive distribution of free time that characterizes pre-urban rural migrants is related to their propensity to recreate rural life in the city. "Workers who come from the peasantry, as a rule, even in the conditions of urban life, to a great degree have plots, gardens, and domestic animals. . . ."[38] This, then, is another way of locating and describing pre-urban rural migrants: those who work on garden plots allocated by the factory. In some cases this population is also ethnically distinct. For example, in the republic of Tadzhikis-tan, 25.8 percent of the urban Tadzhiks farm garden plots, but only 5.3 percent of the urban Russians do so.[39] People who maintain these agricultural pursuits on small plots on the periphery of the city are generally not very well educated, and the adults among them are, on the average, over 40. Many of these rural migrants have not had more than fourth grade education, which is considered to be the threshold of isolation from the values and practices of Soviet society, since people at this educational level are found to lag behind significantly in mass media consumption, initiative at work, and public and social activism. This minimal level of education is also associated with deviance. Studies of those who have been taken to sobering-up stations found that workers with educa-tion up to the fourth grade were two to three times more frequent than in the population at large. Young people with this low level of education are poor prospects for upward social and occupational mobility, spend two to three times more hours (almost 17 hours a week) simply hanging around on the streets than do those with higher levels of education, and there is a strong relationship between this kind of aimless or alienated activity and incidents of criminal and social deviance. In 1973 it was estimated that in the Soviet Union as a whole, some 34 percent of those in nonagricultural employment had fewer than four grades of education.[40]   In one Russian Republic city it was found that up to 15 percent or 20 percent of the population had fourth grade education or less.

People with private urban farming arrangements are likely to be relatively isolated from the official communications system. In one city where a detailed study was made of this population, it was found that about 72 percent of the newcomers to the city who had moved from another city, read the central newspapers daily, but only 52 percent of the migrants from the countryside did so. Sixteen percent of the rural migrants did not read central newspapers at all, but that figure for newcomers from other cities was only 3 percent.[41]  Former urbanites also listen to the radio much more than do former inhabitants of rural areas. Soviet sociologists found they could chart differences in media attention simply by visiting different parts of the city. As they put it: "The accumulation of people not reading even a single newspaper is revealed in defined districts of the city."

Looking more closely at this population of rural migrants in the city, one sees that different members of the migrant family react differently to the city. Women in these families, as most women in the Soviet Union, are usually working women. When, in addition, they have to raise children, the only activity outside of work that draws them into socialist society is television, which they watch three or four times a week. To a much smaller degree, they go to movies, but not more often than once a month. Single women from this environment are somewhat greater consumers of the media, but only insofar as they go more often to the movies—perhaps once a week. Reading, study, and hobbies do not figure in the life-styles of married or unmarried women in this population. The majority do not read books and only intermittently read magazines. The respondents in this group were asked if any had read one book during the past month: 78 percent had not and 42 percent had not opened a magazine. During the course of the year preceding the interview, 72 percent of these women had not been to a concert, theater, museum, or exhibition.[42]  In Leningrad and other major cities, the absence of working women in theater audiences is often attributed to the fact that "a significant part of the working women are migrants from the countryside" and they have no past habit of theater going.[43]

Unmarried women in this group tend not to take advantage of the widespread opportunities to study and improve work qualifications. Only 1 percent of them mix study with work, and when asked how many would study were leisure time to be increased, the respondents registered an increase of only up to 4 percent. The single overriding interest and source of leisure-time expenditure for women of this group, both married and unmarried, is housework. Unmarried young women in this group spend from 40 to 60 percent more time on housework than do other groups of young women in the city. Married women with families spend some four to five hours a day and seven to eight hours on the weekend on housework—and these are all working women. When asked what kinds of activities they would devote more time to if leisure time were increased, some 90 percent of these women spoke of increasing the time spent doing household tasks. For this group of women, however, it should be remembered that housework includes work on urban agriculture. Thus almost all leisure time for the women in this group is spent at home. Two-thirds of these women are mothers, and they spend about 80 percent of their free time at home and looking after children. Unmarried girls still spend some 60 percent of their leisure time doing housework, and another 10 percent of their free time looking after younger brothers and sisters. This combination of disarticulated isolation and constant unspecialized activity creates a pattern for women characteristic of patriarchal, traditional society.

In part, this greater allocation of time spent on household tasks and the desire to do even more, is related to the inferior housing conditions that most of them have. They must spend more time on the rudimentary tasks of making home life livable. Some 40 percent of the families of women in this educational group are poor (maloobespecheny—underprivileged, or poorly provided for), as opposed to 20 percent of those with education beyond this group. Sixty percent live in housing without amenities, as opposed to 40 percent of the rest. But there is another source for the tremendous involvement with housework and urban farming that these women display: they apparently retain the values and traditions of a past culture. They consider housework and agricultural chores not as "a necessary burden, but rather as the fundamental [and] natural occupation of wives and mothers."[44] Even in such a highly developed and sophisticated urban center as Leningrad, it was found that the pattern of life really was very different for the female factory worker who came from the countryside. She maintains a distinct distrust of public catering and cleaning services, for example, and even spurns, when she can afford them, household appliances. She is accustomed to relying on her own labor to get things done and is convinced that this is better than a mechanical device. The only really important appliance to her way of thinking is the sewing machine, which is common in rural areas as well and is part of her culture; in fact, it's more important than a refrigerator. The demands of housework on this woman are great not only because she lacks appliances, but also because in a family such as hers, her husband is far less likely to help around the house than are nonmigrant husbands, those "raised in the spirit of urban culture."[45] On the farm, after all, the husband did far less of the housework than his wife did, and this is the pattern that continues. For example, on farms in the republic of Lithuania, it was found that whereas women spend about 5.1 hours daily on household chores, men contributed about 0.8 hours daily.[46]

Traditional values have proved to be surprisingly durable among the women and girls in this group. One of the most obvious of those traditional values is religion. It is among rural migrants of this type, and especially among the women, that the Baptists have drawn their greatest following. At least six Soviet authors have found that

> Baptists are often newcomers to town life and tend to live on the outskirts of the cities where they try to preserve a rural environment, having their own houses with large kitchen gardens. . . . This strongly urban character of the Baptist sect distinguishes it from other Soviet religious organizations, especially from the Orthodox Church which still has its stronghold in the countryside."[47]

The stress, among Baptists in the Soviet Union, upon providing an entire social life within the religion may account for its appeal to the newly uprooted and unassimilated who do not have the educational and occupational skills to cope with social disorganization.

Among males in this pre-urban population, traditional values have not died out, but they find a somewhat different expression. The traces of their pre-urban psychological orientation are found in the way they spend their leisure time. If they were granted more free time, some 70 percent of these males would use it on their urban farming; among other groups, only 15 to 20 percent would spend more time on household chores. But working on the garden plot is really the only rural activity that the migrant male can continue in the city. For females, endless housework and chores are a constant preoccupation in both the countryside and in the city. For males, although they too may maintain their traditional system of values, their activities in the city are less likely to express those values. Like their women, the males in this group have essentially a single channel to Soviet urban culture, and that is through watching television, which they do about three or four times a week, but for longer periods than do the women. Once or twice a month they see a movie, but they do read newspapers daily. In this they are sharply distinguished from the females in this population. All other forms of cultural activity are limited: 67 percent of this group had not read a single book in the course of the previous month; 42 percent had not read a magazine; 70 percent had not, in the year preceding the interview, gone to the theater, a concert, an exhibition, or a museum. With the important exception of some newspaper consumption, the pattern is one of relative isolation, as with the females. However, media consumption is very unevenly distributed over this population. Married and older people account for a good deal of it. Youth spend half as much time on these forms of cultural and social participation, and their isolation is such that Soviet observers conclude that in their "expenditures of time, contemporary culture (as with women [in this population group]) plays, essentially a negligible role." This is exactly contrary to the observed pattern in the city, where youth spend much more time on these pursuits than do their elders.

The males in this group do, however, spend a relatively great amount of their leisure time just hanging around, doing nothing. In fact, they spend more time on nonactivity than do all other groups in the city. Though they appear to prefer the kind of activity they would have done in the rural setting—and they do some hunting and fishing—they apparently find that opportunities are limited for activities of a rural type, and thus they spend most of their free time on the street. This is especially true of the young men, who spend roughly twice as much time hanging around the streets than do young men in any other category among the youth of the city. With this group of pre-urban young men, virtually all their social activities are carried on in the streets—their territory.

The tensions in the pre-urban way of life are apparently great, and the adjustment to city life is often difficult. Unable to continue in a rural pattern of life—as the females may do to a greater extent—but far from assimilated into an urban culture, the males particularly experience the frustration and alienation so familiar in cities all over the world. Soviet social scientists themselves observe that the way of life of this individual leads to "downright dangerous social consequences." Unable to reconstruct the rural way of life in the city, and not having acquired the ability to live in a new way, "the danger of anti-social conduct in these conditions is especially great."[48] For this type of rural migrant, lack of education and the negative effect it has on mobility and income, and the absence of the informal peer control so characteristic of the countryside, combine to produce what the Soviets call "social disorganization," and the ensuing swelling of the statistics on drunkenness and delinquency.

## NOTES

1. S. N. Ikonnikova, *Molodezh* (Leningrad, 1974), p. 93.

2. O. S. Pchelintsev, "Problemy razvitia bolshikh gorodov," *Sotsiologia v SSSR,* vol. 2, (Moscow, 1966), p. 290.

3. Nicole de Maupeau Abboud and Nicole Ezner, "L'Abandon de la vie rurale," *Migration et Acculturation* (Paris, 1970), p. 90.

4. V. Perevedentsev, "A Sociologist's Commentary," *Sovetskaya kultura,* March 1, 1977, p. 6. Reprinted in *Current Digest of the Soviet Press,* April 13, 1977, p. 5.

5. V. I. Staroverov, "Nekotorye voprosy sravnitelnogo issledovania sotsialnoi struktury selskogo naselenia SSSR," *Izmenenia sotsialnoi struktury sotsialisticheskogo shobchestva* (Moscow, 1976), p. 53.

6. *Rabochaya kniga sotsiologa* (Moscow, 1976), p. 95.

7. R. Paul Shaw, *Migration Theory and Fact,* Philadelphia, Regional Science Research Institute, 1975, p. 18.

8. T. I. Zaslavskaya, *Migratsia selskogo naselenia* (Moscow, 1970), p. 265.

9. R. A. Zlotnikov, *Dukhovnye potrebnosti sovetskogo rabochego* (Saratov, 1975), p. 216.

10. Boris Pavlov, "The Workers' Dormitory," *Molodoi kommunist* (May, June, September 1977). Reprinted in *Current Digest of the Soviet Press,* (February 15, 1978, p. 5.

11. L. A. Gordon and E. V. Klopov, *Chelovek posle raboty* (Moscow, 1972), p. 8.

12. M. I. Talai and N. F. Korienko, "Vneproizvodstvennye faktory tekuchesti molodykh rabochikh na promyshlennykh predpriatiakh," *Problemy vneproizvodstvennoi deyatelnosti trudyashchikhsya* (Moscow, 1976), pp. 113, 115.

13. V. S. Abanesov, B. A. Babin, V. I. Bolgov, I. E. Ermolaev, S. I. Minasyan, S. N.

Tokareva, and V. V. Cherednichenko, "Opyt provedenia oprosov sotsiolnykh grupp molodezhi," *Prognozirovanie sotsialnykh potrebnostei* (Moscow, 1976), p. 102.

14. V. Lozbyakov, "In the Same Room," *Sovetskaya Rossia,* February 10, 1979. Reprinted in *Current Digest of the Soviet Press,* April 18, 1979, p. 14.

15. Iu. M. Antonyan, "Neblagopriatnye uslovia formirovania lichnosti v seme," *Problemy sotsiologicheskogo izuchenia semi* (Moscow, 1976), p. 181.

16. Pavlov, pp. 5-6.

17. Ibid., p. 4.

18. See Lozbyakov.

19. Maupeau Abboud and Ezner (p. 74) write that in their study of French migrants in Caen, it was found that life in the workers' dormitory increased the problem of isolation, that "it is in the group living in young workers' dormitories [foyers de jeunes travailleurs] that one sees most often young people who see only [other] migrants."

20. Pavlov, p. 5.

21. See Lozbyakov.

22. Perevedentsev, p. 4.

23. Ikonnikova, p. 92.

24. V. G. Alekseeva, "Gorodskaya semya i vospitanie lichnosti," *Problemy sotsiologicheskogo izuchenia semi* (Moscow, 1966), p. 19.

25. Perevedentsev, p. 4; Zaslavskaya, p. 250. In some cities, particularly the new towns in Siberia, the jobs open are those that are best suited to men—construction jobs, in particular, and in these cities males predominate. However, where there is light industry and a variety of jobs available, women outnumber men, sometimes to such an extent that the women cannot find husbands and start a family. See A. N. Golubev and V. B. Tabachnikov, "Ekonomiko-demograficheskaya obstanovka: problemy urbanizatsii severo-zapada," *Regionalnye problemy urbanizatsii i rasselenia* (Tashkent, 1976), p. 123. For a discussion of migration to the new towns, see Zh. A. Zaionchkovskaya, *Novosely v gorodakh* (Moscow, 1972).

26. N. G. Iurkevich and G. V. Yakovleva, "K voprosu o vnebrachnoi rozhdaemosti i polozhenie odinokoi materi," *Vzaimootnoshenie pokolenii v seme* (Moscow, 1977), pp. 180-81.

27. Alekseeva, p. 19.

28. I. Iu. Rodzinskaya, "Problema obshchenia semei s sosedyami," *Problemy sotsiologicheskogo izuchenia semi,* (Moscow, 1976), pp. 153-4.

29. Perevedentsev, p. 5.

30. E. S. Menabdishvili and A. Sh. Vacheishvili, *Sotsiologicheskie issledovania* (Tbilisi, 1971), p. 177.

31. Alekseeva, p. 19.

32. Ikonnikova, p. 92.

33. Zaslavskaya, pp. 265-67.

34. Ibid., pp. 266-67.

35. P. P. Litvyakov, *Demograficheskie problemy zanyatosti* (Moscow, 1969), p. 195.

36. Zaslavskaya, pp. 272-76.

37. Zlotnikov, pp. 213, 216.

38. Ibid., p. 213.

39. Iu. N. Pavlova, "Sotsiologicheskie issledovania protsessov sblizhenia natsii v rabochem klasse SSSR," *Izmenenia sotsialnoi struktury sotsialisticheskogo obshchestva* (Moscow, 1976), p. 210.

40. Zlotnikov, p. 174.

41. I. D. Fomicheva, *Zhurnalistika i auditoria* (Moscow, 1976), p. 123.

42. Gordon and Klopov, pp. 282-85.

43. A. G. Kharchev and S. I. Golod, *Professionalnaya rabota zhenshchin i semya* (Leningrad, 1971), p. 105.

44. Gordon and Klopov, p. 285.

45. Kharchev and Golod, pp. 74, 80.

46. Iu. I. Bundzinskene, "Rabochee i svobodnoe vremia kolkhoznikov litovskoi SSR i ego ispolzovanie," *Problemy vneproizvodstvennoi deyatelnosti trudyashchikhsya* (Moscow, 1976), pp. 140-41.

47. Christel Lane, *Christian Religion in the Soviet Union* (Albany: State University of New York Press, 1978), p. 149.

48. Gordon and Klopov, pp. 288-92.

# 8

## THE SUPER-ACTIVISTS: COMMUNIST PARTY MEMBERS

Membership in the Communist Party of the Soviet Union has its rewards. There are many accounts now of the privileges of high party office: the special consumer items, extraordinary housing benefits, including the dacha or summer home, transportation benefits, special medical services, educational benefits, and travel privileges. It appears that there is another side of the coin. Perhaps the best view of the obverse of party privilege is the portrait of Alexander Ivanovich, fictional high party official. This description was written by Victor Erofeev and published abroad in the officially suppressed anthology of Soviet writings called *Metropol*. Erofeev, certainly no apologist for the regime, was one of the editors of the collection. For his part in the illegal undertaking, he was expelled from membership in the Writers' Union, the only channel through which to publish legally. What follows is a description of the daily routine of a member of the party elite in an excerpt from "The Three-Headed Monster-Child."

> [Alexander Ivanovich] relaxed very little . . . but of all people, he really needed rest, working without letup from morning till night. . . . [He works late, comes back home at night to a warmed-up dinner.] He would eat, watching snatches of some television program, then move into his easy chair, pick up "Izvestia" and begin to snore after a few minutes, wake up, pretend he had no idea of sleeping, again stare at the paper, which had fallen out of his hands, and again begin to snore, until his wife would tell him: "Why don't you go to bed, Sasha," and take "Izvestia" away. So, it went almost every day, and,

in addition, receptions, ad hoc meetings, summonses. . . . Or he had to fly somewhere. . . .

And he had to be on time everywhere, not miss anything, check up on everything he was responsible for. And only at the dacha, did he *relax*. He watched movies, preferring comedies. . . , caught up on his sleep, in summer swam in the river and fished, in winter, he regularly skied 15 kilometers. . . . But early Monday morning, a big black car noiselessly pulled up to the dacha . . . and Alexander Ivanovich sped into town, past the saluting puppets, where difficult responsible work with people waited for him, [work] which was pregnant with such unpleasantness as either heart attack or stroke. Well, and that assortment of "privileges" he got, which sometimes evoked fits of envy or sometimes awe in the relatives, . . . appeared to him only as a means for survival. Without a car he wouldn't get anything done. Without his dacha and the clinic on Granovsky Street he would have croaked long ago. *Privileges* were felt by the family. He felt the *burden.*[1]

If there are compensating privileges for the obligations at the top of the party hierarchy, the balance may be less attractive lower down the ladder. In the everyday life of the ordinary party member, benefits are apt to be modest. Party membership "may bring minor privileges such as easier access to lesser material benefits, and improved career prospects, [but] such membership is now enjoyed by some 15 million people, and can hardly be said to bear an elite character."[2]

The Communist Party of the Soviet Union, over 15.5 million adults, is the group of people who monopolize all political recruitment and policy making in the Soviet Union. It is not a mass organization, open to all aspirants. At present, roughly every eleventh person over 18 is a member of the party, about 9.09 percent of the adult population. To get into the party, the prospective member must be recommended by current members who have been in the party at least five years. After a year's probationary period as a candidate member, a two-thirds majority vote of the local party organization is required for the candidate to be admitted to full membership. All youth up to the age of 23 must enter through the Komsomol, the Communist Youth League. Being a party member involves different commitments, depending on the level at which one operates.[3] Most of the many million members carry out party activities as volunteer work, in addition to a regular job. For them, party membership may be the result of ideological fervor or, for the opportunistic, it may simply be the price for holding down a responsible job in education, industry, government work, and a host of other sectors in which the party considers it necessary to have its members present in large proportions. In areas of the economy that the party terms crucial to its goals, saturation by party members is important for purposes of control and policy implementation.[4] But there is also a different kind of party member: the party professional, whose single job is to run the organization. For this person, the "corporate party executive" as it were, the party is the job. Alexander Ivanovich is such a man. It is not known how large this stratum of professionals is, but it is probably less than 5 percent of the organization's membership, concentrated more heavily at the national than the local level.[5] This professional infrastructure of the party is extremely well educated in comparison with the general population. College graduates comprise 96 to 99 percent of these professionals, from the city precinct level of the organization up to the national level, and half of them have completed the Higher Party School, a kind of business school providing instruction in party management and administration.[6]

Those few officials, full-time party functionaries, are the exception; the rule is the rank and file. These ordinary party members are obligated to be super-activists, to ingest more information, perform more public tasks, and "volunteer" for more duties than any other group in the Russian population. They may do so willingly, out of philosophical commitment, or they may just go through the motions. As was noted in the first chapter, the quality of attention is unmeasurable. What we shall look at here are the differences between average party people and the rest of the population. Party members are certainly more attentive to the media than are nonparty people.[7] Party members make up almost half of the subscribers of the national paper, *Pravda* (in the last ten years that proportion has fallen from three-quarters, as the readership has widened), and almost half of the provincial paper, *Buryat Pravda*.[8] Consider that party members are fewer than 10 percent of the population.

Party members also read more of a given issue of the newspaper than do nonparty people. Typically, the average Soviet newspaper reader reads only one-fourth to one-half of the paper; the party member reads many more different and varied types of articles and is much more likely to read them thoroughly. But it is not just that party members read more systematically and cover more material; they also read differently. They follow a specific pattern of reading because they are looking for special insights and instructions in the paper. The surveys bear out what Alexander Solzhenitsyn imagined a typical party member to be thinking as he waited for the newspaper one day on his bed in the *Cancer Ward*. Rusanov, observing that it is the second anniversary of Stalin's death, plans his strategy of how to read the paper:

> Today was a memorable day, a very significant day for the future, and there was a lot he ought to be *working out* and *deducing* from the newspapers. Because your country's future is, after all, your own future as well. Would the whole paper carry a black mourning edge? Or just the first page? Would there be a full-page portrait or only a quarter-page one? And what would be the wording of the headlines of the leading article?[9]

The surveys describe party members as "serious" or "businesslike" readers of newspapers; they are more than twice as likely as nonparty people to begin with the editorial, regarded by officialdom as the "key to an understanding of the entire contents of the newspaper. He who begins reading with the editorial, defines right away the general tone of the newspaper, and it is easier for him to orient himself."[10]

When they pick up a copy of the newspaper, nonparty people turn first to international news, then to sports, science and culture, and the economic news—in that order. Only 1 percent turn first to news of the Communist Party. But party members turn to news of the party before any other story. Stories about ideology and the party and, of course, the editorial, carry special instructions to party members, from which they "work out" or "deduce" their own obligations and political posture. Rusanov knew that, and the surveys show that the reading patterns for these kinds of stories do show strong party-nonparty differences. Only a little more than a tenth of the nonparty newspaper readership read carefully the articles on party organization, but 56 percent of the party readers do. Less than a fifth of the nonparty readers—but 40 percent of the party readers—read the editorial in its entirety. Just under a third of the nonparty readership read to the end the numerous articles on politics and ideology, but over 56 percent of the party readers do so.

A disproportionately large number of letters to newspaper editors come from party members. In a survey of all letters sent from the Russian city of Taganrog to five national newspapers, the local paper, and radio and television stations, it was found that 35 percent were written by party members.[11] Even *Komsomolskaya Pravda,* the newspaper of the Communist Youth League, most of whose members are too young to be in the party, receives from party members almost a third of its letters.[12] Any editor who would judge, from his huge mailbag of letters each day, that the writers were representative of the population would be greatly in error. For party people, but not for people who do not belong to the party, there is a spillover from the newspaper. When Moscow party members finish reading an issue of the newspaper they very often discuss its contents with other people. They do this after lectures and public discussions as well, something nonparty people rarely do.[13]

Whether because they are better educated than the population at large or because they are more active consumers of information, party members read more books than do nonparty people. They are particularly far ahead of the general population in the consumption of social science books. A survey of 840 people in Moscow included some 10 percent who were party members and another 11 percent who were members of the Communist Youth League. This 21 percent accounted for over 50 percent of all books read by the group in the social sciences, 47 percent of the books in technology, 46 percent of the art books, 47 percent of the history books, 48 percent of the Russian literary classics, and 37 percent of the books of contemporary Soviet literature.[14] Libraries do a much brisker business with party members than with ordinary borrowers. A survey of four cities in Bashkiria, an autonomous republic within the Russian Republic, reported that 79 percent of the party members borrowed books from libraries, but fewer than half of the nonparty people did.[15]

Even though the Soviet Union is a vast multi-ethnic state, and even though the media in non-Russian areas include communications in the indigenous languages, there is evidence that members of the Communist Party who are not Russian are keyed into Russian-language communications far more than are their nonparty neighbors. In Latvia a republicwide survey found that about 63 percent of the nonparty Latvians but 95 percent of the Latvians in the party had mastered the Russian language. Latvian party members "in comparison with non-party people were significantly more active in their use of the Russian language in production, culture, and everyday spheres of activity."[16] The assimilation of non-Russian party members is more advanced. Party members are more likely to marry non-Latvians: 15 percent of the Latvians in the Latvian Communist Party married out of their ethnic group, but only 9.7 percent of the nonparty Latvians did. Intermarriage is an indicator of that desired "internationalization," the official vision of the future in which differences among ethnic groups will gradually disappear.

Earlier, in looking at the effects of television viewing in Russia, it was seen that private, housebound relaxation was replacing organized, social activities—what the Soviets call collective leisure. That kind of collective activity is still very much an official value, in part because it breaks down social isolation and creates group effort and, in part, because it fosters doing and creating, rather than mere passive consuming. Much is made in official communications of the hobby circles and amateur arts groups that blanket the country. But it may be, particularly as television watching cuts into these activities, that a relatively small population of activists is keeping these functions going. That survey of 840 people employed in Moscow, of whom a tenth were party members and another tenth were members of the Communist Youth League, looked at who participated in these activities. The party and youth organization activists are more than the backbone; they are also most of the body. They filled up 66 percent of the membership of the dance circles, 65 percent of the amateur theater group, 57 percent of the pop music ensembles, and 56 percent of the choirs in the area.[17] To put it is different terms, these creative activities embrace only a tiny part of the population in the Soviet Union: approximately 7 percent of the population over 14. In the city of Taganrog, between 3 percent and 4 percent participated in these hobby clubs, and this is typical for Russian cities. Activities in hobby clubs are more popular in the countryside (about 7 percent of the adults participate) where there are fewer alternatives, but in the cities, less than 3 percent participation is the rule.[18]

The obligations of being a member of the party do not end here. Nonparty people have close to half of their nonworking hours free for relaxation or entertainment. The party member has less than 30 percent of nonworking time free for relaxation. The party member's free time is reduced by the civic, or public, task. The institution of "volunteer" civic labor is a way for the government to extract production without paying wages. In the Soviet system, there are a host of unpaid jobs for which people may really volunteer or, more often, are required to perform as part of an organized group effort.[19] The kinds of jobs done in this fashion are many: agricultural work, particularly help with the harvest, repairing public buildings, clearing public areas, or contributing free time in one's regular job. Everyone is supposed to do some volunteer work to help society, but party members must do much more of it. For the average nonparty person, the official ideal is about two-and-one-half hours a week of free time committed to these public "volunteer" duties. In fact, the average devoted to these tasks is less than half that, about an hour a week.[20] The party member devotes almost a quarter of his nonworking time to the performance of these civic tasks; the nonparty person, only about 3 percent.[21] Among rural people in Russia and four other republics, over three-quarters did no civic work at all, but only 15 percent of the young party members could get away without volunteering.[22]

Then there are the meetings. Party members, more than all other people, must go to meetings, and they take up a considerable amount of time. Since party members make up the directing core of other organizations, such as the youth organization and the trade unions, their participation is spread wide. For example, in the Young Communist League alone, which has a membership of 36.3 million, there are almost 800,000 members of the Communist Party working as key leaders at all levels.[23] Since the higher level jobs throughout the economy to a greater or lesser degree carry party membership as a kind of prerequisite, the party member-scientist or party member-manager will find that meetings take up a good deal of time during the working day. Research conducted by questionnaire in Moscow found that industrial managers said they wasted as much as 35 percent of their working time in "useless" meetings.[24] At meetings of the mass organizations—the trade unions and the youth organization—it is the party member who, though in the minority, takes over most of the speaking and discussion.[25]

When party members become local party administrators, they have to double or treble the time spent on behalf of the "corporation." At higher levels and in extremely large party organizations (for example, in large industrial plants), a professional will perform the party duty as a paid job. But the overwhelming majority of primary party organizations, the grass-roots level of the party, have fewer than the 150 members needed to qualify for a paid administrator, and a volunteer must assume the title of secretary on a rotating basis. The primary party organization is responsible for the recruitment of new members and maintenance of discipline among the rank and file. It supervises the operation of the propaganda and indoctrination system at the local level, and gathers information to report to higher levels of the organization. The volunteer secretary, who must also hold down a full-time job, spends about two-

and-one-half times more hours during the week doing party tasks than does the ordinary party member.[26] In Leningrad 272 such secretaries were polled about the way they spent their time. Up to 40 percent of their working hours were spent in meetings. Much of this time was not spent at the place of work, but at the higher level precinct party organization. Two-thirds of these administrators spent up to four hours a week at the precinct office, but one-third spent from five to ten hours a week there—all during regular working hours.[27] It is no wonder that the career-minded specialists, who joined the party out of convenience and pragmatism rather than ideological commitment, are reluctant to take on volunteer duties. In Moscow's Lenin district, where some 8,000 people are employed in scientific-research institutes, the party organization has difficulty recruiting scientists and scholars to become primary party organization secretaries. No one wants to pay the price of sharply diminished research time.[28] Professional women are reluctant to take on extra work, when they are already responsible for family and household care.

In addition to these duties, party members are required to study political doctrine and current positions on issues in the party's instruction system. Adult education facilities are, in general, extremely widespread in the Soviet Union, though often unsystematic and disorganized. However, most nonparty people are enrolled in branches that will enable them to upgrade their work qualifications and skill levels. The party instruction system is a separate hierarchy of schools and seminars for the rank and file organized at the place of work, usually after work or on weekends. Leonid Brezhnev announced at the 25th Party Congress in 1976 that there were 20 million people enrolled in the party instruction system, of whom 7 million were nonparty people.[29] Under Brezhnev, the proportion of nonparty people in the system has been low, from 20 percent to 30 percent of the total enrollment, far below what it was in the Khrushchev days when nonparty students swamped the system and party members were in the minority. At that time, the huge influx of nonparty people into the political indoctrination system was a feature of Khrushchev's populist notion that all people should be resocialized in the values of the revolution, and he set into motion plans for all adults to be studying political doctrine all their lives. The component of party members, naturally, shrank to a small proportion. After Khrushchev's ouster, the normal party domination of the system returned.[30] The nonparty people currently in the system are identifiable civic activists, adjunct party members, as it were.[31]

About 22 percent of the leisure time of party members is spent in study after work, more than twice the proportion for the nonparty person. The highly qualified scientists and scholars are not excused. In Moscow's Cheremushkinsky district, every third scientific research fellow is in a party instruction seminar; most study economic issues or party history. About half the seminar participants aver that they are fully satisfied with the seminar discussions; others attend as a matter of form and find the exercise boring and irrelevant. Virtually all the participants say the party instruction system could be improved by providing the participants with more political news.[32]  Staffing this vastinstructional system are over 1.3 million teachers, called propagandists, some 90 percent of whom are college graduates.[33]  They, in turn, are trained and given refresher courses in still other branches of the party education network.

## LECTURES:  THE LEADING ORAL MASS MEDIUM

Party instruction is but a small part of a system the Soviets call "mass oral media."  This network of oral communication includes public lectures, as well as party and youth league instruction.  The system of public lectures is an important part of the official communications system.  The Znanie (Knowledge) Society organizes the lectures nationwide and is responsible for the more than 15.5 million lectures that are given each year for a total attendance figure of more than 775 million.  In Moscow alone in 1976, 818,000 lectures were given by the city branch of the Znanie Society.[34]  In 1966 the audience for these lectures was equal to over five times the entire adult population in the country.[35]  The Taganrog survey found that three-quarters of the entire population of the city attended these lectures.  The reason so many of them go to lectures, they say, is because they find out from the lectures information that is unavailable from newspapers, radio, or television.  This does not mean that the lectures function outside the ideological limits operating elsewhere in the communications system, but rather that the form of this oral medium is such that there is feedback.  The lectures zero in on the specific concerns of the public, and they are relatively unstructured and decentralized.

Lectures usually take place in the evening.  They are conducted by local professors, journalists, or political figures.  A survey of 3,000 such lecturers found that almost two-thirds were party members; most were over 40.[36]  The lectures feature subjects of topical interest:  political or economic events, often in the international arena.  The schedule of lectures given by the Moscow lecture bureau showed the following topics:  philosophy, political economy, military, state and law, international relations, literature and art, pedagogy and psychology, scientific atheism, agriculture, biology, medicine, geology and geography, astronomy, physics and mathematics, chemistry, economics, history of the Communist Party, and Soviet history.  The highest proportion of lectures fell into three categories:  economics, international relations, and party history.[37]  There is time for questions from the audience.

People who go to the lectures say, by a two-to-one margin, that the lecture, compared to the newspaper, provides more objective, precise, and complete information.  But a minority, those who are active consumers of all the media, are less impressed.  They expect new or supplementary information from the lectures and do not find it.  In particular, college graduates and highly skilled professionals are dissatisfied, but industrial workers, white-collar employees, and young people who have not finished high school are both less demanding and more satisfied. The lecture is, by far, the most popular and highly regarded of all oral official communications media, considered more effective and authoritative than the party's own instruction system or the educational system run by the Communist Youth League.[38]

Party officials have had very little systematic information about what goes on in the lectures or how they run. They have been satisfied that the large attendance figures indicate success. In 1969 the decision was made to survey the contents and methods of the lectures conducted in the city of Taganrog. About two-thirds of all lectures were about current events, at home and abroad. Almost three-quarters of all the information relayed related to socialism as a political system; the remaining quarter, to capitalism. When the lecturer talked about capitalism, fully 90 percent of the material he related was negative, such as expansion of American imperialism, the growth of the threatening military-industrial complex, or the catastrophic increase in crime and racial tension. The small proportion of positive information about capitalist systems focused on industrial growth and the organization of production.

What is more surprising is the finding that almost half of the communications about socialist systems were also negative. It is not that the roughly equal positive and negative balance of information about socialism was presented as two sides of a single issue. Instead, what happens is that the positive themes relate to one level of life and the negative to another. When the Soviet Union or friendly socialist countries are described at the national level, as systems, the attributes are always positive, even glowing. The Soviet Union as actor is wholly exemplary. But when talk revolves around life in an individual city or locale, the negatives mount.

Follow, for example, the course of a lecture entitled "About Strengthening the Struggle with Drunkenness," given by a functionary in the city district attorney's (procurator's) office. It begins like this:

> The Soviet People inspired by the tasks set [before it] by the Party Congress, is engaged in peaceful, creative work; it is building the height of human happiness—communism. The Soviet people labor with self-sacrifice at plants and factories, construction sites, [and] farms, [and] acquire knowledge in the field of art and culture. However, this does not mean that we do not encounter facts of anti-social, amoral behavior and violations of legality by individual representatives.

Having spoken in positive, though certainly abstract terms, about the nation as a whole, the speaker shifts to particular instances and switches to negative expressions. He gives some dozen or so instances of the consequences of alcoholism, accompanied by statistical data. He details a picture of a threatening amorality pervading the city and total public indifference to it. Concluding the lecture, he again shifts to the abstract, collective, and wholly positive plane: " 'But, undoubtedly, thanks to the efforts of the state, society, and each citizen of our country, alcoholism will be extinguished, because there is no place for that phenomenon in a society that builds communism.' "[39] All the lectures on social problems—juvenile crime or moral questions—follow this form, in which the positive is both abstract and unconvincing, and the negative is concrete and persuasive. Analyses of 600 lectures in Moscow, Gorky, Volgograd (Stalingrad), and six other cities in Russia show that these results are typical.

The lecture system is so vast and conducts so many presentations nationally, that there is little supervision or evaluation of methods and effects. Not even 1 percent of the lectures on any given subject are monitored by party officials with a view to subsequent critique and correction. Because of the tremendous reach of the system and the large number of presentations, individual lectures cannot be systematically censored before presentation. To this extent, therefore, the Znanie lecture system operates outside the very strict controls characteristic of the other media. This should not be construed as indicating that oral lecture propaganda is free of ideological control. There are apt to be informants in the audience, and anything very controversial would surely reach the party people at the city party organization. Nonetheless, the kinds of controls are, of necessity, looser and far less systematic than those in force in the other branches of the media.[40]

There is another reason why the lectures promote negative observations about the Soviet system. Questions and answers figure importantly in these public lectures. Only 6 percent of the lecturers said they were not asked questions. Over half got at least five questions after a lecture and about a third were asked between six and ten questions. For the most part, the questions related to what was going on currently in the world, the country, and the city. Issues agitating the audience are also brought up in talks with the lecturer before or after the lecture. Some of these one-on-one chats are about matters the press has not covered, and most involve personal problems unrelated to the subject of the lecture. The questions come from people in the audience who have been having problems with housing or their children's education. Attempts to find redress through official procedures have failed to resolve these problems, and in frustration they ask the assistance of the lecturer.

It is the audience participation, the quest for additional and concrete information, which adds to the negative cast with which the lecturer colors the subject. Paradoxically, it is also this element that contributes to the relative popularity of the lecture and to the belief among average cityfolk that they are receiving precise and objective information. The officials in the party deplore the negative thrust of these persuasively concrete examples of everyday life, yet insofar as these examples square with the experience of individual citizens, the authoritativeness of the medium is enhanced. It is again the issue we observed in looking at local newspapers; the possibility of independent verification powerfully affects trust and confidence in the medium. But two qualifications should be kept in mind. First, criticisms and dissatisfactions with one's narrow private existence may have little relation to judgments about politics at the national and international levels. Second, the degree of criticism at these lectures and in discussions afterward may be possible only because the lecture system, as compared to the other media, has not in the past been subject to evaluation. In fact, criteria of efficacy have, up to now, been understood as a single indicator: attendance figures. If the system should become more centralized and more strictly controlled—and that would be a formidable task—its strengths for its audience and its weakness for the regime would be reduced.

The Taganrog survey of the oral media was able to distinguish four categories of audience: highly active (frequent exposure), average, low, and nonaudience (absolutely no exposure). In the first category are people who are also high consumers of all the other media, and for whom oral media are supplementary to what they have already received elsewhere. These people value the oral media particularly because they wish not only to comprehend the issues to which they are exposed, but also to be able to transmit them to others, and in this they are distinguished from all other groups. The overwhelming majority of the people in this group are members of the Communist Party and the Communist Youth League; nine out of ten have party or other civic duties. Two-thirds are between 30 and 40, about half have high school education, and a quarter have some college education. Men make up 70 percent of this category.

In the fourth category, those who are altogether outside of the reach of the oral media by their own choice, women predominate (70 percent). Older people on pensions are a considerable proportion of this nonpublic, but, it is said, "there are not a few young people." The overwhelming majority are nonparty people, many with up to four grades of education or not beyond six; about a third have completed nine grades of education, and 10 percent have gone to high school. Among these people, about a third read no newspapers at all. Why they opt out of the oral media is different for different types in the category. Some are old and infirm, some are illiterate, and some, the women in particular, have too little time and too many tasks. But others in this nonpublic simply do not wish to attend lectures. Compared to the activists profiled above, the nonpublic exhibits a "low level of trust in evaluating the completeness, objectivity, and reliability of the information [and] are highly critical. . . ." They carry out practically no social or civic duties. Only a third said they would sometime in the future go to a lecture. Although there are no aggregate figures for these types, one may imagine that the nonpublic is relatively small, but may still comprise a quarter of the city's adult population. In many ways, they resemble those who live in the pockets of isolation described in the previous chapter.

The super-activists are mainly party members, present or future. Curiously, these highly mobilized people are by no means satisfied with what they hear. The Taganrog researcher says of their evaluation of the oral media: "Considering that the media of mass oral propaganda have greater opportunities to communicate new information, [which] is not contained in newspapers, radio and television, the audience of this type [in the highly active category] nonetheless gives a rather low evaluation to the objectivity, completeness and accuracy of the information, issued by the Media of Mass Oral Propaganda."[41] The super-activists have demands that are greater than those of the average public: they must be able to utilize the information to persuade others, and they must be able to identify the party line for fast-breaking news events or risk deviating from official norms. The dilemma of the lectures, the problem of information and control in conflict, is no less a dilemma for the political elite itself.

# NOTES

1. Victor Erofeev, "Rasskazy i 'Trekhglavoe detishche,' " *Metropol* (Ann Arbor, Michigan: Ardis, 1979), pp. 92(7)-93(8) (emphasis in the original). I am grateful to Professor Denis Mickiewicz for bringing this source to my attention.

2. Mervyn Matthews, *Privilege in the Soviet Union* (London: Allen and Unwin, 1978), p. 53.

3. For a discussion of the determinants of recruitment into the Communist Party of the Soviet Union, see Ellen Mickiewicz, "Regional Variation in Female Recruitment and Advancement in the Communist Party of the Soviet Union," *Slavic Review* 36 (September 1977), pp. 441-54; by the same author, "Regional Social Class Recruitment in the CPSU: Indicators of Decentralization, Power, and Policy," *Soviet Union* 5 (1978), pp. 101-25.

4. T. H. Rigby makes a threefold distinction among party-restricted occupations, high-saturation occupations, and low-saturation occupations. In each, the percentage of party members differs, and that difference becomes a key to the centrality of the profession or occupation itself. For an extended discussion of the issue, see *Communist Party Membership in the USSR, 1917-1967* (Princeton: Princeton University Press, 1968), pp. 412-53.

5. See Frederick C. Barghoorn, *Politics in the USSR*, 2d ed. (Boston: Little Brown, 1966), p. 55.

6. L. A. Slepov, *Vozrastanie rukovodyashchei roli partii v stroitelstve kommunizma* (Moscow, 1972), p. 78.

7. Even earlier, during the 1920s and 1930s, this was true. The Harvard Project, which surveyed refugees from the Soviet Union and asked questions about prewar Russia, found that party members "even though closely matched on age, sex, and occupation with nonmembers, scored substantially higher in exposure to official media, including mass, personalized, and 'aesthetic' media." Alex Inkeles and Raymond A. Bauer, *The Soviet Citizen* (Cambridge: Harvard University Press, 1961), p. 168. However, it should be noted that the subsample of party members, on which this finding was based, was small, numbering no more than 100 respondents.

8. Ellen Mickiewicz, "Evaluation Studies of Soviet Party Members," *Public Opinion Quarterly* 40 (Winter 1976-77), p. 438.

9. Alexander I. Solzhenitsyn, *Cancer Ward* (New York: Farrar, Straus & Giroux, 1969), p. 313 (emphasis added).

10. Mickiewicz, "Evaluation Studies" p. 483.

11. G. D. Tokarovsky, "Pisma trudyashchikhsya kak kanal vyrazhenia obshchest-vennogo mnenia," *Sotsiologicheskie problemy obshchestvennogo mnenia i deyatelnosti sredstv massovoi informatsii* (Moscow, 1976), p. 122. Similar findings are reported in a survey of letters to the Ryazan district newspaper: I. D. Fomicheva, *Zhurnalistika i auditoria* (Moscow, 1976), p. 128.

12. A. I. Verkhovskaya, *Pismo v redaktsiu i chitatel* (Moscow, 1972), p. 156.

13. L. V. Knyazeva, "Vlianie sredstv massovoi ustnoi propagandy na mezhlichnostnoe obshchenie," *Sotsiologicheskie problemy obshchestvennogo mnenia i sredstv massovoi informatsii* (Moscow, 1975), p. 173.

14. S. I. Guryanov, "Dukhovnye interesy sovetskogo rabochego," *Sotsiologia v SSSR,* vol. 2 (Moscow, 1966), p. 169.

15. R. A. Zlotnikov, *Dukhovnye potrebnosti sovetskogo rabochego* (Saratov, 1975), p. 99.

16. A. I. Kholmogorov, *Internatsionalnye cherty sovetskikh natsii* (Moscow, 1970), p. 91.

17. Guryanov, p. 177.

18. L. A. Gordon, E. V. Klopov, and L. A. Onikov, *Cherty sotsialisticheskogo obraza zhizni: byt gorodskikh rabochikh vchera, segodnya, zavtra* (Moscow, 1977), p. 69.

19. For studies of the mobilization of volunteer effort, see such works as William E. Odom, *The Soviet Volunteers: Modernization and Bureaucracy in a Public Mass Organization* (Princeton: Princeton University Press, 1973); Jan S. Adams, *Citizen Inspectors in the Soviet Union: The People's Control Committee* (New York: Praeger, 1977); Allen Kassof, *The Soviet Youth Program* (Cambridge: Harvard University Press, 1965).

20. Gordon, Klopov, and Onikov, p. 137.

21. T. M. Novikova, "Obshchestvennaya rabota v strukture biudzheta vremeni partiinykh aktivistov," *Sotsiologicheskie issledovania,* no. 1 (1976), pp. 149-51.

22. I. M. Slepenkov and B. V. Knyazev, *Rural Youth Today* (Newtonville, Mass.: Oriental Research Partners, 1976), p. 64.

23. The bylaws of the League permit the age limit to be waived in the case of important leadership functions. See M. Perun, "Mesto i rol molodezhi v strategii i taktike kommunistov," *Sotsialnaya aktivnost molodezhi i kommunisty* (Prague, 1975), p. 57.

24. V. T. Davydchenkov, "Organizatsia sotsiologicheskogo obsledovania i vnedrenie poluchennykh rezultatov v tsentralnoi gazete," *Problemy sotsiologii pechati,* vol. 2 (Novosibirsk, 1970), p. 157.

25. V. A. Voinova, "Sobrania v trudovykh kollektivakh i formirovanie obshchestvennogo mnenia," *Sotsiologicheskie problemy obshchestvennogo mnenia i deyatelnosti sredstv massovoi informatsii* (Moscow, 1976), p. 92.

26. Novikova, p. 150.

27. V. Provotorov, "Sotsiologicheskie issledovania v partiinoi rabote," *Partiinaya zhizn,* no. 19 (October 1967), p. 37.

28. I. Lavrov, "Raikom i partorganizatsii nauchnykh uchrezhdenii," *Partiinaya zhizn,* no. 22 (November 1971), p. 22.

29. Cited by I. A. Vinogradov, "Opyt raboty s propagandistami," *Voprosy teorii i metodov ideologicheskoi raboty,* vol. 9 (Moscow, 1978), p. 108.

30. Ellen Mickiewicz, *Soviet Political Schools* (New Haven: Yale University Press, 1967).

31. V. G. Baikova and V. N. Zenkov, "Sotsiologichesky analiz organizatsionnykh problem politicheskogo obrazovania," *Sotsiologicheskie issledovania v ideologicheskoi rabote,* vol. 1 (Moscow, 1974), p. 97.

32. B. N. Chaplin and N. N. Bokarev, "Puti povyshenia effektivnosti ideologicheskoi raboty sredi nauchnoi intelligentsii," *Sotsiologicheskie issledovania,* no. 1 (1974), pp. 127-30.

33. Vinogradov, p. 108.

34. *Moskva v tsifrakh* (Moscow, 1977), p. 161.

35. Ellen Mickiewicz, ed., *Handbook of Soviet Social Science Data* (New York: Free Press, 1973), pp. 171, 173.

36. A. A. Drizul and E. Zh. Zvaigzne, "Ispolzovanie rezultatov sotsiologicheskikh issledovanii v partiinoi propagande," *Sotsiologicheskie issledovania,* no. 3 (1975), p. 125.

37. *Moskva v tsifrakh,* p. 161.

38. L. N. Knyazeva, "Otsenki naseleniem sredstv massovoi ustnoi propagandy kak pokazatel effektivnosti ideologicheskogo vozdeistvia," *Sotsiologicheskie issledovania v ideologicheskoi rabote,* vol. 1 (Moscow, 1974), pp. 59-72.

39. A. A. Vozmitel, "Nekotorye kharakteristiki deyatelnosti lektorov po formiro-vaniu obshchestvennogo mnenia," *Sotsiologicheskie problemy obshchestvennogo mnenia i deyatelnosti sredstv massovoi informatsii* (Moscow, 1976), pp. 45-46.

40. In a symposium on censorship in the Soviet Union, Michael Goldstein, who had been a violinist and composer in the Soviet Union, asserted that he had to submit his lecture on music to prior censorship by officials of the All-Union Society for the Dissemination of Political and Scientific Knowledge, an early name for the Znanie Society. It may be that at the time such prior censorship was practiced, but it seems not to be done very systematically at present. See "Censorship of Music," in *The Soviet Censorship,* ed. Martin Dewhirst and Robert Farrell, (Metuchen, N. J.: Scarecrow Press, 1973), p. 105.

41. L. V. Knyazeva, "Otnoshenie naselenia goroda k sredstvam massovoi ustnoi propagandy kak istochniku informatsii (po materialam konkretnogo sotsiologicheskogo issledovania)," *Sotsiologicheskie problemy sovershenstvovania ideologicheskoi raboty* (Moscow, 1978), p. 60.

# 9

## THE RUSSIAN MEDIA PUBLIC: FROM INVISIBLE TO VISIBLE

A Soviet news analyst associated with the International Information Department of the Communist Party's Central Committee visited the United States
recently. He observed that Americans live in the thrall of television, that the
small screen has created the illusion of reality and Americans no longer have any
other reality. The "average American" reads nothing but newspapers and picture
magazines. "He has forgotten what museums and theaters are." In spite of
their innate sociability, Americans do not often go visiting any more or even
converse with one another very much. Reflecting about his own country, the
correspondent adds a word of caution: "Even with us [the Soviet Union],
television, as is well known, is not free of problems, and some of them—in such
a serious matter, we should not delude ourselves—have not yet attained their
full growth."[1]

The Soviet observer has remarked upon phenomena that, though exag-
gerated, are nonetheless familiar to citizens of the United States. But he has
also pointed to relationships between television watching and other activities
that are increasingly widespread in his own country. His Soviet readers will
surely have noticed the parallels, and he hopes to preempt criticism of his
apparent one-sidedness by noting that similar trends are developing in the
Soviet Union. The reason that his countrymen cannot, as he puts it, delude
themselves any longer results at least in part from the publication of findings
of the recent public opinion surveys in the Soviet Union. Delusions about the
Soviet media public are less likely to be held now because the public has become
visible. Granted, there is still much that we do not know, but what we have

been able to observe by piecing the surveys together has revealed a highly complex, and often contradictory or paradoxical, set of attitudes.

## THE EFFECT OF EDUCATION

One of the most important and complex determinants of media attitudes and exposure is education. We know that the college educated watch less television than all others and are the least satisfied with the programs they do watch. They are the most intensely interested in political and news analysis programs but the least satisfied with the broadcasts. College-educated Russians are avid consumers of newsprint, but most frequently disagree with the editorial viewpoint. The higher the level of education, the greater the demand for information of all kinds. Along with a generalized interest in information goes a demand for more information about foreign countries. Political information that comes through the oral propaganda network of party instruction and lectures is also received most critically by people with high school and college education, among whom members of the Communist Party figure significantly.[2] College graduates are the most critical in evaluating books by contemporary Soviet authors.[3] The more educated young rural workers complain most about working in the countryside and are most likely to leave.[4]

American television studies also find that the educated are more demanding. They want more information about their own country: about social problems, politics and political figures, and more that is educational. But in their evaluation of what they see, they are less sharply distinguished from the average than are their Russian counterparts. American college graduates do tend to be more critical than those with less education; that is, they do not find as many programs as enjoyable. But they are not very different from the less well educated in their dissatisfaction. "Educated viewers take a middling position. Not very many of them think a high proportion of their programs are 'extremely enjoyable' or think a high proportion are 'disappointing.' For most of them, programs are generally 'somewhat enjoyable' or 'just so-so.' "[5] Although they might feel quite strongly that television does not fulfill its potential, American college graduates watch television very nearly as much as do the less well educated, and in their rating of programs they are more lukewarm than either enthusiastic or sharply critical.[6]

In their study of the satisfaction of Americans, Campbell, Converse, and Rodgers found that education, understood as providing an awareness of alternatives, tended to produce a rising level of dissatisfaction. "There is a faint tendency for reported satisfaction to *decline* with advancing education, despite circumstantial evidence that people of better education live in situations which are, from the standard 'objective' view, more desirable."[7] They also found that those on the bottom of the status ladder were inclined to be more satisfied than the observer might have predicted. For example, the lowest income stratum was "more satisfied with its housing than any other segment." The explanation advanced by the analysts:

> We are inclined to imagine that much of the heightened satisfaction which seems associated with low salience of alternatives involves true psychological states, as they are experienced by our informants . . . constricted horizons appear to mean low ceilings on aspirations.[8]

The constricted horizons of the less well educated have, in effect, cancelled out the dissatisfaction.[9]

If, in the American data, there is a slight or faint tendency for criticism and dissatisfaction to increase with education, in the Russian case the tendency is neither faint nor slight. It is clear and observable across all the communications studies. But there is also a more complicated relationship visible. Years ago, in the Harvard Project survey, the researchers found that, in their attitudes, the college educated and the blue-collar industrial workers rather surprisingly resembled one another.[10] In the more recent spate of public opinion polls in the Soviet Union, this peculiar similarity seems to persist: the top of the status ladder and the bottom show the highest, though not identical, rates of dissatisfaction and criticism. In Boris Firsov's Leningrad television survey, it was found that a positive evaluation of television, particularly of news and public affairs

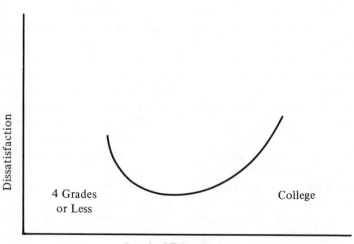

Level of Education

programs, falls with increasing education, but high dissatisfaction was also found among those who had less than four grades of education.[11] In the much broader *Izvestia* survey, it was found that the most critical evaluations came from two groups: people with college education and people with primary education. Most satisfied are people who have had five to ten grades of education. Visually, the relationship is a curve, with high dissatisfaction at the two ends of the U.

It is likely that the dissatisfaction of the college graduates and that of the uneducated are of very different sorts. People with little education are television addicts, but their level of comprehension, particularly of political programs, is very low. Reading newspapers is also difficult for them. Their alienation from the specifically political messages transmitted by the media reflects their inability to plug in the most rudimentary cognitive skills. For those with little education and few prospects for mobility, the relative distance from social integration may be much further than for those at the lower end of the socioeconomic spectrum in the United States.

At the other end of the dissatisfaction curve are people with college education. They presumably do see alternatives and do have high aspirations, and are, accordingly, more critical and dissatisfied. But they are also the privileged who lead, at least in relative terms, the good life, Soviet-style. Their income is the highest, the conditions of life the best, and the status the most desirable. Would this not tend to offset or undercut the dissatisfaction born of wider intellectual perspectives? Perhaps their very awareness of alternatives allows them to measure their well-being against those in other societies, who then become the referents for their aspirations. Or it may be that the probing, critical thrust of the educated mind cannot support constraints that others more passively accept. The most satisfied are those in the middle of the curve, where material conditions are not the worst and education is not so great as to introduce critical perspectives.

Because the dissatisfaction/education relationship with respect to political communications is so clear, the rising level of education of the Soviet population must give pause to the Soviet leaders. Too little is known about the relationship to be able to predict the future, and much may alter the association, such as external threats or changes in levels of domestic consumption. But it is also likely that this is a more profound tension that will increase with increasing education.

The recipient's breadth of experience is related to his evaluation of different types of media messages. Throughout this study it has been seen that the Russian public judges its central media rather differently from its local media. The central press is thought to be far more reliable than the local press; the central press is said to provide more complete coverage than any other medium; and the central press is seen as clearly superior as a purveyor of information on political and social issues. Trust and confidence in the central press are very much higher than in the local press. Although the relationship is weaker, the same vector of confidence is found in American media studies; disagreement tends to increase as the story approaches the personal experience of the respondent. Why does this happen? There are no difinite studies, but it may be a question of dissonance. Where individuals may measure by the standards of reality they see about them, they are more skeptical of the reality portrayed by the media. Naturally, this is more nearly true of stories about and portrayals of everyday, local events. At distances more remote from individual lives, the media "stand in for experience."[12] Thus,

> in general, subject matter which is more distant and more novel, least subject to prior definitions and outside immediate experience responds best to treatment by the campaign. The essential point is that the receiver has no competing sources of information and no personal stake in resisting an appeal or disbelieving information. It is easier to form opinions and attitudes about events abroad than events at home, about unfamiliar than about familiar matters.[13]

The capacity of the media to fill the gap lack of immediate experience creates is not unalloyed. At the very least, it depends on the credibility of the source and upon the quality of attention, which may be diminished by oversaturation with repetitive messages. Within the Soviet communications system, the greatest reserve of trust is that given to the central press.

The whole picture could very well change drastically if and when Soviet broadcast officials utilize the medium of central television to convey in dramatic, visual, "spontaneous" (that is, with the appearance of spontaneity) terms a reality about which Russians know nothing from personal experience. If news and political broadcasts were made up of footage of fast-breaking news events, or if Soviet producers were to go out on location with electronic news-gathering equipment, the degree of confidence accorded the central media would probably rise. The tremendous persuasiveness of what is actually seen would certainly provide an advantage over foreign radio. However, such a shift to on-location news coverage, both at home and abroad, carries with it a certain loss of control. If the editing is not to undercut the credibility of the broadcast, then a reasonably broad range of images is likely to be included, some of them at variance with official censorship norms.[14] It is undoubtedly safer to continue with the present system, in which news is mainly read in the studio, while the army of correspondents, 150 at home and 40 in foreign countries, rarely sign off from location.

The remoteness of international news from the everyday lives of most Soviet citizens results not only in greater trust in those kinds of messages, but also in heightened interest and attention. One of the most striking features of the Russian media public is its intense interest in foreign countries and international news events. It seeks information of this sort at all levels of the media and, in survey after survey, the respondents say that in this area the amount of information provided should be expanded. The thirst for international news cuts across the age, sex, and education variables that differentiate the audience for other kinds of topics. In relative terms (not, of course, in total amount of newspaper space), the Russian public is exposed to rather a high percentage of foreign items in the newspapers. Earlier it was noted that in *Pravda,* about 30 percent of the paper's column inches were devoted to international items. In this category, almost a fifth of the space was devoted to stories about the United States, and another quarter of the total foreign news space to news of NATO and America's European allies. The United States and its allies in Europe were given 44 percent of the international news space, and foreign communist countries only 31 percent. All of this argues for a very heightened salience of the West, and of the United States in particular.

What of the salience of the Soviet Union and communist countries for the American newspaper reader? An analysis of foreign news information in 1977 in four "elite" American dailies—the *New York Times, Chicago Tribune, Miami Herald,* and *Los Angeles Times*—shows that news about the Soviet Union amounted to roughly 4 percent of all foreign news. News about all Communist countries came to 8 percent of all foreign news. Thus the broadest swath of news about communist countries was not more than 12 percent of foreign news, as compared with the 44 percent of the foreign news in *Pravda* devoted to the United States and its European allies.[15] It seems that the salience of foreign political systems for American newspapers depends on their similarities to the U. S. system:

> Like nations attract one another while unlike nations do not attract the attention of one another. Self- or ethno-centrism not poly-centrism seems to shape the pattern of news attention of the U.S. elite press. . . . To compensate for greater distance, occurrences in non-proximate countries will ordinarily have to meet other criteria before being considered newsworthy; they must be perceived threatening to the perceiver or seem to substantially enhance the prospects of something desirable or, at a minimum, they must be spectacular to be valued newsworthy for print.[16]

It is certainly possible that the greater salience of the West for Soviet newspapers may be generated by a greater sense of threat from the U.S. system, or their propagandistic portrayal of the West as threatening, to insure compliance at home. Or it might be the case that for the Soviet Union, the West is simply of greater inherent interest—a system to be imitated or to be used as a measuring stick. That they are more interested in the United States than vice versa appears incontrovertible.

## FOREIGN MEDIA CONSUMPTION

With their heightened interest in foreign political systems and international relations, and with their intensified inclination to be critical and dissatisfied, the college educated might be a likely audience for foreign radio broadcasters.

To some lesser degree, the same might hold true of the dissatisfied less well educated. One would like to be able to estimate the reach of foreign broadcasts: How many Russians listen? What programs do they prefer? What follows is a discussion of what is known and what one may reliably infer about the impact of foreign broadcasting. The overriding conclusion, evident from the beginning, is that one knows very little.

To treat this question, it should be kept in mind that domestic radio listening is a leisure-time activity that has been radically altered by the introduction of television into Russian households.[17] As in the United States, radio listening has been the chief victim of the newer electronic medium, and surveys of radio audiences carried out before television had become widely available should be interpreted with caution. In the big cities especially, exposure to radio has declined dramatically due to television. A Leningrad survey reports that "Television is now far more important than such an important channel of mass communication as the radio. Listening to the radio does not exceed 26-28 minutes a day in any occupational group."[18] In rural areas, radio is both more relevant and more popular, particularly for farming and weather information. To a certain extent, radio listening may be underreported; it, like television watching, is an activity that often takes place while another activity is going on, such as housework or eating or conversation. Another effect of competition from television has been the change in the schedule of radio listening. In rural areas, where radio is more popular than in urban areas, virtually all radio listening is done in the morning before work, and only a miniscule amount in the evening during television prime time.

Among foreign broadcasters, the four major Western radio stations are the BBC, Deutsche Welle (under the Ministry of the Interior of the Federal Republic of Germany), the Voice of America (administered by the American governmental agency, tne International Communications Agency), and Radio Liberty (initially funded by the Central Intelligence Agency and in 1973 placed under legislative control through the formation of the Board for International Broadcasting).[19] The Soviet government has often resorted to jamming, the creation of interfering static, to prevent its citizens from listening to the foreign programs it wishes to censor. From 1963 until the Soviet invasion of Czechoslovakia, large-scale jamming of Western programs was absent, although in 1964 a Soviet program "Mayak" (Beacon) was created to go out at the same time that foreign broadcasts were received (mainly during the late night hours, when broadcasting conditions are most favorable for the Western stations) and interfere with the wavelengths used by the foreign broadcasters.[20] In August 1968 jamming of Western stations was reimposed, to be lifted, once again, in September 1973. Radio Liberty continues to be jammed, no doubt because that station concentrates on internal Soviet matters, broadcasts 24 hours a day, and devotes a good deal of time to ethnic minority problems, religion, and samizdat.

Arriving at an estimate of the Soviet audience for foreign radio with rigorous and reliable methods is very difficult. But these methods are necessary if one is to draw conclusions about the size of the audience and its composition, particularly with respect to the role that education might play in exposure to foreign radio broadcasts. In the course of the first survey of the readership of *Pravda,* which took place in 1968, there were some questions that treated the audience for foreign radio within the context of the total universe of media sources consumed by a given respondent. These results were never published, constituting, as they did, a sensitive issue. However, the principal investigator and head of that project, Vladimir Shlapentokh, has made this information available for the first time on the basis of his recollection of the material.

One of the questions asked respondents to name which sources of information, in addition to the central newspaper, provided them with information (see Table 3). Shlapentokh adds that among the college educated, 10 percent said they received additional information from foreign radio.[21] This question does not ask how much time is spent with these media, but whether the respondent finds information in them. Information may not include, for these Russian respondents,

TABLE 3: Use of Information Sources Other Than the Central Newspaper

| Medium | Respondents (percent) |
| --- | --- |
| Television | 50[a] |
| Local newspaper | 80-90 |
| Radio | 80-90 |
| Oral propaganda (party instruction, lectures) | 30 |
| Friends | 10 |
| Foreign radio | 6-8[b] |
| Foreign newspaper | 2-4[c] |

[a]This percentage is understated with respect to viewing patterns of today. In early 1968, when this survey was taken, the diffusion of television sets was considerably smaller than at present.

[b]This figure may be understated in that it does not include communications from foreign broadcasters that are transmitted by friends and family. This second- or third-hand diffusion of foreign radio broadcasts would tend to increase the audience. It should also be noted that even though this period of survey research was a particularly felicitous one in which respondents were at their most frank, according to those who have worked with opinion polling, it is nonetheless true that a question of this sort—the reach of foreign radio—is a sensitive one. In Shlapentokh's opinion, respondents would be cautious in revealing their attentiveness to foreign stations.

[c]The foreign newspapers generally available to the Soviet public are either those imported from socialist countries or papers published under the auspices of communist parties in nonsocialist countries.

programs of music, which form a large proportion of the programming of the foreign radios. Also, this *Pravda* survey does not analyze the non-Russian republics. Nonetheless, the reach of the foreign radios is considerable and markedly so for college graduates.[22]

There have been attempts to study the Soviet foreign radio audience from afar. These cannot, naturally, utilize survey methods of the sort reported here, but must relax many of the assumptions normally made.[23] For example, Radio Liberty, from its Paris offices, regularly interviews Soviet travelers (not émigrés) in Europe about their exposure to the four major Western radios and their program preference. One's confidence in the Radio Liberty analysis of foreign radio-listening behavior of Soviet citizens rests on the degree to which the travelers are representative of the population of the Soviet Union. In the first chapter it was observed that unless the probability of any individual's falling within the sample is essentially equal to that of any other individual's, one may not draw conclusions about the larger population to which one wishes to generalize. That is, if some bias is present in the sample, then one will be drawing skewed inferences or magnifying that bias when one superimposes it on a parent population. In the instant case, one must believe that there are no serious differences between people who do not leave the Soviet Union and those Soviet citizens who travel in the West, and therefore the behavior of the travelers is not likely to differ markedly from their stay-at-home counterparts. How likely is this assumption to be met?

It is known that travelers, even within a country, are not necessarily representative of the population. A survey of 3,097 passengers on domestic flights in the Soviet Union found that the passengers tended to be repeaters (habitual travelers), far more so than the average Soviet citizen, and that they were drawn disproportionately from higher income levels.[24] For foreign travel, one might expect that these disproportions would be even more prominent. However, an additional factor of political reliability is added to the eligibility of the Soviet citizen for foreign travel. Exit visas are granted selectively. Tourists usually must travel in groups or delegations, and political reliability and control are key elements in the decision to grant an exit visa for tourism or exchanges in foreign countries, particularly in the West. Often the delegations or groups of tourists are made up of people in a single occupation or from a single region. There is often in the delegation at least one ideological watchdog whose duty is to maintain discipline in the group. What the Radio Liberty interviewers do is to conduct in a public place an indirect interview, a conversation with a hidden agenda, but no explicit structure, about listening behavior. Given the circumstances, it may be the only alternative to asking the tourist to fill out a questionnaire or engage in a structured interview. Needless to say, there is a limited choice of respondents, since success depends a good deal on the luck of an encounter. The results obtained from these conversations are then projected onto the population of the Soviet Union on the basis of a computer simulation of Soviet society derived from the sociodemographic characteristics of the tourists interviewed and the population of the Soviet Union. The conclusions are framed in terms of total numbers of Soviet citizens thus estimated to be listening to foreign radio.[25]

If there were no problem in the matter of assumptions, the projecting from a sample onto a larger population from which that sample is drawn is unexceptionable. In this case, though, it is known that certain factors reduce the assumption of independence and randomness to a significant degree. That is, there is something about the population of Soviet foreign tourists that makes them very similar to each other and, in turn, very different from average Soviet citizens; that something is not only economic and social but, more important, political. Even when the delegations are composed of numbers of milkmaids or pipe fitters, the prior political consideration is always present in the granting of the exit visa. In these cases, most probably the visa was a reward for officially desirable behavior at the workplace or in the community. In the complement of Soviet tourists who were interviewed most recently by Radio Liberty, some 23 percent were identified as members of the Communist Party, and for another 11 percent party affiliation was not known. Therefore, in the sample, party members are overrepresented by at least 2.5 times and possibly as much as almost four times their proportion in the population in the Soviet Union.*

The Radio Liberty analysts acknowledge that there may be "potential biases" in their sample:

> On the one hand, travelers might be assumed to come from a more educated (or at least more intellectually curious stratum of the population) and enjoy higher socio-economic status than non-travelers. This might tend to favor such activities as Western radio listening. On the other hand, trips abroad are often taken for professional purposes or as rewards for good work, etc., and there has been evidence of screening of travelers for reliability. . . . This might lead them to minimize certain attitudes and activities such as Western radio listening. We do not know the extent to which these biases may cancel each other out, but are aware that they exist.[26]

That is indeed the problem. Perhaps it is the best that can be done, and it may be a creative and innovative way to squeeze out whatever information is available

---

*A further problem is related to the numbers of tourists who are interviewed. In some categories numbers are so small that even the best estimate is shaky. This is particularly true, as the analysts state, for rural people, very few of whom were encountered by Radio Liberty interviewers. Another problem, one that could be corrected in future interviews, is one of categorization. The Radio Liberty material divides the tourists into the educated (at least high school education) and uneducated (less than complete high school education). In everything seen in earlier chapters, the attainment of higher education is associated with significantly different communications behavior. Similarly, there is another threshold with four grades of education or less. By blurring these distinctions, an important source of information is lost.

and to utilize it to the maximum extent possible. Whether the biases load up or act as counterweights, whether the error is additive or nonadditive, is not known; the problem cannot be resolved.[27]

The results of Radio Liberty audience research profile the foreign radio audience in the Soviet Union and estimate its size. The size of the audience for all Western broadcasters (BBC, Radio Canada International, Deutsche Welle, Israel Radio, Trans-World, Radio-Monte Carlo, Radio Finland, Radio France, Radio Free Europe, Radio Italy, Radio Luxembourg, Radio Sweden, Radio Vatican, Voice of America) they put at 67.3 million Soviet citizens over 16 listening during the course of a year. This amounts to some 37 percent of the adult population of the USSR.[28] Radio Liberty's analysis of program preference is derived from informal, spur-of-the-moment talks with Soviet tourists, since the interviewers do not obtain responses to a checklist of program types. Instead, a notion of program preference had to be distilled from discursive conversation. From this emerged the preference for newscasts, programs on Soviet internal affairs and on samizdat. Such results must be only suggestive at best.

To a very much more limited degree another foreign communications channel is available, but only selectively, to some Russians. There are some foreign movies, particularly movies from the West, that are seen outside the regular movie theater circuit. This audience is counted in very small numbers because the showings are closed and play to a restricted audience. In this case, the foreign product is shown to those whom the officials choose. The audience may include movie industry people and their friends, as well as people from whom favors may be expected, such as medical specialists or officials who have some control over scarce consumer commodities. Two recent examples of such films were *Dr. Strangelove* and *A Clockwork Orange.*[29] Even foreign film festivals held in the Soviet Union play to a restricted audience, and the average Russian would be unable to acquire a ticket. In September 1976 an Italian film festival took place in Moscow. The audience were all drawn from the intellegentsia, the upper social and economic reaches of Soviet society. One of the films they saw was *Suspicion,* by the Italian director, Maselli. Also present was the *Corriere della Sera* correspondent, Piero Ostellino, who described the event:

> When one of the characters in the film "Suspicion"—the action unfolds in 1934—declares that the first duty of every communist is to support the Soviet Union, the only hope for all communists the world over, some of the Soviet spectators ostentatiously left the hall. Others walked out after listening to praise of party discipline even at the cost of sacrificing individual freedom of thought and even of one's own life. In one place, when the characters express doubts about the possibility of building socialism in Italy, someone actually burst out with a yell: "All the better, lucky you!"[30]

## THE EFFECT OF AGE AND LIFE-CYCLE

Another factor that plays an important role in explaining or predicting communications behavior is age. To some degree, it is related to education. The older population in Russia is less well educated than the younger, and therefore is likely to be less actively involved in newspaper reading, which requires cognitive skills. People on pensions are less likely to turn out for the mass lectures that attract so many others. To the extent that it is their lower level of formal education that keeps older people from being exposed to certain kinds of messages, one may assume that in succeeding generations the older people will not differ very much from their younger neighbors.

It is not simple to determine whether one should consider the communications exposure of older people a reflection of generational change or a life-cycle characteristic. If the explanation is generational, then one may expect that with each generation a gradual change occurs in society as older ones die off and new ones grow up. This kind of secular change over generations might well be occurring with respect to the impact of messages relating to World War II. Reactions to movies about World War II show a clear generational difference, and it is unlikely that as today's youth grow older they will acquire an appreciation of and empathy with those themes that now seem to relate hardly at all to their life experiences. On the other hand, some of the relationship between aging and attention to the media is derived from life-cycle factors. Income and mobility both decline with age, and this acts to promote television watching, which is free and takes place at home, while reducing attendance at theaters, movies, lectures, and concerts. Young, unmarried people do the opposite. Eager to socialize and be entertained away from their parents, they are the most active moviegoers in the country.

Between youth and old age comes the most pressured time in the life cycle. The burdens of family obligations, the demands of young children, high expenses, and severe limitations on time all characterize the middle period. This part of the cycle falls particularly heavily on women, and it is not by accident that their exposure to the media in Russia is low. In one survey in Sverdlovsk, at three industrial plants, single women and mothers were compared with respect to the free time at their disposal. It was found that almost 70 percent of the unmarried women went to libraries to read, but only a third of the women with families. Two-thirds of the unmarried women went to the theater, but only a little more than a quarter of the mothers. Almost a third of the single women did some kind of sports, compared to 5 percent of the women with families.[31] A large survey of working women in industry in the large cities of the European part of the Soviet Union came to the following conclusions: at this particular stage in the life cycle, the stage of family with young children, women spend some 30 hours a week on housekeeping chores and another 10 hours caring for children. Almost three-quarters of all nonworking time is spent on household duties. If the hours on the job are added to the hours working at home, then the total working day for an average working mother is between 11 and 12 hours. There is little time left for relaxing with the children, strolling around town, playing with them, reading aloud, or going over homework. Only a third of the mothers said they had done any of these activities in the three days prior to the survey.[32] It is not surprising that women are consistently and sharply underrepresented in media exposure.

A difference in attitude is also associated with age. It was noted that the young are more critical and dissatisfied with media products in Russia than are older people. Satisfaction increases with age. Is this a generational effect that will result in ever more critical cohorts, or is this a life-cycle experience that most undergo as they grow older? In part, the older have less education and are therefore less aware of alternatives and options. With constricted horizons, they are less dissatisfied. To this extent one may imagine that successive generations will not be as likely to be satisfied as is the present older generation. Then, too, the objective world that must have left an imprint on the current older generation was Stalin's Russia and World War II, a time of violence, deprivation, and virtual hysterical personal insecurity. Perhaps the present-day greater satisfaction of the old is to be expected, but may not apply to future generations. But one should not be too quick to grant this assumption; imputing attitudes on the basis of an objective reality is not a reliable undertaking.

Intermixed with these generational effects are those drawn from the life-cycle explanation. In their survey of American satisfaction, Campbell, Converse, and Rodgers suggest that although the differences are not very great, "older people seem to express higher satisfaction with their situations and experiences than the young."[33] A parallel British study showed "the same general trend toward a positive age-satisfaction relationship. . . ."[34] If the source of this relationship is related to the psychology of aging, then one may expect that succeeding generations will also experience it. Although no firm causal explanation may be adduced, it would seem to represent an adjustment or accommodation to a situation—the acceptance of the known, if no turbulent change dispels the fog of familiarity. Two other elements play a role in this relationship: the success that the mobility of an active life has brought (being better off now than when one started out in life), and the "progressive occupancy of niches which are better fitted to the individual's particular needs and tastes," as well as the effect of modifying one's adjustment to those niches.[35] This greater generalized satisfaction of the elderly was expressed irrespective of their conditions of material welfare, indeed even in the face of substandard living arrangements. There is, for the Russian public, nothing like this amount and quality of information. A distinct difference in attitudes does exist between young and old in Russia, sometimes referred to as a new fathers and sons problem, and it might be stronger than in the West. It is, no doubt, both generational and life cycle in origin, but to see further, one shall have to wait longer. Certainly, downward generational mobility, which many of the recent emigres describe, or turbulent change would surely alter particularly these results.

## HOW MALLEABLE IS THE PUBLIC?

Western observers of the vast communications apparatus of the Soviet Union and of the tremendous volume of messages of similar content that go out over the communications network, sometimes conclude that something like brainwashing, or at least powerful persuasive pressuring, must be taking place. But such conclusions fail to separate content and volume of transmissions or columns from content and volume of reception by the individual receiver. With that failure the Soviet communications officials now charge themselves:

> One of the harmful dogmas is to accept silently the notion that people in our society more or less uniformly or equally assimilate the entire mental nourishment that is issued to them. That is, by the way, a profound delusion, because, in the language of cybernetics, the output of propaganda (i.e. that which is assimilated) often turns out not to be what was expected in the input.[36]

The delusions that the "harmful dogmas" produced have come to light with the probing of opinion. For example, communications officials had always thought that people who were religious were people who had not, somehow, been reached by antireligious messages, and that increasing the reach or volume of this propaganda would erase the problem for the regime. However, in a recent survey of several districts in Kostroma, some with and some without churches, it was found that just over a quarter of the population considered themselves strong or moderate believers. What surprised the pollsters was the finding that these people were by no means cut off from the media. Quite the contrary: 88 percent of the strong believers and 95 percent of the moderates regularly read the newspaper, magazines, listen to the radio, and watch television.[37] In another case, before the *Izvestia* readership survey was conducted, a group of experts (journalists, sociologists, economists, and scientists) were asked to predict the result of two questions: Can you remember instances when you did not agree with the newspaper? and With what detail do you read editorials? The experts' predictions were then compared to the actual results. The most prominent journalists predicted that 85 percent of the respondents would say that there were no instances in which they disagreed with the editorial point of view. The survey results showed that only 25 percent gave this answer. The journalists also predicted that 5 percent would cite instances in which they disagreed with the paper, but the actual figure was 11 percent. All of the experts vastly overstated the degree to which respondents did not read editorials. Predictions went from 20 percent to 60 percent, but the survey showed that 9.4 percent of the respondents did not read any of the editorial.[38]

Expert opinion operating in the absence of feedback from the media public is also blamed for the suppression of genres that the audience badly wants. This is what happened with the melodramatic film, which is produced in far smaller quantity than the relatively unpopular contemporary drama. The result is that the audience migrates to imports that are judged inferior by the same Soviet officials who refuse to produce what the public wants. The same is true of the detective genre.

> In the past we were witnesses to many examples when "expert opinion" led to the fact that whole genres were not developed, notwithstanding the enormous demand for them. We cite, for example the detective genre in literature (and also in films) which everyone condemned in all sorts of ways for a long time. Finally, in the conflict of expert and demand, the latter gained the upper hand. Obviously the experts were ignorant of those qualities of this genre which the user valued.[39]

With the development of opinion polling, the officials have found out that the structure of demands and tastes is quite different from what they had imagined or wished, and that the blanketing of the public with constant repetitive messages was not producing the desired effect. There is differential reception. Such attributes as education, income, place of residence, and membership or nonmembership in the party were affecting both the exposure to messages and attitudes toward their credibility. To some extent, the limiting of sources of information might have enhanced the credibility of the media. This might be true, for example, of articles in the central press about international events, where information is beyond the personal experience of most Russians.

A simple strategy, much used in the past, was the nonreporting of an event that is difficult to explain within the confines of the political doctrine, such as deviance, crime, or poverty in Soviet society. But, as has been seen, nonreporting gives rise to explanations from unofficial and sometimes adversarial sources, which, having been first to influence public opinion, then prove more difficult for official explanations to penetrate or replace. Studies of letters received by the central press find that "quite a number of questions addressed to the editors are generated by insufficient knowledge in this or that area. Sometimes they [the questions] result from incorrect interpretations of events, [or] from rumours, the counteracting of which is not always simple or easy."[40] For the first time officials have been shown that their sense of the audience is faulty, and the rather uncomplicated palliatives they have applied in the past have resulted in movements of consumption and opinion over which they have far less control than they would have wished. The tension between user and expert is by no means simply solved, since emphasis on the former leads to inevitable loss of control by the center, and emphasis on the latter leads to the distortions (from the experts' point of view) of consumption and opinion that have now come to light.

## MEDIA AND MODERNIZATION

If I have not used the work "totalitarian" in this study, it has been a deliberate omission. The word has come to stand for a political system in which there is no movement, no change; in which government control is total; in which monopolies of all functions, including the communications function, are held by the leadership; in which the feedback loop has been replaced by a unidirectional movement from the center to an inert and malleable population. I shall not argue here whether or not these notions inhered in the original formulations of the totalitarian "syndrome," as it is properly called. But from the initial delineation of its characteristics, the theory, model, or syndrome of totalitarianism did give rise to these notions. Nor do I accept the modified version of the theory of totalitarianism in which it is treated as a nonexistent limiting case, and one measures, in the real world, something like a "will to become totalitarian." From this notion of totalitarianism comes the tendency to treat rhetoric as reality and to go astray in the welter of varying, far from comparable arrangements that the world's many political systems have devised. I do not use this notion of totalitarianism, because in its original form, which is meant to describe real systems, it does not adequately characterize reality.

It has been seen here that the Russian public is by no means a totally plastic, inert mass. It is doubtful that any group of human beings could ever be so described. Because Soviet reality is far more complex than the totalitarian theory had envisioned does not mean, on the other hand, that the "people's" voice must be heard in high councils. The channels for the transmission of such demands cannot legitimately exist in the Soviet political system. Curiously, it is the opinion poll that comes closest to functioning as such a channel for the broad masses. The immediate political costs of a more efficient and effective communications system may be too high for the Soviet government; it may choose to operate with diminished credibility rather than to cover local events in a realistic and open way; it may opt rather for a dissatisfied population of college-educated audiences than increase the inputs of information. That government has, in the past, incurred tremendous costs in economic and human terms for its policies. Whether those policies were undertaken for the power aggrandizement of the rulers or for the millenial promise of the ideology is moot; one cannot probe that deeply from afar. The clarification of the effect of some of those policies through opinion research may have few, if any, results in changing policy direction or altering its style—not unless efficiency considerations continue to be generated by the pressure of limited resources become far more critical.

While the media have produced these contradictory and conflicting effects even as they blanket and saturate the audience, the question might be raised as to the very role and utility of the mass media system in Russia. In his well-known study of predictors of national political development, Phillips Cutright found that political and economic development indexes were interrelated, and that within the group of indexes expressing economic development, the single best predictor of political development was the index measuring the development of communications in the 76 countries he studied.[41] However, it was also found that some countries represented outlying cases: the Soviet Union and all Soviet-type socialist countries were such deviant cases, in which communications development far exceeded political development. Cutright understands as politically "developed" those systems that have genuinely representative parliaments and a chief executive directly elected in competitive elections.

As noted earlier, the possibilities that communications development presented for a revolution were understood from the beginning by Lenin and his successors. As Soviet Russia has moved from traditional society, the urban population has increased rapidly, and the functions of the media have been both altered and enhanced. The path of communication is no longer within the small group, with its loyalties and identification, but passes through a larger world. Even interpersonal agitation, the talks with fellow workers at the factory, is giving way to public lectures. In the city where the impersonal is the norm, the media, particularly the local newspapers, are charged with the role of integrating the inhabitants of the urban sprawl. At the same time, the standards for media communications are rising. In part, this is a result of the increasing levels of education throughout the population. In part, it might result from the comparisons or alternatives presented by foreign communications. In any case, there is considerable evidence of a continuing upgrading and specialization in the communications function, even among those who disseminate information of a specialized political propaganda sort.[42]

In the early days after the Russian Revolution, the Communist Party, through a network of party schools, served as the general educational system for its many illiterate or poorly educated members. As modernization proceeded, that function was taken over by the developing general educational system. Such a splitting-off of activities, the continual specialization of function and an increasing importance accorded to achievement considerations, has resulted in the proliferation of structures and inputs that are characteristic of the more modernized systems in the world. The restricted fund of information that has in the past been fed back to the ruling elites (that is, to the Communist Party) may have facilitated its domination of these structures. But as information becomes more complex and diffused, the choices become more acute. Among the respondents who acknowledge dissatisfaction with the various media sources, Communist Party members are by no means absent. Indeed, their very distinctiveness as among the most highly educated, suggests that a critical stance might not be a passing phenomenon.

The initial push to develop, even overdevelop, the communications network—pushing it out of balance, as it were, with the level of development of the society—was generated by a desperate need of the revolutionary leadership to effect a revolutionary change, and to integrate a largely premodern society in which there were vast differences across regions, ethnic and linguistic groups, social classes, and traditions. It was a policy that grasped the promise of science and technology and hoped to harness the lines and impulses of messages to persuade and unite the masses of receivers. Western observers, as well as Communist Party leaders, have taken the promise of the policy as the product and have been, perhaps, equally enthralled by the "modernity" of a major policy thrust that was among the first to utilize the new technology. In the absence of information, while the media public was still invisible, such beliefs persisted. Now, however, we have had a glimpse of that public, and what has become clear is that the vigorous and distinctive media policy pursued by the Soviet leaders has had many results—many differing results. They have been contradictory and paradoxical results in many ways; they have borne out official intentions in some areas and directly undermined them in others. They have had different effects on different people. Correspondingly, whether or not media policy changes, the choices must inevitably be more difficult now that the audience has been seen.

## NOTES

1. V. Kobysh, "Zhyt kak po televizoru," *Novy Mir,* no. 11 (1978), p. 277.

2. L. V. Knyazeva, "Otsenka saseleniem sredstv massovoi ustnoi propagandy kak pokazate effektivnosti ideologicheskogo vozdeistvia," *Sotsiologicheskie issledovania v ideologicheskoi rabote,* vol. 1 (Moscow, 1974), p. 66.

3. V. E. Shlyapentokh, "Rost urovnya obrazovania i otnoshenie k sredstvam massovoi informatsii," *Problemy sotsiologii i psikhologii chtenia* (Moscow, 1975), p. 99.

4. R. I. Kalmykov, "Povyshenie obshcheobrazovatelnogo urovnya i professionalnoi podgotovki selskikh truzhenikov kak zakonomernost," *Uchenye zapiski,* vol. 75 (Kursk, 1971), p. 28.

5. Robert T. Bower, *Television and the Public* (New York: Holt, Rinehart & Winston, 1973), pp. 75-80.

6. A recent survey supports this finding and reveals that dissatisfaction, particularly with information programs, is increasing, although viewing time does not decrease. Les Brown, "Viewers' Dissatisfaction with TV Programs Found Increasing," *New York Times,* January 3, 1980, p. C18.

7. Angus Campbell, Philip E. Converse, and Willard L. Rodgers, *The Quality of American Life* (New York: Russell Sage Foundation, 1976), p. 143.

8. Ibid., pp. 147, 149.

9. Ibid., p. 147.

10. Alex Inkeles and Raymond A. Bauer, *The Soviet Citizen* (Cambridge: Harvard University Press, 1961), p. 181.

11. Boris Firsov, "Srednogo zritelya net," *Zhurnalist,* no. 12 (December 1967), p. 44.

12. Denis McQuail, "The Influence and Effects of Mass Media," in *Mass Communication and Society,* ed. James Curran, Michael Gurevitch, and Janet Woollacott (Beverly Hills: Sage Publications, 1979), p. 82.

13. Ibid., pp. 79-80.

14. Rita Cirio, correspondent for the Italian news weekly *L'Espresso,* learned that in a live television interview the noted film director Sergei Parajanov said he had gone to the party's Central Committee to complain that he was not given enough work, and all he saw "were people who were eating caviar by the spoonful." "Chi beve Breznev campa cent'anni,"

*L'Espresso,* Rome, January 29, 1978, p. 81.

15. Communication from Andrew K. Semmel to the author, June 17, 1979. My thanks to Professor Semmel, of the department of political science, University of Cincinnati, for computing this information for me.

16. Andrew K. Semmel, "The Elite Press, Foreign News, and Public Opinion," paper prepared for delivery at the International Studies Association Annual Meeting, March 21-24, 1979, Toronto, Canada, p. 26.

17. For a discussion of the administration and organization of radio in the Soviet Union, see Rosemarie Rogers, "The Soviet Mass Media in the Sixties: Patterns of Access and Consumption," *Journal of Broadcasting* 16 (Spring 1971), pp. 127-46; Gayle Durham Hollander, "Radio and Television," in *Soviet Political Indoctrination* (New York: Praeger, 1972), pp. 99-130. These sources do not treat in detail the changes that television was later to stimulate.

18. Ivan Trufanov, *Problemy byta gorodskogo naselenia SSSR* (Leningrad, 1973), translated as *Problems of Soviet Urban Life* (Newtonville, Mass.: Oriental Research Partners, 1977), p. 89.

19. For studies of the content of the programs beamed to the Soviet Union, see James H. Oliver, "A Comparison of Four Western Russian-Language Broadcasters," *Journalism Quarterly* 54 (Spring 1977), pp. 126-34. See also the various reports published by Radio Liberty and Voice of America.

20. Hollander, pp. 113-14. For an interesting study of official Soviet reaction to foreign broadcasting, see Maury Lisann, *Broadcasting to the Soviet Union: International Politics and Radio* (New York: Praeger, 1975).

21. The author wishes to express her gratitude to Dr. Shlapentokh, of the department of sociology of Michigan State University, for making these data available. The reader should note that since his emigration to the United States in 1979, Dr. Shlapentokh has adopted this transliteration of his name. However, for his works published in the Soviet Union, the reader will undoubtedly find in libraries a different transliteration, such as the one I have used when referring to the published works—Shlyapentokh.

22. In his study of foreign broadcasting in the USSR, Maury Lisann discusses three polls conducted in the Soviet Union that explicitly address these issues. They are early surveys of the mid-1960s. One survey conducted at the University of Vilnius in Lithuania found that about a third of the respondents said they listened to Western Radio. Lisann doubts the representativeness of the sample. A second survey, also with prescientific methods, took place in Estonia and revealed that 66 percent of those surveyed could receive Finnish television. An Estonian radio poll found that among foreign stations, Finnish radio was preferred and the Voice of America's Estonian-language broadcasts were second. Lisann, pp. 129-48.

These surveys predate the methodologically sounder surveys of the period under review in the present study, and it is difficult to generalize from their interesting though methodologically weak conclusions. There are other surveys that, while explicitly asking about foreign listening or viewing behavior, include such categories as "supplementary sources" or "additional sources of information." Although it is tempting to regard these categories as referring to Western radio broadcasts, it is probably not warranted, since word of mouth is such a prominent communications medium in Russia. Of course, that friend's information might well have come from a foreign broadcast, but care should be exercised in drawing conclusions of this sort, especially when international and domestic information are not distinctly separated.

23. Mail that is sent out of the Soviet Union or received from abroad carries the high probability of being read or recorded by internal security authorities. It is not surprising that Voice of America over the course of 18 months, from February 1978 to June 1979, received on the average only about 10.5 letters a month from the Soviet Union and at least six of these per month were innocuous requests for photographs, music, or schedules. An

additional number of letters is collected by the American Embassy in Moscow and sent on to Washington. This was observed twice in the surveyed period, and most of these were also requests for music. One cannot base generalizations about Russian listening behavior on so fragile a foundation.

24. V. E. Shlyapentokh, *Problemy representativnosti sotsiologicheskoi informatsii* (Moscow, 1976), p. 22.

25. For a discussion of the very sophisticated and impressive model and procedure applied in this research, see Ithiel de Sola Pool, "Methodology," Appendix II, "Listening to Radio Liberty in the USSR, 1976-77," Analysis Report 3-78, June 28, 1978, *FRE-RL Soviet Area Audience Research and Program Evaluation*, pp. 4-5.

26. "Listening to Radio Liberty in the USSR, 1976-77," pp. 4-5.

27. Although it is impossible to verify or validate the Radio Liberty audience research directly, the analysts do suggest that the results of domestic Soviet surveys of media behavior at least partially confirm their results and validate their methods. One source of this validation is the Leningrad television survey conducted by Boris Firsov and published in 1967. They find that television-viewing behavior, as reported by Firsov's respondents, roughly coincides with the results of the testimony about television viewing the Radio Liberty interviewers heard from the Soviet tourists in Europe. That is, the figures for exposure were close. Rosemarie Rogers's study found a fairly close match between the findings of a *Komsomolskaya Pravda* write-in survey (self-selected sample) and the information gathered in interviews in Europe with people who had left the Soviet Union between 1956 and 1966.

Does the coincidence of information and exposure to Soviet television create greater confidence in the answers to questions about foreign radio listening? It is difficult to determine. There is no particular political constraint in relating information about watching domestic television programs, but political factors might well enter into testimony about consumption of foreign radio broadcasts. In addition, since the introduction of television on a large scale in the Soviet Union, there have been dramatic changes in communications behavior. Television viewing has severely eroded radio listening. Further, there are now significant disparities between town and country, not only in exposure to radio, but also in exposure to television.

It may be the case that attitudes or opinions make very little difference in exposure. It is said to be "a highly stable phenomenon, quite stable across the population. The choice of programs heard or articles read may differ greatly, but the use of leisure time as between media differs little between subsamples of the population." ("Listening to Radio Liberty in the USSR," p. 12.) We do know that in the Soviet Union, the written media, which depend on cognitive skills, have a highly differentiated audience in terms of level of education. We also know that the electronic media have a much less differentiated audience. It is true, too, as this chapter has shown, that the higher the level of education, the more critical the audience. In television exposure, those with higher education are both lower consumers and greater complainers than the rest of the population. It would seem that exposure is affected, in this case, by attitude. The likelihood of foreign radio listeners to be people with higher education, rather than people with less than college education, suggests that critical opinions may well be a motivating force for turning to the foreign broadcasts. Since the radio-listening habits of Soviet citizens vis-à-vis their domestic broadcasts show an opposite trend—more rural than urban, less well educated than well educated—it becomes problematical as to how really valuable as instruments of verification are results concerning exposure to internal media in the Soviet Union.

28. "Soviet Audiences to Western Radio," Analysis Report 2-79, June 6, 1979, *FRE-RL Soviet Area Audience and Opinion Research*, pp. 4-5.

29. David K. Shipler, "Ticket to U.S. Film a Coveted Item for Soviet Elite," *New York Times*, March 11, 1979, p. 4.

30. Piero Ostellino, *Vivere in Russia* (Milano: Rizzoli Editore, 1977), p. 77.

31. L. N. Kogan, *Khudozhestvenny vkus* (Moscow, 1966), p. 117.

32. L. Gordon, V. Klopov, and E. Gruzdeva, "Etapy zhiznennogo tsikla i byt rabotayushchei zhenshchiny," *Izmenenie polozhenia zhenshchiny i semya* (Moscow, 1977), pp. 146-47.

33. Campbell et al., p. 164.

34. Ibid., p. 158, footnote 4.

35. Ibid., p. 164.

36. Knyazeva, p. 66.

37. B. S. Arkhipov, "Sotsiologicheskie issledovania v rabote oblastnogo komiteta partii," *Sotsiologicheskie issledovania,* no. 1 (1974), p. 115.

38. See Ellen Mickiewicz, "Policy Applications of Public Opinion Research in the Soviet Union," *Public Opinion Quarterly* 36 (Winter 1972-73), p. 573.

39. V. E. Shlyapentokh, "K voprosu ob izuchenii esteticheskikh vkusov chitatelya gazety," *Problemy sotsiologii pechati,* vol. 2 (Novosibirsk, 1970), p. 64.

40. S. I. Igoshin, "Pisma Chitatelei kak vyrazhenie sovetskoi demokratii," *Problemy zhurnalistiki,* vol. 9 (Leningrad, 1977), p. 62.

41. Phillips Cutright, "National Political Development: Measurement and Analysis," *American Sociological Review* 28 (April 1963).

42. Ellen Mickiewicz, "The Modernization of Party Propaganda in the USSR," *Slavic Review* 30 (June 1971).

# INDEX

Academy of Sciences: sponsorship of polls, 3, 16; sociology branches, 3
Akhmadulina, Bella, 20
All-Union Agency for Authors' Rights (VAAP), 91
"Ashes and Diamonds," 78, 79-80

BBC, 21, 33, 138, 142
"Ballad of a Soldier," 78
Baptist religion, 114
"Belorussia Station," 81, 82
Brezhnev, L., 5, 13, 21, 91, 124
*Buryat Pravda*, 120

Campbell, Angus; Converse, Philip; and Rodgers, Willard, 133, 144
*Cancer Ward*, 120
"Caucasian Captive," 76
"The Chairman," 79
"Chapaev," 78
*Chicago Tribune*, 137
Chukhrai, Grigory, 78, 85
"Clear Skies," 85
"A Clockwork Orange," 142
Communist Party of the Soviet Union: Academy of Social Sciences, 3; Central Committee, 4, 68, 73, 132; instruction, 124-25, 148; as lecturers, 125; membership as audience variable, 12, 59, 60, 103, 119-25, 128, 129, 146, 148; officials of, 69, 118-19, 120; primary party organization, 123-24; as subject of media, 43, 60, 121, 125; as subjects of

surveys, 4; volunteer activities, 122-24
Communist Youth League (Komsomol), 43, 119, 121, 122, 123, 126, 128
*Corriere della Sera*, 142
"The Cranes Are Flying," 85
Cutright, Phillips, 147-48

Department of Culture: of Central Committee of Communist Party, 73
De Rita, Lidia, 25
de Sica, Vittorio, 81
Deutsche Welle, 138, 142
dormitories for workers, 105-06, 108, 109
"Dr. Strangelove," 142

"The Entertainer," 79
Erofeev, Victor, 118
"The Experts Investigate," 20

"Family Blood," 78
"Father of a Soldier," 78
Film Section: of Department of Culture, 73
films (*see* movies)
Firsov, Boris, 36, 134
"Flower in the Dust," 80-81
"Forsyte Saga," 21, 33
"The Forty-First," 78
"The Four Days of Naples," 79, 81

# ABOUT THE AUTHOR

ELLEN PROPPER MICKIEWICZ is Dean of the Graduate School of Arts and Sciences and Professor of Political Science at Emory University, Atlanta. Until 1980, she was Professor of Political Science at Michigan State University.

Dr. Mickiewicz edited and contributed to the *Handbook of Soviet Social Science Data* and is the author of *Soviet Political Schools.* She has published widely in the area of Soviet politics and society, and her articles have appeared in the *New York Times, Public Opinion Quarterly, Soviet Union, Slavic Review,* and others. She is editor of the interdisciplinary journal, *Soviet Union.*

Dr. Mickiewicz holds a B. A. from Wellesley College and Ph. D. from Yale University.